es r so doing a
s of the Commonwealth of

was issued to the borrower
below.

OLD BOSTON IN COLONIAL DAYS

OR, ST. BOTOLPH'S TOWN

*FROM THE TIME OF BLACKSTONE, THE
FIRST SETTLER, TO THE OUTBREAK
OF THE AMERICAN REVOLUTION*

Works of
Mary Caroline Crawford

The Romance of
  Old New England Rooftrees $2.50
The College Girl of America   2.50
Among Old New England Inns   2.50
Old Boston in Colonial Days   4.00

THE PAGE COMPANY
53 Beacon Street, Boston, Mass.

BOSTON
PUBLIC
LIBRARY

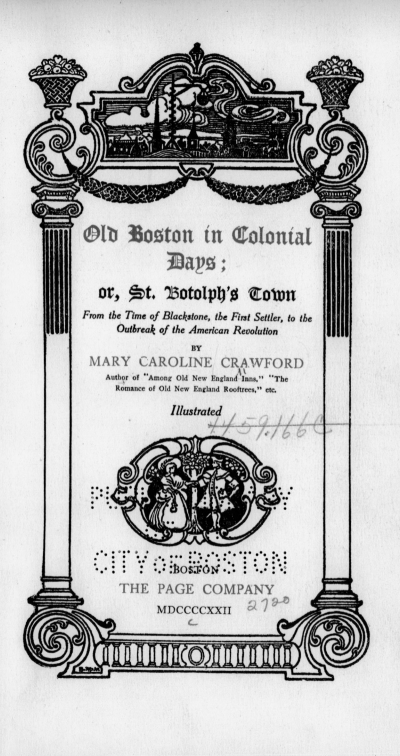

Old Boston in Colonial Days;

or, St. Botolph's Town

From the Time of Blackstone, the First Settler, to the Outbreak of the American Revolution

BY

MARY CAROLINE CRAWFORD

Author of "Among Old New England Inns," "The Romance of Old New England Rooftrees," etc.

Illustrated

44.59.166C

PROPERTY

CITY OF BOSTON

BOSTON

THE PAGE COMPANY

MDCCCCXXII

2720

4459.166C

F73
.4
.C89
1922
copy 4

Dup 3 4459.166
4459.167 (B. H. 5 [3.36])
2 add copies

Copyright, 1908
BY THE PAGE COMPANY

—

All rights reserved

July 28, 1927
I

Made in U.S.A.

PUBLIC LIBRARY
OF THE
CITY OF BOSTON

PRINTED BY C. H. SIMONDS COMPANY
BOSTON, MASS., U.S.A.

4/v/59-xx

FOREWORD

In my student days colonial history never interested me. I did not then understand why but I am now perfectly certain that it was because persons and events were discussed, in most of the books set before me, only as their careers touched New England and hence in so fragmentary a way as to make them appear mere puppets with tiresome dates attached. The treatment usually accorded Sir Harry Vane offers an excellent example of what I mean. He flashed before us, in the history books, as a brilliant, handsome youth who espoused the cause of Mrs. Hutchinson, — and then disappeared for ever from view. Because his wonderful career in England was deemed to have nothing to do with the subsequent history of Massachusetts we were deprived of the great privilege it would have been to make his inspiring life-story a part of our mental equipment! If this volume errs in the other extreme

v

by talking over-much of Vane and of La Tour
after their connection with Boston has ceased
the fault may be attributed to a reaction from
my own defective education.

The truth is that it is biography rather
than history which really allures me; history
seems to me worse than useless unless it illus-
trates the times of which it writes *as* those
times affected the lives of its men and women.
A book like this has no justification, to my
mind, save as it makes us understand just a
little better the part New England, in the person of its chief town, has played in the mighty
drama of nations made up of thinking, feeling
men and women.

Up to the time of the Revolution, of course,
Boston was the biggest place in all the colonies
as well as the chief settlement of Massachusetts. This numerical preëminence needs to be
borne in mind if we would understand many
acts on both sides of the ocean. To understand
the America of to-day, too, we must needs know
the Boston of the fathers. So only can we be
sure that the excrescences of modern government are no essential part of that Christian
state of which Winthrop dreamed and for
which Vane was glad to die.

The books consulted in the preparation of

this work have been many and, for the most
part, are named in the text. But sweeping
credit is here due to the invaluable " Memorial
History of Boston " and to the " Boston An-
tiquities " of Samuel Drake. I have to thank
also Mr. Irwin C. Cromack of the engineering
department, City of Boston, for kindly aid
given and the editor of the Canadian Magazine
for permission to incorporate in the chapter
" How Winthrop Treated With the La Tours "
my article on the " Fight Between La Tour
and D'Aulnay " contributed to his magazine
last year.   M. C. C.

"ST. BOTOLPH'S Town! Far over leagues of land
And leagues of sea looks forth its noble tower,
And far around the chiming bells are heard:
So may that sacred name forever stand
A landmark and a symbol of the power
That lies concentred in a single word."
— LONGFELLOW.

"THE distinctive characteristic of the settlement of the English colonists in America is the introduction of the civilization of Europe into a wilderness without bringing with it the political institutions of Europe. The arts, sciences, and literature of England came over with the settlers. . . . But the monarchy did not come, nor the aristocracy, nor the church as an estate of the realm. Political institutions were to be framed anew such as should be adapted to the state of things." — DANIEL WEBSTER.

"THE spirit of that age was sure to manifest itself in narrow cramping measures and in ugly acts of persecution; but it is, none the less, to the fortunate alliance of that fervid religious enthusiasm with the love of self-government that our modern freedom owes its existence." — JOHN FISKE.

"THOU, too, sail on O ship of State!
Sail on, O Union, strong and great!
Humanity with all its fears,
With all the hopes of future years
Is hanging breathless on thy fate!" — LONGFELLOW.

CONTENTS

List of Illustrations

OLD BOSTON IN COLONIAL DAYS:

OR, ST. BOTOLPH'S TOWN

————◆————

I

AS IT WAS IN THE BEGINNING

To Sir Ferdinando Gorges, the intimate friend of Sir Walter Raleigh and a man of much more than common interest in the history of Elizabethan England, is due the credit of the first enduring settlement in the environs of Boston. John Smith had skirted the coast of New England and looked with some care into Boston Harbour before Gorges came; Miles Standish had pushed up from Plymouth to trade with the Indians of this section; and Thomas Weston, soldier of fortune, had established a temporary trading-post in what is now Weymouth. But it remained for Gorges and his son Robert to plant firmly upon our shores the standard of England and to reiterate that that was the country to which, by

1

virtue of the Cabots, those shores rightly belonged.

The Cabots, to be sure, had come a century
and a quarter before and, since their time, ex-
plorers of several other nations had ventured
to the new world — one of them even going so
far as to carve his name upon the continent.
But an English king had fitted out the " carvels " of John and Sebastian Cabot; and English kings were not in the habit of forgetting
incidents of that sort. The letter in which
Sebastian Cabot relates the story of those Bris-
tol vessels is very quaint and interesting.
" When my father," he writes, " departed
from Venice many yeers since to dwell in England, to follow the trade of merchandizes, he
took me with him to the city of London, while
I was very yong, yet having, nevertheless, some
knowledge of letters, of humanity and of the
Sphere. And when my father died in that
time when news was brought that Don Chris-
tofer Colonus Genuse [Columbus] had discovered the coasts of India whereof was great
talke in all the court of King Henry the
Seventh, who then raigned, inso much that all
men with great admiration affirmed it to be
a thing more divine than humane, to sail by
the West into the East where spices growe, by

a way that was never known before; by this
fame and report there increased in my heart a
great flame of desire to attempt some notable
thing. And, understanding by reason of the
Sphere, that if I should saile by way of the
Northwest winde, I should by a shorter track
come into India, I thereupon caused the king
to be advertised of my devise, who immediately
commanded two Carvels to bee furnished with
all things appertaining to the voiage, which
was, as farre as I remember, in the yeere 1496,
in the beginning of Sommer.

"I began therefore to saile toward the
Northwest, not thinking to find any other land
than that of Cathay, and from thence to turn
toward India, but after certaine dayes I found
that the land ranne towards the North, which
was to me a great displeasure. Nevertheless,
sailing along the coast to see if I could find any
gulfe that turned, I found the land still continuing to the 56 deg. under our pole. And
seeing that there the coast turned toward the
East, despairing to find the passage, I turned
back again, and sailed down by the coast of
that land towards the Equinoctiall (ever with
intent to find the said passage to India) and
came to that part of this firme land which is
now called Florida, where my victuals failing, I

departed from thence and returned into England, where I found great tumults among the
people, and preparation for warrs in Scotland:
by reason whereof there was no more consideration had to this voyage." But barren of
immediate results as this voyage undoubtedly
was it is of immense importance to us as the
first link in the chain which, for so long, bound
America to England.

The next link was, of course, forged by Captain John Smith to whom New England as well
as Virginia owes more than it can ever repay.
About one year before the settlement of Boston
by the company which came with Winthrop
Smith recapitulated the affairs of New England in the following lucid manner: " When
I went first to the North part of Virginia, [in
1614] where the Westerly colony [of 1607] had
been planted, which had dissolved itself within
a yeare, there was not one Christian in all the
land. The country was then reputed a most
rockie barren, desolate desart; but the good
return I brought from thence, with the maps
and relations I made of the country, which I
made so manifest, some of them did beleeve
me, and they were well embraced, both by the
Londoners and the Westerlings, for whom I

The portraictuer of Captayne Iohn Smith Admirall of New England. Æta 37 A.º 1616

BOSTON PUBLIC LIBRARY

CAPTAIN JOHN SMITH

had promised to undertake it, thinking to have joyned them all together. Betwixt them there long was much contention. The Londoners, indeed, went bravely forward but in three or four yeares, I and my friends consumed many hundred pounds among the Plimothians, who only fed me but with delayes promises and excuses, but no performance of any kind to any purpose. In the interim many particular ships went thither, and finding my relations true, and that I had not taken that I brought home from the French men, as had beene reported; yet further for my paines to discredit me and my calling it New England, they obscured it and shadowed it with the title of Cannada, till, at my humble suit, king Charles confirmed it, with my map and booke, by the title of New England. The gaine thence returning did make the fame thereof so increase, that thirty forty or fifty saile, went yearely only to trade and fish; but nothing would be done for a plantation till about some hundred of your Brownists of England, Amsterdam and Leyden, went to New Plimouth, whose humourous ignorances caused them for more than a yeare, to endure a wonderful deale of misery with an infinite patience; but those in time doing well diverse others have in small handfulls undertaken to goe there, *to be severall Lords and Kings of themselves.* . . . "

The Gorges project, certainly, aimed at nothing short of a principality and was begun in all pomp and circumstance. To Greenwich on June 29, 1623, came the Dukes of Buckingham and Richmond, four earls and many lords and gentlemen to draw lots for possessions in the new country. This imposing group was called the Council for New England and had been established under a charter granted in 1620 to the elder Gorges and thirty-nine other patentees. Gorges had had the good luck to acquaint Raleigh with the conspiracy of the Earl of Essex against Queen Elizabeth and James I had valid reason, therefore, to appoint him governor of Plymouth in Devonshire. It was while pursuing his duties in Plymouth that his interest in New England was excited, by the mere accident, as he relates, of some Indians happening to be brought before him. At much pains he learned from them something of the nature of their country and his imagination was soon fired with the vision of golden harvests waiting in the western continent to be reaped by such as he. Naturally sanguine and full of enthusiasm he succeeded in interesting

in his project Sir John Popham, Lord Chief
Justice of the King's Bench, through whose
acquaintance with noblemen and connection at
Court the coveted patent for making settle-
ments in America was ere long secured.

Then the success of the Greenwich assembly
— King James himself drew for Buckingham!
— seems to have decided both Sir Ferdinando
and his son to go at once to their glittering new
world; and, a few weeks later, the latter sailed
forth, armed with a commission as lieutenant
of the Council with power to exercise jurisdiction, civil, criminal and ecclesiastical, over the
whole of the New England coast. The plan
was for him to settle not too far from Plymouth, absorb as soon as might be the little
group of men and women who were really laying there the foundations of a nation and begin in masterful fashion the administration of
the vast province which was undeniably his —
on paper.

At Weymouth Thomas Weston had left a
rude block-house and this Robert Gorges and
his comrades immediately appropriated. In
their company were several mechanics and
tillers of the soil who proceeded to make themselves useful in the new land; but of most interest to us because of their after-history, were

three gentlemen colonists, Samuel Maverick, a young man of means and education who established at what is now Chelsea the first permanent house in the Bay colony, Rev. William Morrell, the Church of England representative in the brave undertaking and William Blackstone, graduate of Cambridge University and destined to renown as the first white settler of what we to-day know as Boston.

It was in September, 1623, that Robert Gorges landed in Weymouth. In the spring of 1624 he returned to England taking with him several of his comrades. Governor Bradford, whom he tried in vain to bully into obeisance observes mildly that Gorges did not find " the state of things heare to answer his Qualitie and condition." So he stayed less than a year. Some of those who had come with him were for trying the thing longer, however. Even the Rev. Mr. Morrell put in a second bitter winter before giving up the attempt. Though he speaks feelingly of the hard lot of men who are " landed upon an unknown shore, peradventure weake in number and naturall powers, for want of boats and carriages," and being for this reason compelled with a whole empty continent before them " to stay where they are first landed, having no means to remove them-

selves or their goods, be the place never so
fruitlesse or inconvenient for planting, building houses, boats or stages, or the harbors
never so unfit for fishing, fowling or mooring
their boats,'' — yet Morrell was none the less
very favourably impressed, as Smith and all
the others had been, with the natural charms
of New England. As the fruit of his sojourn
we have a Latin poem in which the country is
described in a genial and somewhat imaginative
way.

The year that Morrell returned to England
(1625) was in all probability that in which
William Blackstone took up his abode across
the bay, in Shawmut, opposite the mouth of
the Charles. And it was in that same year,
too, that Captain Wollaston and his party established themselves at the place since known
as Mount Wollaston, in the town of Quincy.

Among Wollaston's companions was one
Thomas Morton '' of Clifford's Inn, Gent.,'' a
lawyer by profession and an outlaw by practice.
In the rather dull pages of early New England
history Morton's escapades supply '' colour,''
however, for which we cannot be too grateful
to him. The staid Plymouth people soon came
to speak of him as the '' Lord of Misrule '' and
there is no evidence whatever that he failed

to deserve the title.   When Wollaston departed
to Virginia on business he proceeded to become
captain in his stead and, naming the settlement
Mare Mount, — Merry Mount, — he invited all
the settlers to have a good time. They did so,
according to Morton's own account — in the
mad glad bad way ever dear to roystering Englishmen. Not only did he and his followers
drink deep of the festal bowl but they made the
Indians with whom they traded welcome to
drink deep also. To the men savages were
given arms and ammunition while to the women
was extended the privilege of becoming the
mates of the conquering English. The May
Day of 1627 was celebrated in revelry run riot.
Morton has left us a minute description of the
pole used on this occasion " a goodly pine tree
of 80 foote long . . . with a peare of bucks
horns nayled one, somewhat neare unto the
top of it," while Governor Bradford says
they " set up a May-pole, drinking and dancing aboute it many days togither, inviting the
Indean women for their consorts, dancing and
frisking togither (like so many fairies, or
furies rather) and worse practices."

Bradford not unnaturally failed to appreciate the " colour." Moreover, the settlers
could not, of course, have the natives furnished

with firearms. So Morton was, after some difficulty, made a prisoner and shipped off to England. But he came back again the next year and for a considerable time was a veritable thorn in the flesh to Endicott and his companions at Salem.

The Salem settlement was in the nature of a rescuing party. For while Sir Ferdinando and his friends had been exhausting themselves upon the pomps and ceremonies of colonization John White, a Dorchester clergyman, had established a little group of " prudent and honest men " in a kind of missionary settlement near what is now Gloucester. Of these men Roger Conant with three others had stayed on in the face of much discouragement after their companions returned to England, finally removing to Naumkeag (Salem), — where Endicott found them when he landed early in the fall of 1628.

The rights of Endicott's men to territory in New England were obtained by purchase from Sir Ferdinando's Council of Plymouth. The name adopted by them was that of " the Massachusetts Company." Very wisely, however, as matters turned out, Endicott and his friends insisted that a charter be obtained from the Crown confirmatory of the grant from the

Council of Plymouth. And though they sailed before the charter passed the seals, when it did so, March 4, 1629, the rights of the colonists were defined as they never before had been, — and Charles I had placed in the hands of mere subjects powers which many a king who came after him would have given much to revoke.

Though Endicott was the " Governor of London's Plantation in the Massachusetts Bay of New England " Matthew Cradock was the governor, — i. e. the executive business head, — in the old country; and Cradock it was who, in July, 1629, submitted to his fellow-members in England certain propositions, conceived by himself, which, reinforced as they were by the charter, were destined to work a veritable revolution in the colonization of New England. Up to this time there seems to have been no thought whatever of transferring to the new land the actual government of the Company but Cradock made the startling proposal that just this should be done to the end that persons of worth and quality might deem it worth while to embark with their families for the plantation. There is still standing in Medford, near Boston, a house bearing the name of this governor and built for his use though he never came to occupy it. Between the suggestion

OLD HOUSE IN MEDFORD, BUILT BY GOVERNOR CRADOCK

BOSTON PUBLIC LIBRARY

of Cradock's plan at Deputy Goffe's house in
London, in August, 1629, and its adoption a
month later every member of the Company
gave deep thought to the change involved.
And, gradually, they came to see in it a way
of escape from persecution and oppression.
Reforms in England, whether of Church or
State, seemed impossible. Strafford was at
the head of the army and Laud in control of
the Church. Illegal taxes were being levied on
all hands and it looked as if Charles were resolved to rule the kingdom in his own stiff-
necked way, disdaining the coöperation of any
Parliament. Little hope indeed did the Old
World offer to the liberty-loving, religious men
who made up the bulk of the Puritan party!

The document by which these men finally
emancipated themselves has come down to us
as the Cambridge Agreement, so called because
it was signed beneath the shadows and prob
ably within the very walls of that venerable
university whose traditions it was destined to
transplant into a new world. It bore the date,
August 26, 1629; and was in the following
words: —

" Upon due consideration of the state of the
Plantation now in hand for New England,
wherein we whose names are hereunto sub-

scribed, have engaged ourselves, and having
weighed the work in regard of the consequence,
God's glory and the Church's good; as also in
regard of the difficulties and discouragements
which in all probabilities must be forecast upon
the prosecution of this business; considering
withal that this whole adventure grows upon
the joint confidence we have in each other's
fidelity and resolution herein, so as no man
of us would have adventured it without the
assurance of the rest; now for the better en-
couragement of ourselves and others who shall
join with us in this action, and to the end that
every man may without scruple dispose of his
estate and affairs as may best fit his preparation for this voyage; it is fully and faithfully
agreed among us, and every one of us doth
hereby freely and sincerely promise and bind
himself, in the word of a Christian and in the
presence of God, who is the searcher of all
hearts, that we will so really endeavor the
prosecution of this work, as by God's assistance we will be ready in our persons, and with
such of our several families as are to go with
us, and such provision as we are able conveniently to furnish ourselves withal, to embark
for the said Plantation by the first of March
next, at such port or ports of this land as shall

be agreed upon by the Company, to the end to pass the Seas (under God's protection) to inhabit and continue in New England: Provided always, that before the last of September next, the whole Government, together with the Patent for the said Plantation, be first, by an order of Court, legally transferred and established to remain with us and others which shall inhabit upon the said Plantation; and provided also, that if any shall be hindered by such just or inevitable let or other cause, to be allowed by three parts of four of these whose names are hereunto subscribed, then such persons for such times and during such lets, to be discharged of this bond. And we do further promise, every one for himself, that shall fail to be ready by his own default by the day appointed, to pay for every day's default the sum of £3 to the use of the rest of the company who shall be ready by the same day and time.

(Signed)

RICHARD SALTONSTALL,	THOMAS SHARPE,
THOMAS DUDLEY,	INCREASE NOWELL,
WILLIAM VASSALL,	JOHN WINTHROP,
NICHOLAS WEST,	WILLIAM PINCHON,
ISAAC JOHNSON,	KELLAM BROWNE,
JOHN HUMFRY,	WILLIAM COLBRON."

As important to this epoch-making agreement as the Prince of Denmark to the play of Hamlet is the sentence '' Provided always, that before the last of September next, the whole Government, together with the Patent for the said Plantation, be first by an order of Court, legally transferred and established to remain with us and others which shall inhabit upon the said Plantation.'' This was the great condition, we must bear clearly in mind, upon which Saltonstall, Dudley, Winthrop and the rest agreed to leave the land where they had been born and bred, and '' inhabit and continue '' in a new land of which they knew nothing. Two months later John Winthrop was chosen head of the enterprise, with the style and title *Governor of the Massachusetts Bay Company.* Emphatically, Boston has now '' begun.''

II

FROM every point of view that was a remarkable group of men who boldly declared at Cambridge their resolution to found a state in the new world. Sir Richard Saltonstall was descended from a former lord mayor of London and occupied a place of no little importance in the England of his time; the ancestors of Thomas Dudley had all been men honoured in English history; John Nowell was related to the dean of St. Paul's in the reign of Elizabeth; John Humfrey married a daughter of the Earl of Lincoln; William Vassall was endowed with a positive genius for trade; William Pynchon possessed unusual learning and piety; Isaac Johnson was a man of very large wealth and another son-in-law of the Earl of Lincoln, and Thomas Sharpe, Michael West, Killam Browne and William Colbron were all English country gentlemen of no inconsiderable fortune and of university breeding. But the greatest

17

man of the group was, of course, John Winthrop, who had been chosen to be its head. And
his peer in every womanly respect was Margaret, his noble wife.

As a lad Winthrop had received a good education and had been admitted in 1602 into
Trinity College, Cambridge. An early love-
match prevented him from staying to take his
degree, however, and when only a youth of
eighteen, we find him living at Great Stam-
bridge in the County of Essex with his first
wife's family, — very wealthy people for that
day and of high standing in the community.
Six children were born to the happy young
pair and then, when the husband and father
was only twenty-five, he was left a widower.
Within a year he was married again, according
to the customs of that period. Then, in another
year, this wife and her infant child were also
committed to the grave. Up to this time Winthrop's profession had been that of a lawyer
but these successive and severe bereavements
made him full of misgivings as to his religious
condition and he seriously contemplated the
abandonment of the law with a view to taking
orders as a clergyman. His introspection at
this stage of his development is recorded in a
manuscript of " Religious Experiences " which

JOHN WINTHROP

BOSTON PUBLIC LIBRARY

covers a period of three years and makes intensely interesting reading.

To understand these " Religious Experiences " and the subsequent life of the man who wrote them it is necessary to appreciate the fact that Winthrop came of intensely religious parentage. Adam Winthrop, his father, was a man of deep personal piety and Anne Winthrop, his mother, could not live happily away from the daily inspiration of her Bible, as we see from a letter sent to her husband before their son was born. The mingling of love for God with ardent human affection which we shall find to be a constant trait in the letters of her son is present here also: " I have reseyved, Right deare and well-beloved," she writes her absent husband, " from you this week a letter, though short, yet very sweete, which gave me a lively tast of those sweete & comfortable wordes, whiche alwayes when you be present with me, are wont to flowe most aboundantlye from your loving hart — wherebye I perseyve that whether you be present with me or absent from me, you are ever one towardes me, & your hart remayneth allwayes with me. Wherefore layinge up this perswaision of you in my brest, I will most assuredlye, the Lord assistynge me by his grace, beare al-

wayes the lyke loving hart unto you agayne,
untyll suche tyme as I may more fully enjoye
your loving presence: but in the meane tyme
I will remayne as one having a great inherit-
aunce, or riche treasure, and it beinge by force
kept from him, or hee beinge in a strange Con-
trey, and cannot enjoye it; longethe contyn-
ually after it, sighinge and sorrowinge that hee
is so long berefte of it, yet rejoyseth that hee
hathe so greatt tresure pertayninge to him, and
hopeth that one day the tyme will come that
hee shall enjoye it, and have the wholle benyfytt
of it. So I having a good hoope of the tyme to
com, doe more paciently beare the time present,
and I praye send me word if you be in helthe
and what sucesse you have with your letters.
. . . I send you this weke by my fathers
man a shyrte and fyve payer of hoses. . . .
I pray send me a pound of starch by my fathers
man. You may very well send my byble if it
be redye — thus with my verye hartye com-
mendacions I byd you farewell comittinge you
to almightye God to whom I commend you in
my dayle prayers as I am sure you doe me, the
Lord kep us now & ever Amen

          " Your loving wife
            " Anne Winthrop "

From his mother, then, Winthrop inherited a nature of quite unusual affectionateness for a man of his time and from his father an enduring tendency toward introspection and stern self-discipline. His Diary, as frank and often as pathetic as Amiel's, constantly displays the warring of a passionate tendency with a consecrated other-worldliness. " The Love of this present world! " he exclaims in the course of an exquisite love-letter to the wife from whom his work has parted him, " how it bewitches us & steales away our hearts from him who is the onely life & felicitye. O that we could delight in Christ our Lord & heavenly husband as we doe in each other, & that his absence were like greivous to us! " Winthrop *could* leave home and friends, yes, even his adored Margaret, — to come to a foreign land. But it would not be easy for him. The step would be taken in that same frame of mind which his Diary of Jan. 1, 1611, reflects when it says: " Beinge admonished by a christian freinde that some good men were ofended to heare of some gaminge which was used in my house by my servants I resolved that as for my selfe not to use any cardings etc, so for others to represse it as much as I could, during the continuance of my present state, & if God bringe me once more to be whollye by my selfe, then to banishe all togither." This resolution is particularly interesting when placed alongside of the first New England temperance pledge later fathered by Governor Winthrop.[1]

When in the heydey of his youthful vigour (he was then only twenty-five!) Winthrop wrote, " Finding that the variety of meates drawes me on to eate more than standeth with my healthe, I have resolved not to eate of more then 2 dishes at any one meale, whither fish, flesh, fowle or fruite or whittemeats etc: whither at home or abroade; the lorde give me care & abilitie to performe it." A year later when, by the death of his second wife's father, he had come into considerable wealth and therefore felt again keen temptation to self-indulgence he makes twelve resolutions, so interesting in the light of his after life that I give them here in full:

" 1.   I doe resolve to give myselfe, my life, my witt, my healthe, my wealthe to the service of my God and & Savior, who by givinge himselfe for me & to me, deserves whatsoever I am or can be, to be at his Comandement & for his glorye:

" 2.   I will live where he appoints me.

[1] See p. 9 " Old New England Inns."

" 3. I will faithfully endeavour to discharge that callinge wch he shall appoint me unto.

" 4. I will carefully avoide vaine & needless expences that I may be the more liberall to good uses.

" 5. My property, & bounty must goe forthe abroade, yet I must ever be careful that it beginne at home.

" 6. I will so dispose of my family affaires as my morning prayers & evening exercises be not omitted.

" 7. I will have a speciall care of the good education of my children.

" 8. I will banish profanes from my familye.

" 9. I will diligently observe the Lords Sabaoth bothe for the avoidinge & preventinge worldly business, & also for the religious spendinge of such tymes as are free from publique exercises, viz. the morninge, noone, & evening.

" 10. I will endeavour to have the morninge free for private prayer, meditation & reading.

" 11. I will flee Idlenes, & much worldly busines.

"12. I will often praye & conferre privately wth my wife."

Just here seems as good a place as any to observe that Winthrop was wonderfully fortu-

nate in each of the three women whom he successively called " my wife." The bride of his
youth, the wife of his young manhood, — with
whom he lived only one short year, — and Margaret, who was his faithful spouse for more
than a quarter of a century, were all women
who could respond richly to the aspirations of
his soul as well as to the cravings of his heart.
Margaret, of course, was peculiarly his mate.
The daughter of Sir John Tyndal, knight, she
it was who made him what he now became.
" From the day that his faith was plighted
to her " as one sympathetic historian has said
. . . " he learned to step boldly out among
his equals, to take his share in the world's
work."

After his marriage and up to the time when
he engaged upon the New England enterprise
Winthrop's business was that of an attorney
practising in London and on the circuit. This,
naturally, took him much away from Groton
where Margaret and his young children lived
and as a result we find in the correspondence
which passed between Groton Manor and the
" Chamber at the Temple Gate " an almost
complete record of the temporal, spiritual and
affectional development of this remarkable
pair. Tender love-letters, every one of these

epistles! " I wish thy imployments coulde
suffer thee to come home," writes the wife, to
which her husband responds promptly, " such
is my love to thee my deare spouse, as were it
not that my imployment did enforce me to it,
I could not live comfortably from thee halfe
thus long. . . . so I kiss my sweet wife &
rest alwayes Thy faithfull husband

" JOHN WINTHROP "

For a dozen years of this correspondence
there is, however, no thought that Winthrop's
" imployment " would ever be such as to put
the ocean between them. He was not a member of the original Massachusetts Company;
one may search in vain for his name along
with those of Cradock, Saltonstall and Endicott
on the Massachusetts Charter of March, 1629.
But the early summer of that year found him
thinking very seriously of emigration as one
sees between the lines of a letter to Margaret
dated June 22, 1629. " My comfort is that thou
art willinge to be my companion in what place
or condition soever, in weale or in woe. Be it
what it may, if God be with us we need not
feare; his favour, & the kingdome of heaven
wilbe alike & happiness enough to us & ours
in all places." Evidently the writer of this

felt a crisis to be at hand both in the affairs
of his country and in his own personal life.
But it was not in John Winthrop's nature to
lightly decide upon any serious step. From his
paper " General Considerations for the Plantations of New England " it is plain that he
thought carefully and prayerfully upon every
phase of the enterprise.

Then finally it became to him clear that he
had fallen upon disastrous times; that foun-
tains of learning in his own country were cor-
rupted; that all arts and trades were carried
on in such deceitful and unrighteous ways that
it was well-nigh impossible for a good man to
live by any of them; that the land was weary
of her inhabitants; that man had become of less
importance than beasts, children, — who ought
to have been considered blessings, — being
counted the greatest burdens; that the kingdom
of anti-christ was increasing; that, in a word,
the Lord had begun to frown upon England
and cut its inhabitants short. To John Winthrop, therefore, New England seemed a place
provided by God " to be a refuge for many
whome he meanes to save out of the generall
callamity."

His friends, of course, were not nearly so
sure as he was that the new country was beck-

oning him and Robert Ryece, whose advice he
asked in the matter, replied in a letter which is
full of interest because it marshals all the prudent considerations which should have persuaded Winthrop to stay just where he was
and let other people be pioneers in this difficult
and dangerous enterprise. '' The Church &
Common welthe heere at home,'' he begins,
'' hathe more neede of your beste abyllytie in
these dangerous tymes then any remote plantation, which may be performed by persons of
leser woorthe & apprehension. . . . Agyne,
your owne estate wylbe more secured in the
myddest of all accidents heere at home, than in
this forreine expedition, which discovereth a
1000 shipwrackes which may betyde. All your
kynsfolkes & moste understandinge friendes
wyll more rejoyce at your stayenge at home
with any condition which God shall sende, then
to throwe your selfe upon vayne hopes, with
many difficulties & uncertaynties. Agayne, you
shalbe more acceptable in the service of the
Hieste, & more under His protection whiles you
walke charely in your vocation heere at home,
then to goe owte of your vocation, comyttinge
your selfe to a woorlde of dangers abroade.

'' The pype goeth sweete, tyll the byrde be
in the nett; many bewtifull hopes ar sett before

your eyes to allewer you to danger. Plantations ar for yonge men, that can enduer all
paynes & hunger. Yf in your yewthe you had
byn acquaynted with navigation, you mighte
have promised your selfe more hope in this
longe vyadge, but for one of your yeeres [Win-
throp was now forty-two] to undertake so large
a taske is seldome seene but to miscarry. To
adventure your wholle famylly upon so mani-
feste uncerteynties standeth not with your wys-
dome & longe experience. Lett yonger yeeres
take this charge upon them, with the advyse
of that which elder yeeres shall directe them
unto, the losse shalbe the lesse yf thay mys-
carry; but there honor shalbe the more if thay
prosper. So long as you sytt at the helme,
your famylie prospereth, but yf you shoold
happen to fayle, your flocke woolde be at the
least in hazarde, if not totally to myscarrye.
Yonge men directions thowghe sometymes with
some successe, do not all wayes succeede.
These remote partes will not well agree with
your yeeres; whiles you are heere you wyll be
ever fytter by your understandings & wisdome
to supply there necessities. But if it shoolde
happen that you shoolde gett safely thither,
you shall soone fynde, how necessitie wyll calle
for supplies from these parts. I pray you par-

don my boldnes, that had rather erre in what
I thinke, then be sylente in what I shoolde
speake. How harde wyll it bee for one
browghte up among boockes & Learned men,
to lyve in a barbarous place, where is no
learnynge & lesse cyvillytie. . . . "

This counsel of prudent cowardice was written just a fortnight before the memorable com-
pact at Cambridge. But it did not deter Winthrop from signing that brave Agreement.
For, in the meantime his son, — that John Winthrop who was afterwards renowned as Governor of Connecticut, — returned from a pro-
tracted journey in foreign lands and heartened
him with these words: " For the business of
New England, I can say no other thing, but that
I believe confidently, that the whole disposition
thereof is of the Lord. . . . And for myself, I have seen so much of the vanity of the
world, that I esteem no more of the diversities
of countries, than as so many inns, whereof the
traveller that hath lodged in the best or in the
worst, findeth no difference, when he cometh to
his journey's end; and I shall call that my
country, where I may most glorify God, and
enjoy the presence of my dearest friends.
Therefore, herein I submit myself to God's
will and yours, and with your leave, do dedicate

myself . . . to the service of God and the
Company. . . . "

Best of all the gentle Margaret did not fail
her husband in this hour of need. Letters full
of cheer and sympathy found their way to him
from Groton Manor and in them all she expressed conviction that the good Lord would
" certainly bless us in our intended purpose."
His tender appreciation of her pluck is reflected
in all the letters he sent her during the months
preceding his departure. " I must now begin
to prepare thee for our long parting, which
grow very near," he writes early in January,
1629. " I know not how to deal with thee by
arguments; for if thou wert as wise and patient
as ever woman was, yet it must needs be a great
trial to thee and the greater because I am so
dear to thee; " and then he goes on to point out
that she must find her comfort in religion, as
where else could she find it, poor thing! when
the husband with whose soul hers was peculiarly knit was for venturing to a foreign land,
leaving her behind. Her replies to his brave
attempts at consolation are indeed touching,
and immensely pathetic also are his answers.
He has been arranging to leave with friends
fifteen hundred pounds for her support until
she should be able to follow him to the New

World and now he writes, " MY SWEET WIFE,
The Lord hath oft brought us together with
comfort, when we have been long absent;
and if it be good for us he will do so still.
When I was in Ireland he brought us together
again. When I was sick here in London he restored us together again. How many dangers,
near death, hast thou been in thyself! and yet
the Lord hath granted me to enjoy thee still.
If he did not watch over us we need not go over
sea to seek death or misery: we should meet it
at every step, in every journey. And is not he
a God abroad as well as at home? Is not his
power and providense the same in New England as it hath been in Old England? . . .
My good wife, trust in the Lord, whom thou
hast found faithful. He will be better to thee
than any husband and will restore thee thy
husband with advantage. But I kiss my sweet
wife and bless thee and all ours and rest Thine
ever Jo. WINTHROP

February 14, 1629 — *Thou must be my valentine* . . . "

The picture of him whom we are wont to call
" the stern John Winthrop " remembering,
even in the midst of hurried and troubled pre-
parations to embark for the New World
woman's perennial sentiment concerning such

festivals as St. Valentine's Day is so striking
as to be worth bearing in mind. And when we
have placed alongside of it the series of farewell letters sent to his wife from Cowes and
the Isle of Wight where the ships were detained
by bad weather, we have a complete compre-
hension of one side of the man's character.
" Mondays and Fridays, at five of the clock
at night, we shall meet in spirit till we meet in
person," he promises her. Shakespeare, not
long before, had put the same thought into the
mouth of Imogen, when, on having parted with
Posthumus, she complains that they had been
torn apart

> " Ere I could tell him,
> How would I think on him, at certain hours,
> Such thoughts, and such;
>   . . . or have charged him,
> At the sixth hour of morn, at noon, at midnight,
> To encounter me with orisons; for then
> I am in heaven for him."

But Posthumus, as Robert C. Winthrop, the
editor of his progenitor's remarkable letters,
points out, was not in his forty-third year, as
was the Governor of the Massachusetts Bay
Colony; nor Imogen in her thirty-ninth. Moreover, one can scarcely fancy either of Shakespeare's lovers admitting, as Winthrop does in

one of the first New England letters which he
sent his wife, " I own with sorrow that much
business hath made me too often forget Mondays and Fridays."

III

NOWADAYS embarking from old England for
the new seems no great matter. But in that
spring of 1630 when Winthrop's little fleet
sailed from Cowes travelling was quite a different proposition. For it was certain that the
voyage would be very long and usually it was
dangerous also. On this particular occasion it
took seventy-six days and was attended by all
those "perils of the deep" against which
some of us still have the good sense to pray.
Winthrop's vessel was called the Arbella in
compliment to Lady Arbella Johnson, who was
one of its passengers, and among the other
ships which brought over this Company of
some eight hundred souls was the Mayflower,
consecrated in every New England heart as the
carrier, a decade earlier, of the Pilgrims of
Plymouth. During the voyage Governor Winthrop wrote the simple beginnings of what is
known as his "History of New England," a

journal from which we glean the most that we know of the early days of the colonists.

Being rather impatient, however, just as its compiler probably was, actually to land in the New World we will quote here only that paragraph which describes the end of the voyage: " Saturday 12. About four in the morning we were near our port. We shot off two pieces of ordnance and sent our skiff to Mr. Peirce his ship. . . . Afterwards Mr. Peirce came aboard us, and returned to fetch Mr. Endecott, who came to us about two of the clock and with him Mr. Skelton and Captain Levett. We that were of the assistants and some other gentlemen and some of the women and our captain returned with them to Nahumkeck, where we supped with a good venison pasty and good beer, and at night we returned to our ship but some of the women stayed behind. In the mean time most of our people went on shore upon the land of Cape Ann, which lay very near us and gathered store of fine strawberries.''

The initial landing, this makes clear, was not at Boston at all but at Salem where Endicott's band had already settled. Things were not very rosy in this colony just then, however, as we see from the following passage in Dudley's letter to the Countess of Lincoln: " We found the colony in a sad and unexpected condition, about eighty of them being dead the winter before, and many of those alive weak and sick; all the corn and bread amongst them all hardly sufficient to feed them for a fortnight, insomuch that the remainder of a hundred and eighty servants we had the two years before sent over, coming to us for victuals to sustain them, we found ourselves wholly unable to feed them by reason that the provisions shipped for them were taken out of the ship they were put in; and they who were trusted to ship them in another failed us and left them behind whereupon necessity forced us, to our extreme loss, to give them all liberty, who had cost us about £16 or £20 a person furnishing and sending over." So, far from being able to take in more people, Salem had to relinquish almost two hundred of those already there! Small wonder that Dudley comments dryly, " Salem, where we landed, pleased us not."

Accordingly, Winthrop and his friends moved farther south along the coast until they came to the spot now dear to our country as the town which shelters Bunker Hill Monument. Here they established their settlement. And here, on the thirtieth of July, 1630, Winthrop, Dudley, Johnson and the pastor John

Wilson adopted and signed a simple church covenant which was the foundation of the independent churches of New England. Before leaving England this band of colonists had made it clear that they were not " Separatists from the Church of England " though they admitted that they could but separate themselves from the corruptions in it in order that they might practise the positive part of Church reformation and propagate the Gospel in America. We must remember this in order to justify the stand taken by Winthrop, a little later, in dealing with Roger Williams. But it is necessary also to bear clearly in mind the fact of this established church at Charlestown. To set up a state in which there should be no established church was as far from the minds of these men as to set up a state in which there should be no established government. None the less they esteemed it their honour, as Winthrop expressly said, " to call the church of England our dear mother."

By August the little company was apparently settled for good in Charlestown, for the first Court of Assistants had now been held and recommendations as to " how the minister should be maintained " adopted. As a further step towards permanency Governor Winthrop,

as we are told in the town-records, " ordered
his house to be cut and framed there."

Then sickness came upon them, the Lady
Arbella and her husband being among the first
to pass away in the land from which they had
hoped so much. Of the lady Cotton Mather has
said quaintly that " she took New England in
her way to Heaven." She was only one of the
many who died. Johnson in his " Wonder-
Working Providence " records that " in almost
every family lamentation, mourning and woe
were heard, and no fresh food to be had to
cherish them. It would assuredly have moved
the most lockt up affections to tears, had they
past from one hut to another, and beheld the
piteous case these people were in; and that
which added to their present distress was the
want of fresh water. For, although the place
did afford plenty, yet for present they could
find but one spring, and that not to be come at,
but when the tide was down."

Enter, thereupon, Mr. William Blackstone,
as the saviour of the enterprise! Blackstone
was one of those who had come over with
Sir Robert Gorges and had remained in spite
of untoward conditions. On Shawmut (afterwards Boston) he possessed large holdings by
virtue of a title Winthrop and his men later

acquired by purchase. Now, therefore, "he came and acquainted the Governor of an excellent Spring there; withal inviting him and soliciting him thither. Whereupon after the death of Mr. Johnson and divers others, the Governor, with Mr. Wilson, and the greatest part of the church removed thither; whither also the frame of the Governor's house, in preparation at this town, was also (to the discontent of some) carried; where people began to build there houses against winter; and this place was called Boston." Thus does the record incorporated in Frothingham's "History of Charlestown" tell the tale of Boston's actual birth. There are those who maintain that the story of our city's growth could very effectively be told by a series of historical tableaux; for the initial number on the program they name with excellent judgment the picture of Blackstone, the gentle recluse, exhibiting to John Winthrop the "excellent spring" of his own domain.

This act of Blackstone's was the more praiseworthy because he was a "solitary" by nature and frankly disliked men even remotely of Puritan stripe. He was at this time about thirty-five and had dwelt in his lonely hut on the west slope of what is now Beacon Hill, not

far from Beacon and Spruce streets, for about
five years, spending his quiet days in trade with
the savages and in the cultivation of his garden.
Just why he had left England is not more clear
than just why he later left Boston. But when
he died in Rhode Island (May 26, 1675) he left
behind him " 10 paper books " in which it is
believed he may have told the story of his mys-
terious life. These were unfortunately destroyed by the Indians when they burned his
house, however, and all that we further know
of him is that he returned to Boston, after he
had ceased to be an inhabitant of the place, and
married the widow of John Stephenson, who
lived on Milk street, on the site of the building in which Franklin was born.

In regard to a name for the new settlement
there seems to have been absolute unanimity.
By common consent it was called after the
old-world city, St. Botolph's town, or Boston, of Lincolnshire, England, from which the
Lady Arbella Johnson and her husband had
come and in whose noble parish church
John Cotton was still preaching. The order
of the Court of Assistants, — Governor Winthrop presiding, — " *That Trimontaine shall
be called Boston* " was passed on the 17th of
September, 1630, thus giving the death blow

ST. BOTOLPH'S CHURCH, BOSTON, ENGLAND

BOSTON PUBLIC LIBRARY

to Carlyle's picturesque statement in his book
on Cromwell concerning Cotton's share in the
matter: " Rev. John Cotton is a man still held
in some remembrance among our New England friends. He had been minister of Boston
in Lincolnshire; carried the name across
the ocean with him; fixed it upon a new small
home he found there, which has become a large
one since, — the big busy capital of Massachusetts, — Boston so called. John Cotton, his
mark, very curiously stamped on the face of
this planet; likely to continue for some time."
This is superb writing, of course, but exceedingly lame history. Cotton did not come
to the new world until nearly four years after
this settlement was named Boston.

But, since it is a fact that the St. Botolph's
town, in which Cotton was still living, exercised
a profound influence upon that to which he
presently came let us turn aside and make a
little pilgrimage there. Hawthorne did this
during one of his trips abroad and he printed
the result in the Atlantic Monthly of January,
1862. We cannot do better, I think, than to
follow as he leads: " In mid-afternoon we beheld the tall tower of Saint Botolph's Church
(three hundred feet high, the same elevation
as the tallest tower of Lincoln Cathedral) loom-

ing in the distance. At about half-past four we reached Boston (which name has been shortened, in the course of ages, by the quick and slovenly English pronunciation, from Botolph's town) and were taken by a cab to the Peacock, in the market-place. It was the best hotel in town, though a poor one enough; and we were shown into a small stifled parlor, dingy, musty, and scented with stale tobacco smoke, — tobacco smoke two days old, for the waiter assured us that the room had not more recently been fumigated. An exceedingly grim waiter he was, too, apparently a genuine descendant of the old Puritans of this English Boston.

" In my first ramble about the town, chance led me to the riverside, at that quarter where the port is situated. . . . Down the river I saw a brig, approaching rapidly under sail. The whole scene made an odd impression of bustle and sluggishness and decay, and a remnant of wholesome life; and I could not but contrast it with the mighty and populous activity of our own Boston, which was once the feeble infant of this old English town; — the latter, perhaps, almost stationary ever since that day, as if the birth of such an offspring had taken away its own principle of growth. I thought of Long

JOHN COTTON'S VICARAGE

Wharf and Faneuil Hall, and Washington
street and the Great Elm and the State House,
and exulted lustily, — but yet began to feel
at home in this good old town, for its very
name's sake, as I never had before felt in
England.''

The next day Hawthorne visited " a vacant
spot of ground where old John Cotton's vicarage had stood till a very short time since. According to our friend's description it was a
humble habitation, of the cottage order, built
of brick, with a thatched roof. In the right-
hand aisle of the church there is an ancient
chapel, which at the time of our visit was in
process of restoration, and was to be dedicated
to Cotton, whom these English people consider
as the founder of our American Boston. . . .
The interior of St. Botolph's is very fine and
satisfactory, as stately almost as a cathedral,
and has been repaired — as far as repairs were
necessary — in a chaste and noble style. . . .
When we came away the tower of St. Botolph's
looked benignantly down; and I fancied that
it was bidding me farewell, as it did Mr. Cotton, two or three hundred years ago, and telling
me to describe its venerable height and the
town beneath it, to the people of the American
city, who are partly akin, if not to the living

inhabitants of old Boston, yet to some of the dust that lies in its churchyard.''

It is of this tower with its beacon and its bells that we hear in Jean Ingelow's touching poem, '' High Tide On the Coast of Lincolnshire.'' St. Botolph, the pious Saxon monk of the seventh century, who is believed to have founded the town, received his name, indeed, — Bot-holp, i. e. Boat-help, — from his service to sailors; and the high tower was originally designed to be a guide to those out at sea, six miles down the river. An account of the town written in 1541 tells the whole story in one terse paragraph: '' Botolphstowne standeth on ye river of Lindis. The steeple of the church ' being quadrata Turris ' and a lanthorn on it, is both very high & faire and a mark bothe by sea and land for all ye quarters thereaboute.''

Perhaps it was remembrance of what the beacon in St. Botolph's tower had meant to the people of Lincolnshire which caused the Court of Assistants, assembled in new Boston, to pass the following resolution March 4, 1634: '' It is ordered that there shalbe forth with a beacon sett on the Centry hill at Boston to give notice to the Country of any danger, and that there shalbe a ward of one pson kept there from the first of April to the last of September;

and that upon the discovery of any danger the
beacon shalbe fired, an allarum given, as also
messengers presently sent by that town where
the danger is discov'red to all other townes
within this jurisdiction."

Hawthorne hints, too, that it is to the influence of the old St. Botolph's town that the
winding streets of our modern city may be attributed. "Its crooked streets and narrow
lanes reminded me much of Hanover street,
Ann street, and other portions of our American
Boston. It is not unreasonable to suppose that
the local habits and recollections of the first
settlers may have had some influence on the
physical character of the streets and houses
in the New England metropolis; at any rate
here is a similar intricacy of bewildering lanes
and a number of old peaked and projecting-
storied dwellings, such as I used to see there
in my boyish days. It is singular what a home
feeling and sense of kindred I derived from
this hereditary connection and fancied physi-
ognomical resemblance between the old town
and its well-grown daughter."

Somewhat less romantic but still appealing
is the explanation of our crooked streets volun-
teered by Bynner. "The first houses [of the
colonial period] were necessarily of the rudest

description and they seem to have been scattered hither or thither according to individual need or fancy. The early streets, too, obedient to the same law of convenience, naturally followed the curves of the hills, winding around their bases by the shortest routes and crossing their slopes at the easiest angles. To the pioneer upon the western prairie it is comparatively easy to lay out his prospective city in squares and streets of unvarying size and shape, and oftentimes be it said, of wearying sameness; to the colonist of 1630 upon this rugged promontory of New England it was a different matter. Without the power of leisure to surmount the natural obstacles of his new home, he was contented to adapt himself to them.

" Thus the narrow winding streets, with their curious twists and turns, the crooked alleys and short-cuts by which he drove his cows to pasture up among the blueberry bushes of Beacon Hill, or carried his grist to the windmill over upon Copp's steeps, or went to draw his water at the spring-gate, or took his sober Sunday way to the first rude little church, — these paths and highways, worn by his feet and established for his convenience, remain after two centuries and a half substantially un-

changed, endeared to his posterity by priceless
associations. And so the town, growing at first
after no plan and with no thought of proportion, but as directed and shaped by the actual
needs of the inhabitants, became a not unfitting
exponent of their lives, — the rough outward
garb, as it were, of their hardy young civilization.''

Truth, however, demands the statement that
our forefathers made brave efforts to compel
a ship-shape city. In 1635 it was ordered:
'' That from this day there shall noe house at
all be built in this towne neere unto any of the
streetes or laynes therein but with the advise
and consent of the overseers . . . for the
more comely and commodious ordering of
them.'' At a subsequent meeting in the same
month John Gallop was summarily told to improve the alignment of the '' payles at his
yard's end.'' Very likely he fought off the
order, however; and very likely dozens of
others did the same, regulating their homes in
the fashion attributed to those settlers of Marblehead who are said to have remarked, each
to the other, '' I'm a'goin' to set here; you can
set where you're a mind to.'' Apparently just
that had happened in the old St. Botolph's
town; not improbably that was what also happened in the new.

IV

THE earliest and, in many ways, the best
account of Boston life in the winter immediately following the naming of the town was
that sent by Thomas Dudley in a letter to the
Countess of Lincoln, mother of Lady Arbella
Johnson. The explanation of this letter's
origin is found in a note which Dudley sent
with it " to the righte honourable, my very
good Lady, the Lady Bryget, Countesse of
Lincoln " in the care of Mr. Wilson, pastor
of the First Church, who sailed from Salem,
April 1, 1631. " Madam," he wrote, " your
ltt'res (which are not common or cheape) following me hether into New England, and bringing with them renewed testimonies of the accustomed favours you honoured mee with in
the Old, have drawne from me this Narrative
retribucon, (which in respect of your proper
interest in some persons of great note amongst
us) was the thankfullest present I had to send

over the seas. Therefore I humbly intreat
your Honour, this bee accepted as payment
from him, who neither hath nor is any more
than your honour's old thankful servant,

"THOMAS DUDLEY."

Chronologically, the narrative trips in places
for it was written, as Dudley himself says, by
the fireside on his knee, in the midst of his
family, who " break good manners, and make
me many times forget what I would say and say
what I would not," at a time when he had " no
leisure to review and insert things forgotten,
but out of due time and order must set them
down as they come to memory." None the less
the plain unvarnished descriptions in this letter make it a very telling one and when we put
along with it Winthrop's brave notes to his
son we have a vivid picture of the hardships
of that first winter. " I shall expect your
mother and you and the rest of my company
here next spring, if God will . . ." wrote the
governor. " Bring some good oil, pitch and
tar and a good piece of an old cable to make
oakum; for that which was sent is much lost.
Some more cows should be brought, especially
two new milch, which must be well mealed and
milked by the way, and some goats, especially

sheep, if they can be had. Bring some store
of garlick and onions and conserve of red
roses, alum and aloes, oiled skins, both calf and
sheep and some worsted ribbing of several
sizes.''

The middle of August, 1631, found Margaret
Winthrop under sail for the new world and
early in November the married lovers were re-
united after their sad season of parting. In
honour of the joyful occasion Governor Bradford of Plymouth came up to visit the head of
the Massachusetts Colony and '' divers of the
assistants and most of the people of the near
plantations '' came also to bid the lady Margaret welcome, bringing with them '' great
store of provisions, as fat hogs, kids, venison,
poultry, geese partridges etc so as the like joy
and manifestation of love had never been seen
in New England. It was a great marvel that
so much people and such store of provisions
could be gathered together at so few hours'
warning,'' recorded the happy husband.

The resources of the settlement, as the last
sentence of this entry clearly shows, were still
very meagre. And the governor was no more
prosperous than a number of his associates.
In fact, he was poorer than they, if anything,
for he had no assured income from his office

and he was under the constant necessity of spending money for the common good. In the fall of 1634 Winthrop presented a detailed account of his pecuniary relations to the Massachusetts colony for " the four years and near an half " in which he had held the office of chief magistrate and this document is so interesting that it is here given entire from the Records of the Colony. It speaks more eloquently than we could in many pages of the severe simplicity of those early days in Boston.

" Whereas, by order of the last general court, commissioners were appointed, viz., Roger Ludlow, Esq. the deputy governour, and Mr. Israel Stoughton, gent. to receive my accompt of such things as I have received and disbursed for public use in the time of my government; in all due observance and submission to the order of the said court, I do make this declaratory accompt ensuing: —

" First, I affirm, that I never received any moneys or other goods committed to me in trust for the commonwealth, otherwise than is hereafter expressed.

" Item, I acknowledge I have in my custody certain barrels of common powder, and some match and drumheads, with some things be-

longing to the ordnance; which powder, being
landed at Charlestown, and exposed to the in-
jury of the weather, I took and bestowed first
in a tent which I made of mine own broadcloth, (being then worth eight shillings the
yard but in that service much spoiled). After I
removed it to my storehouse at Boston, where
it still remains, save that some of it hath been
spent in public service, and five barrels I sold
to some ships that needed them, which I will
allow powder or money for. The rest I am
ready to deliver up to such as shall be appointed to receive them.

" I received also some meal and peas, from
Mr. White of Dorchester in England, and from
Mr. Roe of London, which was bestowed upon
such as had need thereof in the several towns;
as also £10 given by Mr. Thomson. I received
also from Mr. Humfrey, some rugs, frieze
suits, shoes, and hose, (the certain value
whereof I must know from himself,) with letters of direction to make use of the greatest
part thereof, as given to help bear out my
charge for the public. I paid for the freight
of these goods and disposed of the greatest
part of them to others; but how I cannot set
down. I made use, also, of two pair of carriage wheels, which I will allow for: I had not

meddled with them but that they lay useless
for want of the carriages which lay in England. For my disbursements, I have formerly
delivered to the now deputy a bill of part of
them, amounting to near £300, which I disbursed for public services divers years since,
for which I have received in corn at six shillings the bushel, (and which will not yeild me
above four shillings) about £180, or near so
much. I disbursed also for the transportation
of Mr. Phillips his family which was to be
borne by the government till he should be
chosen to some particular congregation.

" Now, for my other charges, by occasion of
my place of government, it is well known I
have expended much, and somewhat I have received towards it, which I should have rested
satisfied with, but that, being called to accompt,
I must mention my disbursements with my re-
ceipts and, in both, shall refer myself to the
pleasure of the court.

" I was first chosen to be governour without
my seeking or expectation (there being then
divers other gent. who for their abilities every
way, were far more fit.) Being chosen I furnished myself with servants and provisions accordingly, in a far great proportion than I
would have done had I come as a private man,

or as an assistant only. In this office I continued four years and near an half, although I earnestly desired in every election to have been freed. In this time I have spent above £500 per annum, of which £200 per annum would have maintained my family in a private condition. So, as I may truly say, I have spent by occasion of my late office, above £1,200. Towards this I have received by way of benevolence, from some towns about £50 and by the last year's allowance £150 and by some provisions sent by Mr. Humfrey, as is beforementioned, about £50, or, it may be, somewhat more.

" I also disbursed, at our coming away, in England, for powder and great shot, £216, which I did not put into my bill of charges formerly delivered to the now deputy, because I did expect to have paid myself out of that part of Mr. Johnson's estate, which he gave to the public; but, finding that it will fall far short, I must put it to this accompt.

" The last thing, which I offer to the consideration of the court, is, that my long continuance in the said office hath put me into such a way of unavoidable charge, as will be still as chargeable to me as the place of governour will be to some others. In all these things, I refer myself to the wisdom and justice of the court, with this protestation, that it repenteth me not of my cost or labour bestowed in the service of this commonwealth; but do heartily bless the Lord our God, that he hath pleased to honour me so far as to call for anything he hath bestowed upon me for the service of his church and people here, the prosperity whereof and his gracious acceptance, shall be an abundant recompense to me. I conclude with this one request, (which in justice may not be denied me) that, as it stands upon record that, upon the discharge of my office, I was called to accompt, so this my declaration may be recorded also; lest, hereafter, when I shall be forgotten, some blemish may lie upon my posterity, when there shall be nothing to clear it. JOHN WINTHROP."

" *September 4, 1634.*"

The person who had unconsciously precipitated all this calling to account was none other than Winthrop's old friend, Rev. John Cotton, who, almost immediately after landing in Boston, preached a sermon in which he maintained that a magistrate ought not to be turned into a private man without just cause. This was a view of civil government not at all palatable to the Massachusetts worthies of that day and, as if to assert, once for all that they wished to be entirely free in their choice of a supreme officer they chose for the highest office in their gift, not Winthrop who had so far served them continuously, but Thomas Dudley, his former deputy. Winthrop entirely acquiesced in this result and after entertaining the new governor handsomely in his own house rendered the above account of his stewardship, which had been demanded of him. Three years later he was again chosen chief magistrate. During twelve of the nineteen years of his life in Boston, indeed, he served his fellow colonists in this capacity.

No doubt the Rev. John Cotton was sorely perplexed and not a little chagrined at the change in the government which his first effort in his new pulpit had brought about. But his had been an exciting life and he was fairly well used to changes. Born in 1585, a son of Rowland Cotton, a lawyer of Derby, England, he had entered Trinity College, Cambridge, when only twelve years of age and soon became noted for his acquirements. At nineteen he was admitted to the degree of Master of Arts. Soon afterwards he received the appointment of head lecturer, dean and catechist of Em-

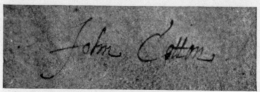

BOSTON PUBLIC LIBRARY

Photographed from the Boston Parish Register

SIGNATURE OF JOHN COTTON, 1620

manuel College. Here he came to be greatly
loved by his students for his sweet and gentle
disposition and prodigiously admired by the
distinguished divines of the time for his grasp
upon the doctrines of Calvin. His theological
bent being what it was it is difficult to understand how he should have been called to St.
Botolph's until one learns that this came about
through a mistake on the part of the Mayor
who voted for him when he intended to vote
against him. And so great was the tact of the
new clergyman that he was able to hold for
many years a place gained in this extraordinary way! In his marriage as in many other
things Cotton was fortunate, for Elizabeth
Horrocks, with whom he lived eighteen years,
brought him on his wedding day the " assurance of his spiritual redemption; hence it was
a day of double marriage to him." After her
death he married " one Mrs. Sarah Story, a
vertuous widow, very dear to his former wife."

Eventually the news of Cotton's non-con-
formity got to the ears of those on the lookout
for heresy, and complaint being entered at the
High Commissioned Court that " the Magistrates did not kneel at the Sacrament " and
that some other ceremonies were also unob-
served " letters missive were dispatched in-

continently to convene Mr. Cotton " before
that " infamous " Court. Some time previously the Earl of Dorset had promised to do
what he could for Cotton should he be persecuted as others before him had been, but now,
when appealed to, he replied " that if Mr. Cotton had been guilty of drunkenness, of unclean-
ness, or any such lesser fault, he could have
obtained his pardon; but inasmuch as he had
been guilty of Nonconformity and Puritanism,
the crime was unpardonable and therefore he
must fly for his safety! "

Accordingly, Mr. Cotton travelled in disguise to London and while hesitating between
Holland, Barbadoes and New England decided
to set sail for the last-named place. To this
decision he was no doubt much influenced by
the pressing invitations of friends and by
" letters procured from the Church of Boston
by Mr. Winthrop, the Governor of the Colony." Boston in New England was certainly
very glad to welcome him. It was a figurative
saying there for many years that the lamp in
the lantern of St. Botolph's ceased to burn
when Cotton left that church to become a shining light in the wilderness of New England.

His ascendency seems to have been a purely
personal one, however. Though Hutchinson

says that he was more instrumental in the settlement of the civil as well as the ecclesiastical polity of New England than any other person one finds little in his writing to explain his power. And the "insinuating and melting way" which Hubband attributed to him is conspicuous chiefly by its absence from the published sermons which have come down to us. He became the progenitor of many of the best and most useful citizens Boston has had, and these good people are ever zealous to link the Old Boston to the new. This very winter of 1908, for instance, they have been approached by the mayor of the old-world city to help repair a portion of St. Botolph's church as a sign of love for its "shining light."

The request this functionary made seems rather odd until one has heard what our Boston gladly did in this respect more than fifty years ago. The story is told briefly in a sounding Latin inscription written by the Honourable Edward Everett and engraved upon a memorial plate in the southwest chapel of St. Botolph's, now called Cotton Chapel, in honour of him who was once minister of the church. Put into English it reads:

"In perpetual remembrance of John Cotton who, during the reigns of James and Charles was, for many years, a grave, skilful and laborious vicar of this church. Afterward, on account of the miserable commotion amongst sacred affairs in his own country, he sought a new settlement in a new world, and remained even to the end of his life a pastor and teacher of the greatest reputation and of the greatest authority in the first church of Boston in New England, which city received this venerable name in honour of Cotton. Two hundred and twenty-five years having passed away since his migration, his descendants and the American citizens of Boston were invited to this pious work by their English brethren in order that the name of an illustrious man, the love and honour of both worlds, might not any longer be banished from that noble temple in which he diligently, learnedly and sacredly expounded the divine oracles for so many years; and they have willingly and gratuitously caused this shrine to be restored, and this tablet to be erected, in the year of our recovered salvation, 1855."

Those who then subscribed to the chapel have, almost all of them, descendants bearing the same names who are to-day living in and about Boston. These people it is, no doubt, who will gladly respond to the request of the

COTTON CHAPEL, ST. BOTOLPH'S, BOSTON, ENGLAND

BOSTON PUBLIC LIBRARY

English mayor. For the original contributors
were, in the majority of cases, either descendants of John Cotton, or husbands of wives so
descended. To the former class belonged John
Eliot Thayer, who gave $250; Edward, Gor-
ham, Sidney and Peter C. Brooks, who gave
$100 each, and John Chipman Gray, who gave
$50. Among the husbands of Cotton's women
descendants who contributed were Charles
Francis Adams, Edward Everett and Langdon
Frothingham, each of whom gave $100. Other
well-known names on the list of donors are
Nathan and William Appleton, George Ban-
croft, Martin Brimmer, Abbott Lawrence, John
Amory Lowell, Jonathan Phillips, Jared
Sparks, Frederic Tudor and John Collins
Warren.

The good feeling between the two Bostons,
which was cemented by these generous gifts
toward the Cotton Chapel, seems to date from
the reopening of the church, two years earlier,
for which occasion several gentlemen from our
Boston were invited to England, at least four
of whom were able to be present.

In our public library may be found a curious
little sheet which gives an account of the exercises. In print so poor and so small as to
nearly ruin the eyes are there recorded the

speeches of the day. One of these, made by Col. T. B. Lawrence of this city, expresses regret that " the domestic institutions of the states of the south " were being warmly debated in the English drawing-rooms of that time. Happily, Cotton's Boston descendants did not all think alike on this important subject!

V

THOMAS DUDLEY, whom Cotton's zeal had
caused to be chosen as Winthrop's successor,
was himself left out of the governorship at
the election of May, 1635, and John Haynes
elected in his stead. Then there arrived in
Boston two men of very different character
both of whom, however, were destined to make
a deep mark in the history of their time and
eventually to die on the scaffold for allegiance
to the truth as they saw it. These two men
were Hugh Peters and Sir Harry Vane.
Peters had been the pastor of the English
church in Rotterdam and had there been persecuted by the English ambassador. Vane
was heir to Sir Harry Vane, Comptroller of
the king's household, a man of great importance in the politics of the time. And his son
has a personality of so much interest that I
am resolved to trace his life fom its bright
beginning to its glorious end even if, in so

doing, I run somewhat ahead of my narrative
and carry my readers far away from Boston
in New England. The fact is that one usually
encounters only the Massachusetts segment of
Vane's wonderful life and so is deprived of
opportunity to judge his career in its whole-
ness and to realize that he, more than any
other man, is the " link that binds together
the severed divisions of the English-speaking
race."

One American writer, Charles Wentworth
Upham, has pointed out in the preface to his
really capital " Life of Sir Harry Vane," that
there is an interesting parallel between the
career of this hero and that of Lafayette.
Both were scions of an aristocratic house and
might easily have passed their youth following the pleasures of court life and indulging
in those enervating relaxations commonly associated with young aristocrats. Instead,
however, both yearned towards America,
Lafayette because he saw in the new land a
chance to realize the vision of political freedom which illumined his young soul, Harry
Vane because he thought to find here " freedom to worship God." Both paid dearly in
youth and in middle life for their devotion to
an ideal, and Vane finally suffered death upon

the block. But because of them American history contains at least two highly romantic chapters and is more deeply inspiring than it could ever have been without them. For each served in his own era to point the truth that the only really great man is he who, with never a thought of self, unswervingly " follows the gleam " even when it leads to exile, prison and death.

Sir Harry Vane was born in 1612, one of a very numerous family of children. His father had been knighted by James I and though only in the early twenties at the time of the younger Harry's birth, was already on the way to eminence in the government of England. At the preparatory school in Westminster and while at Magdalen College in Oxford young Vane bade fair to follow a similar career along the line of least resistance. He was gay, addicted to pleasure and, as he himself says, fond of " good fellowship." But when he was about seventeen he began to interest himself in theology and, the fascination of this subject growing rapidly upon him, he pursued it further and further, at the same time alienating himself as a natural result from the form of worship and doctrine established by law. When the period of his matriculation arrived he declined to take the oath of allegiance and, leaving Oxford, passed over to Holland and France, finally settling down for some time in Geneva.

Residence in the stronghold of Calvinism naturally strengthened the young man's bent towards doctrinal speculations and spiritual exercises and as it was never part of his habit to conceal his opinions, the king was soon being informed by his bishops that the heir of an important family, closely connected with the throne, had conceived a dislike for the discipline and ceremonies of the Church of England. Whereupon, Laud was instructed to expostulate with the young Puritan and wean him back to the true faith. The young dissenter had learned his new lesson well, however, and he was much more than a match for Laud in theological discussion. Perceiving which, the haughty prelate lost his temper and tried to threaten where he could not persuade. This naturally did not endear his doctrines to Harry Vane, whose ardent soul was aflame with love for the meek and gentle One Laud only professed to serve. Accordingly he announced his purpose of going to New England, where those who believed as he did stood ready to give him a warm welcome and, although his

HARRY VANE
Afterwards Sir Henry Vane

BOSTON
PUBLIC
LIBRARY

father at first opposed the plan, he soon assented to it, having found the king to be quite in favour of removing the aristocratic heretic.

The excitement occasioned by the coming to the colony of this brilliant youth, not yet twenty-three, who was heir to a title and a fine estate, whose hand had not yet been pledged in marriage and who was, besides, exceedingly handsome and distinguished-looking, can be better imagined than described. That he should at such an age, after visiting foreign capitals and witnessing all the splendours and enticements which the gay and brilliant world holds out to those of his rank and condition, voluntarily take up the self-denying uneventful life of the Boston of that day was held to mean, as indeed it did mean, deep desire to realize himself spiritually. Accordingly Winthrop and the rest gave him the right hand of fellowship without any of the usual delays and, within a month after his arrival young Vane found himself an honoured member of John Cotton's congregation.

A year later he was chosen governor of the colony, Winthrop, who was twice his age, being appointed his deputy. '' Because he was son and heir to a Privy Councillor in England, the ships congratulated his election with a volley

of great shot,'' comments the Journal. But
Vane deserved the salutes of the cannon on
his own account as well as on his family's.
He was a remarkable youth. In the perplexing
civil and religious controversies which now
came crowding thick and fast, he soon found
scope, however, for all the tolerance and good
judgment he could possibly command.

The most appealing of these controversies,
from the point of view of those who care
chiefly for the human side of history, was
that which centred about Mrs. Hutchinson. A
later chapter will discuss this matter in some
detail, so we will here touch upon it only so
far as it concerns the young governor, precipitated, at twenty-four, into disputes that would
have made many an older head ache with their
complexities. Like a youth he took the generous and what proved to be the wrong (?)
side of the question. And this, added to the
fact that his sudden elevation had nursed deep
jealousies of him, proved his undoing in Massachusetts. Naught did it avail that he showed
great sagacity in dealing with the Indians and
extraordinary tact in smoothing the ruffled
sensibilities of the older magistrates. The fact
remained that he was too popular with the
masses, too young, too handsome, too zealous

for liberty of conscience to be acceptable to those who had borne the burden and heat of colonization and who saw their hard-won peace threatened by people with opinions subversive of theirs.

Even the noble Winthrop indulged, on at least one occasion, in jealousy of Vane's popularity. The case in point occurred after the elder man had again been elected governor and so would, in the natural order of things, have entertained all distinguished visitors from abroad. But Lord James Ley (afterwards the Earl of Marlborough) snubbed his advances. He was then only a youth of nineteen and he made no secret of preferring the society of the magnetic Vane to that of the dignified Winthrop. Vane had no house of his own for, upon arriving in Boston, he went to live with Mr. Cotton and there, or in an addition made to the parsonage, stayed throughout his sojourn in Boston. But if he could not entertain Lord Ley in his own mansion he could put him up at the inn of a friend, which he at once proceeded to do, Winthrop at the moment being away on a two-days' visit to Lynn and Salem. The inn in question was that of Mr. Cole[1] and when the governor, upon his

[1] See "Among Old New England Inns."

return, proffered hospitality to Lord Ley, the latter politely declined, saying he " came not to be troublesome to any and the house where he was, was so well governed that he could be as private here as elsewhere." That Winthrop deeply resented this and an incident that followed is shown by an entry in his Journal under date of July, 1637: " The differences grew so much here," he wrote, referring to the religious troubles, " as tended fast to a separation; so as Mr. Vane being among others, invited by the Governor to accompany the Lord Ley at dinner, not only refused to come, alleging by letter that his conscience withheld him, but also, at the same hour, he went over to Noddle's Island to dine with Mr. Maverick, and carried the Lord Ley with him." This happened at the end of Vane's stay in America, however, and we are only at the beginning.

The first act of his administration, accomplished within a week of his induction into office, was one at which no one could cavil. It was an amicable arrangement by which all inward-bound vessels agreed to come to anchor below the fort in the harbour and wait there for the governor's pass; further, the captains agreed to submit their invoices to the inspection of the government before discharging

their cargoes; and, in addition, they gave their
word that their crews should never be permitted to remain on shore after sunset except
under urgent necessity. These measures, all
of which made for the preservation of order
in the community, were exceedingly important;
but only a Vane could have carried them
through, for they required the kind of han-
dling no previous governor could give.

Soon, however, there arose a complication
which no human creature could have solved
to the satisfaction of everybody. A contuma-
cious mate of the British vessel Hector, observing that the king's colours were not displayed at the fort, declared, on the deck of his
vessel and in the presence of many of the
townspeople then visiting her, that the colonists were all " traitors and rebels." Of
course, the government had to take cognizance
of this and, equally of course, the mate was
made to apologize. But, after the dignity of
the colony had been vindicated, the fact still
remained that the king's colours were *not* fly-
ing at the fort and the British officers could
not say that they were should news of the affair be wafted back to England and the king
moved to ask questions about the matter.
Would not the governor, then, be so kind as

to run up a flag, just to save their consciences?

Now, on the surface, this seemed an exceedingly reasonable request for British officers to make of a colony which held a charter from the crown and resented as an insult the imputation that they were "rebels." But the English flag displayed a "papal cross," an abomination no Puritan could bear! And on the board of magistrates who were requested to hoist this ensign sat John Endicott who, in a fit of insensate rage against the "emblem of papacy," had cut the red cross out of the flag! The issue was for a time deferred by the explanation that the whole colony contained not a single flag. But when the unsuspecting captains courteously offered to present a flag to be hoisted at the fort, the magistrates, unable longer to dodge the issue, had to explain how matters stood. But they promised to display the king's colours on the king's fort, though protesting that they were fully persuaded that the cross in those same colours seemed to them idolatrous. The matter being thus adjusted to the satisfaction of everybody, the conference was brought to a close.

But the clergy, who had a finger in every pie, were yet to be reckoned with, and when the case was submitted to them, that evening,

BOSTON
PUBLIC
LIBRARY

JOHN ENDICOTT

in accordance with the practice of the government upon all important and difficult questions, they gave it as their opinion that the magistrates had erred in saying that a flag bearing the badge of Romish superstition should be displayed on any terms whatever over Puritan soil. Whereupon the poor captains were ordered to appear next morning, the whole matter was again threshed out and the board voted, on reconsideration, *not* to display the flag. Governor Vane, though as conscientious a Puritan as any of them, could not sympathize with such proceedings. They seemed to him not only inconsistent but absurdly overscrupulous. Mr. Dudley agreed with him and, the magistrates obstinately adhering to their last determination, the flag was displayed without the authority of the government and upon the personal responsibility of Mr. Vane and Mr. Dudley. In this case, as in dozens of crises which came later in his life, Sir Harry exhibited an admirable sense of proportion and justified Milton's characterization of him as " Vane, young in year, but in sage counsel old." For had he not taken the action which he did on this occasion the colony would without doubt have been precipitated into enormous difficulties with which it was in no posi-

tion then to cope. But, of course, he had to
pay the price of his diplomacy. Had he not
begun his career by defying the clergy? The
attitude which he took in the Mrs. Hutchinson
affair naturally did not help his cause. He
believed with all his soul in religious liberty
and, into the bargain, he admired Mrs. Hutchinson as a woman of unquestionable piety as
well as talent. Moreover, he was fresh from
Geneva, where the impress of Calvin was still
sharp and inclined all interested in intellectual
pursuits to a delight in fine-spun theological
discussion.

The occasion of his break with the ruling
powers was, however, a law passed after Winthrop was again governor to the effect that a
heavy penalty should be imposed upon any
person who should receive into his house a
stranger coming with intent to reside, or let
to such an one a lot or habitation, without, in
every instance, obtaining particular permission of one of the standing council, or two of
the assistant magistrates; and a large fine was
also to be levied upon any person, which should
without such permission, allow a stranger a
residence. This law was aimed to prevent the
reception into the colony of several friends of
Rev. John Wheelwright, who would have

joined the Hutchinson faction, but it was felt
by many beside Harry Vane to be a violation
of the rights of the people. So incensed were
the inhabitants of Boston that they refused
to meet the governor, as was their custom,
when he returned from the legislature. Vane's
stand in the matter was the broad liberty-loving one of a man cosmopolitan by nature, Winthrop's that of a colonist bent, above everything else, upon preserving peace in the country for which he had given his all. Both were
honest with themselves and right from their
own standpoint, only Vane had the far view
as against Winthrop's short sight. In all justice to the latter, however, it seems fair to remember that he had suffered much more than
Vane for the peace he was bent upon securing.
Nor could he sail away, as Vane soon did, to
a glorious career elsewhere. It is good, in this
connection, to be able to record that Vane
never forgot the country to which he had dedicated his ardent youth, and that Winthrop has
left to posterity this cordial eulogy of the man
who, for a time, utterly eclipsed him in a community of which he was founder and patri-
arch: '' Although he might have taken occasion against us for some dishonor, which he
apprehended to have been unjustly put upon

him here, yet he showed himself at all times a true friend to New England and a man of noble and generous mind.''

Soon after returning to England Vane married, and for a time it seemed as though he would remain in retirement and lead the quiet happy life of an English country-gentleman. But in the spring of 1640 he was induced to enter Parliament and, soon after, he was made Treasurer of the Navy and knighted by King Charles. Almost immediately, as a result of this preferment, he was singled out for vengeance and insult by Sir Thomas Wentworth, afterward the Earl of Strafford. The means chosen by Wentworth to incense Sir Harry seems rather clumsy to us of to-day. The family seat of the Vanes was Raby Castle, and it was here that Sir Harry's father had been wont to entertain King Charles with such feudal splendour and princely pageantry as Scott has described for all time in '' Kenilworth.'' To this castle the younger Sir Harry Vane would naturally fall heir, and so, purely out of contempt, as Wentworth's own biographer admits, the Earl of Strafford had his patent to the peerage made out with the style and title Baron Raby of Raby Castle, '' an act of the most unnecessary provocation and one which was the chief occasion of the loss of Strafford's head.''

For the elder Sir Harry Vane was not of a forgiving nature and, from now on, he pursued Lord Strafford with a fixed and deadly hostility. His son, on the other hand, felt himself free of embarrassing loyalties to a king who would permit his father to be so insulted and he forthwith devoted himself openly to the advocacy of those principles of freedom for which he had always contended. When Charles dissolved Parliament because it had not voted him the supplies he had asked for our Sir Harry was immediately reëlected. And as he was now in the Long Parliament (so called in consequence of an act which it passed early in its session, and which the king was infatuated enough to sign, by which the body was assured against its own dissolution, except by its consent in both houses), the young member for Kingston upon Hull was for quite a term of years in a position greatly to influence the England of his time.

Here, as in the Massachusetts colony, he soon came to be a leader. Hallam, in his Constitutional History of England, accounts for this fact thus: '' He was not only incorrupt but disinterested, inflexible in conforming his public conduct to his principles, and averse to every sanguinary and oppressive measure; qualities not common in revolutionary chiefs.'' This very temperate dictum gives one rather a chill for the fact of the matter was that Vane was positively heroic in his contention for peace and liberty of conscience and abhorred every form of persecution and bigotry. Great as was his personal dislike for all that Papacy implied, he so exerted himself in the cause of Catholic emancipation as to bring down upon his head denunciations from Protestants whose cause he would have died for. Similarly, in the negotiations between Charles and the Parliament, he struggled with all his might for such terms as would assure to the people the rights which they had lost. And yet, when Colonel Pride forcibly ejected the members opposed to his views and principles he would not stay with '' The Rump,'' preferring retirement to a triumph gained in so illegal a manner. Of all the republicans he alone refused to profit by power thus gained.

Consequently Sir Harry Vane cannot be held in the least degree responsible for the impeachment, trial and execution of King Charles. He heartily disapproved of the whole proceeding. And when Cromwell came to him in February,

1649, to urge the purity of his intentions as a reason for Vane's becoming a member of the Council Sir Harry only reluctantly agreed to accept the honour and would not take the oath of office until the clause which approved of the trial and condemnation of Charles was struck out.

In the foreign wars which followed Vane bore a glorious part and when the people felt as too oppressive the taxes these struggles entailed he voluntarily relinquished the profits of his office as treasurer and commissioner for the navy. Later, when Cromwell followed the desperate determination which had insidiously taken possession of him and on April 20, 1653, grasped once for all the power with which he had been dallying, Vane was the first to leap to his feet in stinging rebuke of his treacherous course. We are not surprised to read in history that Oliver's retort to this was the exclamation, in a fit of unbounded passion, " Sir Harry Vane! Sir Harry Vane! Good Lord deliver me from Sir Harry Vane." After which he seized the records, snatched the bill from the hands of the clerk, drove the members out at the point of the bayonet, locked the doors, put the key in his pocket and returned to Whitehall to observe that the spirit of God had been too strong upon him longer to be resisted.

Tyranny once more having the upper hand in England there was nothing for Sir Harry Vane to do but again to retire to Raby Castle and pursue his philosophical and theological studies while awaiting a time when he could again serve the " good cause," as he termed it, of the people's rights and liberties. The occasion for which he longed came duly. Following his policy of giving a sanctimonious face to each new encroachment upon liberty the Protector, as a step in his plan to make himself king and settle upon his descendants forever the crown he had wrested from its rightful owner, published, on March 15, 1656, a declaration calling upon the people to observe a general fast to the end that counsel and direction might come to the government from Providence concerning the best ways of promoting peace and happiness in England.

To Cromwell's unbounded surprise and indignation Sir Harry Vane took him at his word and composed a paper entitled " A Healing Question propounded and resolved, upon Occasion of the late public and seasonable Call to Humiliation in order to Love and Union amongst the honest Party, and with a Desire

Oliver Cromwell

BOSTON
PUBLIC
LIBRARY

to apply Balm to the Wound, before it become
incurable. By Henry Vane, Knight.'' With
perfect good faith he transmitted his paper
privately to Cromwell before giving to the
world any hint of the advice therein contained.
But when, after the lapse of a month, the manuscript was returned without comment Sir
Harry immediately issued it from the press
together with a Postscript in which allusion
was made to the fact that it had been previously communicated to Cromwell.

Now, whether Cromwell had read the manuscript or not we shall never know, but he was
furious at its publication and sent Vane a peremptory and harshly-worded summons to appear at once before the Council on the ground
that his paper tended to the disturbance of the
present government and the peace of the Commonwealth. Of course it did, for in this, one
of the most remarkable documents ever penned
by man, Vane had asserted, for the first time
in history, the need of a written constitution
or body of fundamental laws by which the government itself should be controlled! In answering the dictatorial summons of the Council
Vane added fuel to the flames by remarking,
'' I cannot but observe, in this proceeding with
me, how exactly they tread in the steps of the

late king, whose design being to set the government free from all restraint of laws, as to our persons and estates, and to render the monarchy absolute, thought he could employ no better means to effect it, than by casting into obloquy and disgrace all those who desired to preserve the laws and liberties of the nation." His letter concludes: " It is no small grief to be lamented that the evil and wretched principles by which the late king aimed to work out his design, should now revive and spring up under the hands of men professing godliness." For this and the pamphlet which preceded it Vane was imprisoned in Carisbrook Castle on the Isle of Wight and, when Oliver feared longer to keep him in durance, was hunted down on his own stamping-ground and unlawfully deprived of his estates.

Then, in the fall of 1658, Oliver went to meet a King whom he could not bully and Richard Cromwell assumed the Protectorate. This was more than even Sir Harry Vane could stand with patience. Oliver had at least been a foe worthy of his steel; but that the opportunity for a republic should be set aside in order that this feeble creature should hold office was too much for any man with high hopes of England to bear. Sir Harry again offered himself for

Parliament and, when he had been cheated out of two elections given him by the franchises of the people, he tried in a third district, that of Whitchurch in Hampshire, and was returned in spite of the machinations of his enemies. Then he made in Parliament what seems to me one of the best short speeches I have ever read:

" Mr. Speaker, Among all the people of the universe, I know none who have shown so much zeal for the liberty of their country, as the English at this time have done. They have, by the help of Divine Providence, overcome all obstacles and have made themselves free. We have driven away the hereditary tyranny of the house of Stuart, at the expense of much blood and treasure, in hopes of enjoying hereditary liberty, after having shaken off the yoke of kingship, and there is not a man amongst us who could have imagined that any person would be so bold as to dare attempt the ravishing from us that freedom which has cost us so much blood and so much labour.

" But so it happens, I know not by what misfortune, we are fallen into the error of those who poisoned the Emperor Titus to make room for Domitian, who made away Augustus that they might have Tiberius and changed Claudius for Nero. I am sensible these examples are foreign from my subject since the Romans in those days were buried in lewdness and luxury; whereas the people of England are now renowned all over the world for their great virtue and discipline, — and yet suffer an idiot without courage, without sense, nay, without ambition, to have dominion in a country of liberty.

" One could bear a little with *Oliver* Cromwell, though contrary to his oath of fidelity to the Parliament, contrary to his duty to the public, contrary to the respect he owed to that venerable body from whom he received his authority, he usurped the government. His merit was so extraordinary that our judgement and passions might be blinded by it. He made his way to empire by the most illustrious actions. He held under his command an army that had made him a conqueror and a people that had made him their general.

" But as for *Richard* Cromwell, his son, who is he? What are his titles? We have seen that he has a sword by his side, but did he ever draw it? And, what is of more importance in this case, is he fit to get obedience from a mighty nation who could never make a footman obey him? Yet, we must recognize this man as our

king under the style of Protector — a man
without birth, without courage, without conduct. For my part, I declare, sir, it shall never
be said that I made such a man my master.''

Following this remarkable triumph of oratory Richard Cromwell was forced to resign,
the famous Long Parliament was reassembled,
and Sir Henry Vane was appointed one of the
Committee of Safety, to whom the supreme
and entire power of the country was entrusted
until Parliament could make further arrangements. Later he was made President of the
Council. And if General George Monk had not
sold the army to Prince Charles for the title
of a duke Vane's dream of a republican England would in all probability have been realized. As it was, Charles the Second was
crowned and England given over to the scourge
of an unbridled tyranny.

Of course Sir Harry Vane was among the
first to fall a victim to the treachery of the army
and of Parliament. He was imprisoned, first
in his own castle and then on the island of
Sicily, while the king waited until he should
be strong enough to claim his life. Then he
kept him for another season in the Tower. In
the Declaration of Breda Charles had proclaimed amnesty to all not especially excepted

by Parliament and as Sir Harry had not been
one of his father's judges and was a well-known
opponent of the action taken by the regicides,
it had been supposed that he would be quite
secure from the vengeance of the new monarch.
Moreover, the two Houses of Parliament had
been assured through the Lord Chancellor that,
" If Vane were ever convicted, execution as
to his life should be remitted." It was because
this appeared to be sufficient that Sir Harry
Vane's name was excepted from the Act of Indemnity and Oblivion which the Commons
framed.

When a new Parliament came in, however,
and, stimulated by desire to get a share of Sir
Harry's great estate, pushed matters vigorously against him, the king had either to redeem or break his pledge. Characteristically
he shifted the burden of decision upon his
Chancellor in the following letter which shows,
as well as a whole volume of history could, the
manner of man who now ruled England:

" HAMPTON COURT, Saturday,
" Two in the afternoon.
" The relation that has been made to me of
Sir Henry Vane's carriage yesterday in the
Hall, is the occasion of this letter; which, if

SIR HARRY VANE'S HOUSE, STILL STANDING IN HAMPSTEAD, LONDON

BOSTON PUBLIC LIBRARY

I am rightly informed, was so insolent as to
justify all he had done, acknowledging no supreme power in England but a Parliament, and
many things to that purpose. You have had
a true account of all and if he has given new
occasion to be hanged, certainly he is too dangerous a man to let live, if we can honestly put
him out of the way. Think of this and give
me some account of it to-morrow, till when I
have no more to say to you.   C. R."

The end soon came. Sir Harry was by this
time in the Tower and the king was thirsting,
as he very well knew, for his blood. When it
was suggested to Vane that he might save his
life by making submission to Charles he answered simply, "If the king does not think
himself more conserved for his honour and
word than I am for my life let him take it."
And indeed nothing could have availed. His
trial was long but unfair from beginning to
end and, even when he came to the block, looking very handsome in his black clothes and
scarlet waistcoat, he was given none of the
privileges usually accorded those about to die.
Pepys, who was on hand for the execution as
for most other interesting spectacles that happened during his lifetime, describes, with every

mark of admiration, the bearing of the prisoner, adding further, loyalist though he was, that " the king lost more by that man's death than he will get again for a good while." Another loyalist exclaimed in admiration, as he watched the dignity of those last moments, " He dies like a prince." To which I can only add, after reading his wonderful prayer for those who had betrayed him, that he died like *the* Prince, — that Prince of Peace whose principles he had all his life advocated and whose sublime example he followed even in the hour of his death.

VI

SCARCELY had Winthrop been chosen governor for the fourth time when (June, 1643) there came to Boston to entreat help against his rival, Charnissay D'Aulnay, Charles La Tour, one of the lords of New France and perhaps the most picturesque figure in the early history of this continent. The manner of this powerful Frenchman's arrival in Boston was most disconcerting to the Puritans. For he came in a French armed ship and sailed straight up the harbour, past a fort in which there was not a single person to answer his military salute! Had he been an enemy he might easily have sacked the town.

As it was, he made his début in Boston in a charmingly simple fashion. For coming toward his ship as it sailed up the bay was discerned a boat containing Mrs. Gibbons, the wife of Captain Edward Gibbons, going with her children to their farm. One of the gentle-

men on La Tour's vessel recognized her and
told La Tour who she was. Whereupon the
lord of New France had a boat of his own
fitted out and proceeded to follow the lady to
her landing-place. Mrs. Gibbons, not knowing
the strangers, hastened from them as fast as
she could and put in at Governor's Island, so
called because it was the summer home of the
Winthrops. But it happened that the governor
and some of his family were on the island at
the time, so La Tour was able, by having pursued her, the more speedily to get in touch with
the very person whom he had come to see!
While he was telling his story over the hos-
pitable supper-table, Mrs. Gibbons returned
to town in the governor's boat and spread the
news of the stranger's informal arrival, so that
when La Tour, later, took the governor up to
Boston in his own boat, they were met by three
shallops of armed men, come out to escort them
ceremoniously into the town.

Before proceeding to describe the negotiations which went on between Winthrop and
this representative of a foreign state, let us,
however, digress a bit and learn who this La
Tour was and why he had come to Boston.
To make the matter clear one must go back
to the very beginnings of the settlement of

New France and retrace the story of Champlain's second expedition to the St. Lawrence, when in 1604 he sailed under De Monts (to whom the King of France had granted the land), in company with Baron de Poutrincourt, Pontgravé and divers merchants, priests and Huguenot ministers. This variously assorted company on exploration and colonization bent settled on St. Croix Island, in the mouth of St. Croix River, now the boundary between Maine and New Brunswick. There they passed their first winter in America. But the next year they crossed the Bay of Fundy and founded Port Royal on the wooded shore of Annapolis Basin, in the very heart of that country where

> . . . the murmuring pines and the hemlocks,
> Bearded with moss, and in garments green, indistinct in
>   the twilight,
> Stand like Druids of old, with voices sad and prophetic,
> Stand like harpers hoar, with beards that rest on their
>   bosoms.

It was a wonderfully peaceful land which they found; and so it continued to be — even when the colonists suffered most from want and privation — until the passions of ambitious men and the schemings and counter-schemings of rival branches of the priesthood

availed to transform it into a scene of feudal-
istic strife.

Champlain's men had been content to work
hard and deny themselves, to live cleanly and
to beguile their days with gardening, verse-
making and a *nonchalant* Christianization of
the Indians. Not so their sons. Poutrincourt's son cared chiefly for war, and soon
built among the rocks and fogs of Cape Sable
a small fort to which he gave the name Fort
Lomeron. This fort descended at his death to
Charles La Tour, one of his adventurous retainers, and was by him called Fort St. Louis.

La Tour, by improving to the utmost every
chance that came his way and by winning the
alliance of both English and French, soon made
himself a terrifying power in the Acadian land.
To his first fort he ere long added another
variously called to-day Fort La Tour and Fort
St. Jean — the latter from its situation at the
mouth of the river, in the centre of the present
city of St. John, N. B.

Strong as Charles La Tour had succeeded in
becoming, an even stronger man was soon to
arrive from France. Under Claude de Razilly
(a knight of Malta, charged by Louis XIII to
seize the Acadian possessions), had sailed
D'Aulnay Charnissay, a gentleman of birth,

and to him in 1635 there came by Razilly's
death royal power in Acadia. D'Aulnay made
his headquarters at Port Royal, and nobody
thought of disputing his authority, so clearly
could it be traced to the king — nobody, *except* La Tour. That adventurer, having papers
from both the English and the French, and
having besides an indomitable spirit and inex-
haustible craft, made D'Aulnay's situation
from the very beginning well-nigh unbearable.

In position and qualities the two rivals were
poles apart. D'Aulnay came of an old and
distinguished Touraine family, and he prided
himself above all things upon his character of
gentilhomme français. He was a consistent
Catholic, too, while La Tour's religion — like
his family — was obscure. The rivalry, which
had always been keen, appears to have grown
into positive bitterness, when, five years after
his first coming to Acadia, D'Aulnay returned
from a visit to France, bringing with him a
charming wife. The plucky bride was a daughter of the *Seigneur de Courcelles,* and was well
fitted by birth and breeding to transmute, by
her gentlewoman's touch, the rough settlement
into an orderly colony. What with old settlers
and new, about forty families were now gathered at Port Royal and on the river Annapolis.

And over these D'Aulnay ruled, '' a kind of feudal Robinson Crusoe.''

A scene for an artist, as Parkman points out, was the Port Royal of those days, with its fort, its soldiers, its manor-house of logs, its seminary of like construction, and its twelve Capuchin friars, with cowled heads, sandaled feet and the cord of St. Francis! The friars were supported by Richelieu; their main business — and they were pretty successful in it — was to convert the Micmac and Abenaki Indians into loyal vassals of France and earnest subjects of the Church.

But Charles La Tour was not so easily dealt with. He who had before felt himself the chief man in Acadia was now fairly aflame with jealousy of this French *seigneur* who dwelt just across the intervening Bay of Fundy, surrounded by loyal retainers and solaced by a loving wife. Wives, however, were certainly to be had even if settlers were not; and since D'Aulnay had given evidence, by bringing over a woman, that he had no intention of abandoning his claim, La Tour resolved that he, too, would set up a home in Acadia. His agent was thereupon instructed to pick out in France a girl worthy to share his heart and fort. Accordingly, Marie Jacquelin, daughter of a bar-

ber of Mans, was selected to join La Tour at
Fort St. Jean. She proved to be an Amazon.
With passionate vehemence she took up her
husband's quarrel, and where D'Aulnay's lady
heartened her lord by gentle words and soft
caresses, Lady La Tour threw herself into the
thick of the fight and became a force greatly
to be feared in the Acadian land.

From this time on events march. Goaded
by his wife, La Tour grew more and more con-
tumacious, until that day when the King of
France, losing all patience, ordered D'Aulnay
to seize his rival's forts and take their com-
mander prisoner. In accordance with these instructions, we find D'Aulnay (in 1642) an-
chored at the mouth of the St. John and endeav-
ouring to arrest the outlaw. Then it was that
La Tour, rendered desperate, defied the king
as well as his representative, and — Catholic
though he claimed to be — turned for help to
the heretics of Boston.

Boston was in no position, as we have seen,
to help and La Tour's coming provided highly
disturbing matter for debate. Though he was
hospitably received by Governor Winthrop and
the Reverend John Cotton, many there were
who wished him well out of the way. Even his
unimpeachable gravity of demeanour when he

attended church with Winthrop on Sunday could not make him acceptable to these clear-sighted souls. Still, his men were not only allowed to come ashore, but permission was granted them to drill on Boston common, along with the town militia, — to the accompaniment of the ambitious band and the industrious frog chorus.

One very amusing incident is connected with the " land leave " granted the La Tour men. Winthrop, writing the next year, tells the story, not without some sense of its humour: " There arrived here a Portugal ship with salt, having in it two Englishmen only. One of these happened to be drunk and was carried to his lodging; and the constable (a godly man and a zealous against such disorders) hearing of it found him out, being upon his bed asleep; so he awaked him and led him to the stocks, there being no magistrate at home. He, being in the stocks, one of La Tour's gentlemen lifted up the stocks and let him out. The constable hearing of it, went to the Frenchman (being then gone and quiet), and would needs carry him to the stocks; the Frenchman offered to yield himself to go to prison, but the constable, not understanding his language, pressed him to go to the stocks; the Frenchman resisted

and drew his sword; with that company came
in and disarmed him and carried him by force
to the stocks; but soon after the constable took
him out and carried him to prison, and presently after, took him forth again and delivered
him to La Tour. Much tumult there was about
this."

The magistrates looked into the case and
decided that the gentleman must return to
prison until the Court met. Some Frenchmen
offered to go bail for him, but since they were
strangers their offer was declined. "Upon
this," continues Winthrop, "two Englishmen,
members of the church of Boston, standing by,
offered to be his sureties, whereupon he was
bailed till he should be called for, because La
Tour was not like to stay till the Court. This
was thought too much favour for such an offence by many of the common people, but by
our law bail could not be denied him; and beside the constable was the occasion of all this
in transgressing the bounds of his office, and
that in six things: 1. In fetching a man out
of his lodging that was asleep on his bed and
that without any warrant from the authority.
2. In not putting a hook upon the stocks nor
setting some to guard them. 3. In laying
hands upon the Frenchman that had opened

the stocks when he was gone and quiet, and
no disturbance then appearing. 4. In carrying him to prison without warrant. 5. In de-
livering him out of prison without warrant.
6. In putting such a reproach upon a stranger
and a gentleman when there was no need, for
he knew he would be forthcoming and the magistrate would be at home that evening; but
such are the fruits of ignorant and misguided
zeal.''

The clever La Tours lost no time in pushing
the business upon which they had come. Showing papers which would seem to prove the
doughty Charles a lawful representative of the
King of France, the governor was asked for
such aid as would enable him to bring to his
fort the ship, containing supplies, which D'Aulnay would not permit to proceed up the bay.
Very adroitly La Tour then suggested that he
at least be permitted to *hire* four vessels, each
fully armed and equipped, with which to defend
his rights in Acadia.

Winthrop finally gave bewildered consent to
this arrangement, and his action was approved
by a majority of those in authority. But in the
ensuing discussion over this arresting departure, the '' inevitable clergy '' joined hotly, and
texts being the chief weapons of the debate,

various Old Testament worthies were brought
forward to prove that Massachusetts would
have done much better to keep out of the fight.
John Endicott stoutly maintained that La Tour
was not to be trusted, and that he and D'Aulnay would much better have been left to fight
it out by themselves. In this opinion several
chief men of the colony concurred, saying in
the famous " Ipswich letter " that they feared
international law had been ill observed, and
declaring in substance, that the merits of the
case were not clear, that the colony was not
called upon in charity to help La Tour (see 2
Chronicles xix, 2, and Proverbs xxvi, 17); that
this quarrel was for England and France; that
endless trouble would come if D'Aulnay were
not completely put down, and that " he that
loses his life in an unnecessary quarrel dies the
devil's martyr."

This letter, trenching as it did upon Winthrop's pride of office, stung the governor into
vehement retort. But he soon had the candour
to admit that he had been in fault in three
things: first in answering La Tour too hastily,
next in not sufficiently consulting the elders,
and lastly in not having opened the discussion
with prayer.

But La Tour had meanwhile received his

ships, and was able with them to rout D'Aulnay's three vessels. His lady alertly followed up this advantage, visiting France to help strengthen his cause, and coming back by way of Boston. This visit on the part of the redoubtable madam seems not to have been of her planning, however. She had engaged Captain Bayley to transport her from London to Acadia whither she was anxious to bring, as soon as might be, stores and munitions which should aid her husband. But Bayley chose to put in at Boston.

Promptly Madam La Tour sued him for damages, alleging that the six months consumed by the voyage had been an unreasonable length of time and that he had not taken her to Acadia as bargained for. The jury awarded her £2,000, for which Captain Bayley's ship was attached. This proved to be worth only £1,100, however, and it cost the Lady about £700 to hire vessels to convey her and her effects to Acadia. The colony, too, had ultimately to pay the damages it had awarded her. For the owners of the ship and cargo which Lady La Tour had attached promptly seized a Boston ship in London to indemnify themselves and, when it became doubtful whether they would be able to hold her, attached the bodies of Stephen Winthrop, the governor's son, who happened to be then in London, and of Captain Joseph Weld, who had been on the jury when the La Tour damages were awarded. Sir Harry Vane nobly came to the rescue of the Bostonians, thus winning from Winthrop the acknowledgment that "both now and at other times Mr. Vane showed himself a true friend of New England and a man of a noble and generous mind."

Meanwhile Lady La Tour had arrived back at her stamping-ground and had offered her husband a very shrewd piece of advice. "Go to Boston, declare yourself to be a Protestant," she counselled, "ask for a minister to preach to the men at the fort, and promise that if the Bostonians help us to master D'Aulnay and conquer Acadia, we will share our conquests with them." This Machiavellian suggestion La Tour seized with avidity, and sailed gaily forth.

Scarcely had he gone when his lady, falling one day into a transport of fury at some unpleasant turn of events, so berated and reviled the Récollet friars at Fort St. Jean, that they refused to stay under her roof, and set out for Port Royal in the depth of winter, taking with them eight strong soldiers, who were too good

Catholics to remain longer in such a hotbed of heresy. At Port Royal this little party was most warmly received. D'Aulnay paid the eight soldiers their long overdue wages and lodged the friars with his own priests. Then he plied them all with questions and, learning that La Tour had gone to Boston, leaving only forty-five men to defend his wife and his fortress, he saw Heaven's smile at last, and leaped to seize the golden opportunity opened to him.

Every man about Port Royal was hastily mustered into action. Then D'Aulnay crossed the Bay of Fundy with all his force, erected a fort on the west side of the river, and, after delaying for a time in an attempt to win over more of La Tour's men (capturing incidentally a small vessel which had been sent from Boston loaded with provisions and bearing a letter to tell Lady La Tour that her husband would join her in a month), he brought his cannons into position, and made as if he would batter down the fortress. The garrison was summoned to surrender, but when for answer they hung out a red flag and " shouted a thousand insults and blasphemies," accompanying the same with a volley of cannon shots directed by the intrepid Amazon, D'Aulnay could do nothing but fight the thing to a finish. In spite of the gallant

FORT LA TOUR (OR ST. JEAN), ST. JOHN, NEW BRUNSWICK, FROM
A DRAWING BY LOUIS A. HOLMAN

defence of Madame La Tour, D'Aulnay's superior numbers prevailed. All resistance was overcome; the fort was pillaged, and all the survivors of the garrison, including Madame La Tour, were taken prisoners. At first the lady was left at liberty, but after she had been detected in an attempt to communicate with her husband by means of an Indian, she was put into confinement. Then, and then only, did she fall ill. Three weeks later she was dead.

D'Aulnay had now robbed his rival of his wife and captured Fort St. Jean, the best trading station in Acadia. The King complimented him highly, and when he demanded reparation for the part Boston had taken against him his right to satisfaction was indirectly admitted. Winthrop had learned his lesson. D'Aulnay's stay as described in the governor's Journal makes interesting reading:

" It being the Lord's day [of September, 1646] and the people ready to go to the assembly after dinner, Monsieur Marie and Monsieur Louis, with Monsieur D'Aulnay [and] his secretary arrived at Boston in a small pinnace and Major Gibbons sent two of his chief officers to meet them at the waterside who conducted them to their lodgings without noise or bustle. The public worship being ended the

Governor repaired home, and sent Major Gibbons with other gentlemen and a guard of musketeers to attend them to the Governor's house, who meeting them without his door carried them into his house, where they were entertained with wine and sweetmeats, and after a while he accompanied them to their lodgings being the house of Major Gibbons, where they were entertained that night.

" The next morning they repaired to the Governor, and delivered him their commission, which was in form of a letter directed to the Governor and magistrates. . . . Their diet was provided at the ordinary, where the Magistrates used to diet in Court times; and the Governor accompanied them always at meals. Their manner was to repair to the Governor's house every morning about eight of the clock, who accompanied them to the place of meeting; and at night either himself or some of the Commissioners, accompanied them to their lodgings."

A great deal of ceremony surely for a little place like Boston! But then, D'Aulnay had asked £8,000 indemnity and the government had to look as if it *could* pay in case it had to. The Commissioners, though, sturdily denied " any guilt " on their part maintaining that

they had only permitted La Tour to *hire* the
vessels. And they brought counter-charges
against D'Aulnay. Finally, it was agreed that
the matter be settled amicably and that Boston
" send a small present to D'Aulnay in satisfaction." A treaty was accordingly signed. In
due time the proposed " small present " was
sent. It consisted of a sedan chair which the
marauding Captain Cromwell had taken as a
prize and presented to Winthrop a few months
before. Winthrop gave it to D'Aulnay, as he
frankly says, because it was of no value to him!

But the suite of the victorious French lord
was sent off with all possible honours just the
same " the Governor and our Commissioners
accompanying them to their boat, attended
with a guard of musketeers, and gave them five
guns from Boston, three from Charlestown,
and five from Castle Island; and we sent them
aboard a quarter cask of sack and some mutton. . . ." D'Aulnay was evidently satisfied
with the results of his visit. For he had not in
the least expected the large sum of money for
which he had asked. All that he wished to
make clear to the Puritans was that they
should fit out no more expeditions for La Tour.
And now, when he had made this point, forced
Fortune to crown his life-work and saw ahead

of him promise of a thriving trade and a constantly growing colony,

"Death stepped tacitly and took him."

On the 24th of May, 1650, as he and his valet were canoeing in the basin of Port Royal, not far from the mouth of the Annapolis, their frail craft overturned, and though they clung to it and got astride of it, one at either end, in an endeavour to save themselves, they could not. At the end of an hour and a half D'Aulnay was dead, not from drowning but from cold, for the water still retained the chill of winter. So Father Ignace, the Superior of the Capuchins, found him. With fitting ceremonies he was buried in the chapel of the fort at Port Royal in the presence of his soldiers, his tenants and his sorrowing wife.

That poor, poor wife! For she still had Charles La Tour to deal with, and with him her own life was destined to be linked. That La Tour had friends in France she soon came to know only too well. Through false papers, intrigues and dastardly treachery Port Royal was promptly wrested from her, and she was even persuaded to return to La Tour Fort St. Jean, which her husband had taken fairly in a well-fought fight. Beset with insidious ene-

mies and tortured beyond endurance by fears
for her eight young children, the brave spirit
of this lovely woman broke with her heart, and
three years after the death of her noble husband she *married* (February 24, 1653) the man
who had so long been her tormentor. With
him she took up her abode at Fort St. Jean.
Of the children for whose sake she had sold
herself the four boys were killed in the wars
of Louis XIV, and the girls all became nuns.
So no single trace of D'Aulnay's blood may
to-day be found in the land for which he gave
his life and wealth out of the great love he
bore France and the Church.

The significant lesson of this whole episode
so far as Boston history is concerned lies, however, in the fact that what was, properly speaking, an international matter took place wholly
within the borders of the town; and that Massachusetts assumed, throughout, the attitude
of a completely independent government, dealing with D'Aulnay and La Tour just as inde-
pendently and in the same manner as Charles
and Buckingham dealt with the Huguenots and
the French monarchy. We shall do well to
recall this incident later on in Boston's history
and contrast it with the claims made by England in regard to her attitude of '' protection.''

VII

FREEDOM TO WORSHIP GOD

CRITICS of the Puritans, taking their text from Mrs. Heman's poem, are disposed to judge harshly, on the ground of inconsistency, that band of earnest Christians, who, coming here because they had been persecuted in England persecuted in their turn those who ventured upon a spiritual angle in any degree different from their own. Such critics are, however, confusing the ideals cherished by our forefathers with their own ideals for them. *They* never claimed that their object in coming here was to secure for all men the boon of freedom in religion. On the contrary, they said quite plainly that the object of their emigration was to escape oppression for *themselves*. Upon that they laid the emphasis; and with that they stopped.

Far from being inconsistent they adhered through fire and water to their own self-defensive principle. All their legislation, all the

arrangements of their society were framed to
secure this object. It was in accordance with
this that they reserved to themselves the right
of admitting only whom they pleased as freemen of the colony; and it was to this end that,
a little more than a year after their arrival,
they " ordered and agreed that, for time to
come, no man should be admitted to the freedom of the body politic, but such as are members of some of the churches within the limits
of the same." To them such an ordinance
seemed the one and only way of forming the
Christian republic towards which their hearts
yearned, a community in which the laws of
Moses should constitute the rules of civil life
and in which the godly clergy should be the
interpreters of those rules.

Of course, the weakness of the system lay
in the fact that the clergy were only men. And
being men, of like passions with ourselves, they
grew, by the very deference they fed upon,
into creatures insatiate for power. But piti-
fully narrow though they were, revoltingly
cruel though they soon came to be, it should
nevertheless be borne in mind that they were,
in almost every case, sincere. They believed
that they were conserving the great good of
Christian amity in persecuting relentlessly all

who differed from them, — and so, girding up
their loins, they gave still another turn to the
screw!

And now, having said in their defence all,
as I honestly believe, there is to be said, I can
with a clear conscience, record their persecutions and paint as darkly as I must the horrors
of that terrible era. To understand it all we
must bear in mind the fact that, not only was
the number of clergy among the emigrants to
Boston and vicinity large, but being men of unusual gifts, that they of necessity exercised an
enormous influence in this '' Christian republic.'' Moreover, the magistrates themselves
were, in a large number of cases men imbued
with what we may call the ecclesiastical feeling. When Governor Dudley, for instance,
came to die, there were found in his pocket
these lines which showed his own cast of mind
to have been fiercely bigoted:

" Let men of God in Courts and Churches watch
O're such as do a Toleration hatch,
Lest that Ill Egg bring forth a Cockatrice,
To poison all with heresie and vice."

The '' cockatrice '' which most powerfully
agitated Boston was Mrs. Anne Hutchinson,
delicately characterized by the Reverend

Thomas Welde as "the American Jezebel."
To students of history calmly examining to-
day the testimony on both sides, Mrs. Hutchinson stands out however as a gentlewoman of
spotless life, kind heart, brilliant mind and
superb courage. That she had a good deal of
that intellectual vanity possessed by most
clever women is also plain. And she had besides — and it was this which more than anything else occasioned her banishment — a
tongue which could and did lash furiously
those whom she disliked. Comparing with her
own clergyman — the Reverend John Cotton
— the host of other clergy then in the Massachusetts colony, she found between them a
great gulf fixed; and she said this quite distinctly to the groups of people who used to
come to her house opposite the place where
the Old South Church now stands, to hear her
discuss Mr. Cotton's sermons.

Mrs. Hutchinson came to the colony (in the
autumn of 1634) primed for religious discussion. Her father had been Francis Marbury,
a minister, first in Lincolnshire and afterwards
in London, and in the scholarly and theological
atmosphere of his house she had, for years,
been accepted as the intellectual equal of his
ministerial friends. Theology, indeed, was as

the breath of life to her and she hinted in no uncertain way to some Puritan ministers who were on the vessel during her journey to New England that they might expect to hear more from her in the new world. For she regarded herself as one with a mission.

William Hutchinson, the husband of this lady, was the type of man who is always married by strong-minded magnetic women. Winthrop has nothing but words of contempt for him, but there is little doubt that a sincere attachment existed between the married pair and that Hutchinson possessed sterling character and solid worth as well as a comfortable estate. In their Lincolnshire home the two had been parishioners of the Reverend John Cotton and regular attendants at St. Botolph's Church. When Cotton fled to escape the tyranny of the bishops, the Hutchinsons decided to follow, and when the Reverend John Wheelwright, who had married Mrs. Hutchinson's daughter, began to be persecuted in his turn their departure was naturally hastened.

Promptly upon their arrival in Boston both Hutchinsons made their application to be received as members of the church. This step was indispensable to admit the pair into Christian fellowship and to allow Mr. Hutchinson

the privilege of engaging in business and
otherwise exercising the rights of a citizen.
He came through the ordeal easily enough but,
in consequence of the reports already spread
concerning her extravagant opinions, his wife
was subjected to a most searching examination. Finally, however, she, too, was pronounced a " member in good standing " of the
congregation over which her beloved John
Cotton served as associate pastor. And now
she was ready to enter upon the career which
soon divided Boston into two violently opposed
factions and which ended by the withdrawal to
England of the brilliant young Governor Vane
and by the banishment from the colony of her
with whom he had sympathized.

Even so far back as 1635 Boston seems to
have been capable of great enthusiasm over a
woman who could persuasively present " some
new thing." The doctrine advanced by this
woman was certainly an arresting one for that
day. For, cleverly interwoven with what was
ostensibly only a recapitulation of the sermon
preached the Sunday before, ran constantly the
astonishing proclamation that there are in this
world certain " elect " who may or may not
be ordained clergy and that to them are given
direct revelations of the will of God. Now the

ministers of New England were formalists to
the core and the society which they dominated
was organized upon the basis that if a man had
a sad countenance, wore sombre garb, lived an
austere life, quoted the Bible freely, attended
worship regularly and took off his hat to the
clergy he was a good man. Such a man alone
might be a citizen. To admit, therefore, that,
in place of these convenient signs of grace, —
" works " as they were called, — one must rest
salvation upon the intimate and so necessarily
elusive relation between man and his God was
to preach political as well as spiritual revolution. The logical result of accepting Mrs.
Hutchinson's doctrines would have meant nothing less than the annihilation of those convenient earmarks by which the " good " and the
" bad " in the community could be readily distinguished, — the " good " marked for civic
advancement and the " bad " for the stocks
and banishment.

At first the far-reaching import of the lady's
views seems not to have struck her hearers.
All the leading and influential people of the
town flocked to her " parlour talks " and, for
a time, she was that very remarkable thing —
a prophet honoured in her own community.
For the matter of her " lectures " was always

pithy and bright, the leader's wit always ready
and " everybody was there," — which counted
then for righteousness just as it does now.
Hawthorne's genius has conjured up for us
the scene at one of these Hutchinson gatherings so that we, too, may attend and be among
the " crowd of hooded women and men in steeple hats and close-cropped hair . . . assembled
at the door and open windows of a house newly-
built. An earnest expression glows in every
face . . . and some pressed inward as if the
bread of life were to be dealt forth, and they
feared to lose their share."

Unfortunately Mrs. Hutchinson found the
transition between the abstract and the con-
crete as easy as every other *descensus Averni*.
From preaching against a doctrine of
" works " she soon dropped into sly digs at
the pastors who defended this belief. " A
company of legall professors," quoth she, " lie
poring on the law which Christ hath abolished." No wonder it began to be noised
abroad that the seer was casting " reproach
upon the ministers, . . . saying that none of
them did preach the covenant of free grace
but Master Cotton, and that they have not the
seale of the Spirit and so were not able ministers of the New Testament."

It was, however, in Cotton's house and not
in her own that Mrs. Hutchinson made the
fatal admission for which she had afterward
to pay so dear. The elders had come to Boston in a body to see how far Cotton " stood
for " the things his gifted parishioner was
preaching and, in the hope of clearing the
whole matter up, the clergyman had suggested
a friendly conference with Mrs. Hutchinson at
his house. The interview took place, the lady
cleverly parrying all attempts to make her say
indiscreet things. But finally, the Reverend
Hugh Peters having besought her to deal
frankly and openly with them, she admitted
that she saw a wide difference between Mr.
Cotton's ministry and theirs and that it was
because they had not the seal of the Spirit that
this difference arose. If Mrs. Hutchinson had
not thought herself in confidential intercourse
with those who were men of honour as well as
clergymen, she would never have put the thing
thus bluntly. But the event proved that her
confession was treasured up to be used against
her, — and that there were many in the colony
who chafed as she did, under the power of
those preaching this " covenant of works."
For promptly the liberals, whose mouthpiece
she had unconsciously become, blossomed out

into a sturdy political party led by the enthusiastic Vane. The part which he played in the
controversy has already been touched upon in
the previous chapter and the brave way in
which he fought against the decree which
would banish the incoming friends of Wheelwright there described.

But it all availed nothing. The theocracy
had been attacked and the clergy sprang like
one man to its defence. Even Cotton, after a
little, ranged himself on the side of his order
as against the woman who lauded him above
his brethren. The " trial," in the course of
which Mrs. Hutchinson was condemned, is one
of the ghastliest things in the history of the
colony. The prisoner, who was about to become a mother, was made to stand until she
was exhausted, the while those in whom she
had confided as friends plied her with endless questions about her theological beliefs.
Through two long weary days of hunger and
cold she defended herself as well as she could
before these " men of God," but her able
words availed nothing; she had " disparaged
the ministers " and they were resolved to be
revenged. Though Coddington pointed out
that " no law of God or man " had been broken
by the woman before them, she was none the

less banished " as unfit for our society." So
there was driven out of the city she had adopted
the most remarkable intellect Boston has ever
made historic by misunderstanding.

Roger Williams was another great and good
man of whom the city founded by Winthrop
soon proved itself unworthy. Just here seems
as good a place as any to attempt some explanation of the change that had come about
in Winthrop's character. His letters to his
wife show him to have been tender and gentle,
but he was certainly relentless in his attitude
towards Mrs. Hutchinson, — though all the
time more than half persuaded that what she
said was true. The fact is that Winthrop's very
amiability made him subject to men of inflexible will. His dream had been to create on
earth a commonwealth of saints whose joy
should be to walk in the ways of God. But in
practice he had to deal with the strongest of
human passions and become himself intolerant
for the sake of leading an intolerant party.
The exigencies of life in America seem to have
made him more and more narrow as the years
went by, but he appears to have repented, at
the last, of his tendency towards intolerance;
for, being requested on his death-bed to sign
an order for the banishment of some person

Roger Williams

BOSTON PUBLIC LIBRARY

for heterodoxy, he waved the paper away, saying, "I have done too much of that work already."

Williams, though, was one whom he persecuted with a will. He had been glad to have
him come to Boston and he recorded his arrival — in the Journal of February, 1631 — as
that of "a godly minister." But he did not
then know what startling doctrines the new
arrival was to set forth or how iconoclastic to
the state would prove this clergyman's earnest
conviction that, in all matters of religious belief and worship, man was responsible to God
alone. Scarcely had Williams set foot in Boston when things began to happen. In the first
place, he was thoroughly convinced that the
Puritans had done wrong in holding communion with Church of England folk, whose power
and resources were constantly employed in
crushing the spirit of true piety. So he refused to join with the church at Boston until
its congregation had declared repentance for
having had communion with the churches in
England.

His chief offence against the state, however,
was in immediately promulgating the principle
for which he all his life contended, i. e. that the
magistrates had no right whatever to impose

civil penalties upon those who had broken only church rules. From the point of view of Bostonians of that day any man holding this opinion was by that very fact unfitted for the office of a minister among them. Consequently, the magistrates opposed with all the authority at their command the settling of Williams in the Salem pulpit to which he had now been called. His history from this time on does not properly belong to a book about Boston; but it is worth noting that he was persecuted for being, among other things, a believer in adult baptism and that against the Anabaptists, as they were called, were directed some of the most cruel persecutions ever waged in the Saint Botolph's Town of New England.

One can scarcely believe the records as one follows the story of the way President Dunster of Harvard College was treated for the crime of believing in adult baptism. Because he would not baptize infants he was deprived of his office (in October, 1654), and when he asked leave to stay for a few months in the house he had built, on the ground that

" 1st. The time of the year is unseasonable, being now very near the shortest day and the depth of winter.

" 2nd. The place into which I go is unknown

THE WELLS - ADAMS HOUSE, ON SALEM STREET, WHERE THE BAPTISTS HELD SECRET
MEETINGS

BOSTON
PUBLIC
LIBRARY

to me and my family, and the ways and means
of subsistence. . . .

" 3d. The place from which I go hath fuel
and all provisions for man and beast laid in for
the winter. . . . The house I have builded upon
very damageful conditions to myself, out of
love for the college, taking country pay in lieu
of bills of exchange on England, or the house
would not have been built. . . .

" 4th. The persons, all beside myself, are
women and children, on whom little help, now
their minds lie under the actual stroke of
affliction and grief. My wife is sick and my
youngest child extremely so and hath been for
months, so that we dare not carry him out of
doors, yet much worse now than before. . . ."

Still slight heed was paid to him. For in
answer to these pathetic demands Dunster was
reprieved only until March and then, with what
was due him still unpaid, he was driven forth,
a broken man, to die in poverty and neglect.
Clearly Massachusetts was not a comfortable
place for the Baptists. You see the eminent
John Cotton had declared that the rejection
of infant baptism would overthrow the church;
that this was a capital crime and that therefore, those opposing this tenet were " foul
murtherers! " The offence was plainly enough

admitted to be against the clergy rather than
against God. When John Wilson — of whom
in his venerable old age Hawthorne has given
us a pleasing portrait in " The Scarlet Letter " — was in his last sickness he was asked
to declare what he thought to be the worst sins
of the country. His reply was that people
sinned very deeply in his estimation when they
rebelled against the power of the clergy.

Upon the Quakers, who absolutely refused
to conform, and who promulgated the doctrine
that the Deity communicated directly with men,
were naturally visited the worst of all the religious persecutions. The first Quakers who
came to Boston were women, Mary Fisher and
Ann Austin, the former being a person whose
previous experience enabled her to compare
unfavourably the manners of New England
Christians with those of Turkish Mahometans!
For, some time before setting out for Boston,
Mary Fisher had made a romantic pilgrimage
to Constantinople for the purpose of warning
the Turks to " flee from the wrath to come."
This was at a time when the Grand Vizier was
encamped with his army near Adrianople, to
whom this astonishing person having jour-
neyed " 600 miles without any abuse or in-
jury " had herself announced as " an Eng-

lishwoman bearing a message from the Great God to the Great Turk.'' She was promptly given an audience and treated with great respect, an escort being even offered to her when the time came for her to depart.

As for her treatment in Boston, let us read Sewel: '' It was in the month called July, of this present year (1656) when Mary Fisher and Ann Austin arrived in the road before Boston, before ever a law was made there against the Quakers; and yet they were very ill-treated; for before they came ashore the deputy governor, Richard Bellingham (the governor himself being out of town), sent officers aboard, who searched their trunks and chests and took away the books they found there, which were about one hundred and carried them ashore, after having commanded the women to be kept prisoners aboard; and the said books were, by an order of the council, burnt in the market-place by the hangman. . . . And then they were shut up close prisoners and the command given that none should come to them without leave; a fine of five pounds being laid upon any that should otherwise come at or speak with them, tho' but at the window. Their pens, ink and paper were taken from them and they not suffered to have any candlelight in the night season; nay, what is more, they were stript naked under pretence to know whether they were witches, tho' in searching, no token was found upon them but of innocence. And in this search they were so barbarously misused that modesty forbids to mention it. And that none might have communication with them a board was nailed up before the window of the jail.

"And seeing they were not provided with victuals, Nicholas Upshal, one who had lived long in Boston and was a member of the church there, was so concerned about it (liberty being denied to send them provision) that he purchas'd it of the jailor at the rate of five shillings a week lest they should have starved. And after having been about five weeks prisoners, William Chichester, master of a vessel, was bound in one hundred pound bond to carry them back, and not suffer any to speak with them, after they were out on board; and the jailor kept their beds and their Bible, for his fees."

The lack of laws touching the Quakers was now at once supplied. Those who brought in members of this sect were fined and those who entertained them deprived of one or both ears. In 1656 an act was passed by which it cost

five shillings to attend a Quaker meeting and
five pounds to speak at one. In October of the
same year the penalty of death was decreed
against all Quakers who should return to the
colony after they had been banished. When
Nicholas Upshall, the kindly innkeeper [1] who
had befriended Mary Fisher and her comrade,
protested against such legislation he was fined
and finally banished. Then, to provide a fillip
to zeal, constables who failed vigorously to
break up Quaker meetings were themselves
fined and imprisoned, a share of the fine imposed being given to the informer. The object
of this last-named legislation was to sustain
the atrocious custom of "flogging through
three towns," a privilege established by the
Vagabond Act, so called, of May, 1661, in which
it was provided that any foreign Quaker or
any native, upon a second conviction, might
be ordered to receive an unlimited number of
stripes, the whip for such service being a two-
handled implement, armed with lashes made
of twisted and knotted cord or catgut. The
last Quaker known to have been whipped in
Boston was Margaret Brewster, whose offence
Samuel Sewall has chronicled in the following
paragraph: "July 8, 1677, New Meeting

[1] See "Among Old New England Inns."

House Mane: In sermon time there came in
a female Quaker, in a canvas frock, her hair
disshevelled and loose like a Periwigg, her face
as black as ink, led by two other Quakers and
two others following. It occasioned the greatest and most amazing uproar that I ever saw.
Isaiah i. 12, 14.'' Whittier has put the scene
into verse for us and made us poignantly to
feel its horror:

> "Save the mournful sackcloth about her wound,
>   Unclothed as the primal mother,
> With limbs that trembled and eyes that blazed
>   With a fire she dared not smother. . . .
>
> "And the minister paused in his sermon's midst
>   And the people held their breath,
> For these were the words the maiden said
>   Through lips as pale as death: . . .
>
> "Repent! repent! ere the Lord shall speak
>   In thunder and breaking seals!
> Let all souls worship him in the way
>   His light within reveals.
>
> "She shook the dust from her naked feet
>   And her sackcloth closer drew,
> And into the porch of the awe-hushed church
>   She passed like a ghost from view."

The meeting-house which provided the background for this very dramatic scene was the
predecessor on the same site of the present Old

South Church.[1]   Thither Margaret Brewster
had travelled a long distance for the express
purpose of protesting against further persecutions of her sect. At her trial, she said some
brave words that effectually stirred — after an
interval — the consciences of her persecutors.
John Leverett was then chief magistrate and
to him she appealed thus: " Governour, I desire thee to hear me a little for I have something to say in behalf of my friends in this
place: . . . Oh governour I cannot but press
thee again and again, to put an end to these
cruel laws that you have made to fetch my
friends from their peaceable meetings, and
keep them three days in the house of correction, and then whip them for worshipping the
true and living God: Governour, let me entreat thee to put an end to these laws, for the
desire of my soul is that you may act for God,
and then would you prosper, but if you act
against the Lord and his blessed truth, you
will assuredly come to nothing, the mouth of
the Lord hath spoken it. . . ."

" Margaret Brewster," came the stern reply, " you are to have your clothes stript off
to the middle, and to be tied to a cart's tail
at the South Meeting House, and to be drawn

[1] See " Romances of Old New England Churches."

through the town, and to receive twenty stripes upon your naked body.''

But though Margaret Brewster suffered last she did not suffer most. Mary Dyer paid the extreme penalty in 1660 because she insisted on coming back to Boston after she had been reprieved from death and banished. In no case better than here may we see illustrated the lengths to which religious enthusiasm will carry the person possessed by it. For with William Robinson and Marmaduke Stevenson she had been condemned to hang on the Common, but '' after she was upon the ladder with her arms and legs tied and the rope about her neck she was spared at the earnest solicitation of her son and sent out of the colony.'' But, because she thought she must needs die for the triumph of her cause she came back a year later to be executed.

Josiah Southwick, eldest son of Lawrence and Cassandra Southwick, was another who '' appeared manfully at Boston in the face of his persecutors '' after he had been shipped to England. As punishment, he was '' sentenced to be whipt at a cart's tail, ten stripes in Boston, the same in Roxbury and the same in Dedham.'' The peculiar atrocity of flogging from town to town lay in the fact that the victim's wounds became cold beween the times of punishment, and in winter often froze, the resulting torture being intolerably agonizing.

The case of the Southwicks is particularly interesting as an extreme example of the far-reaching ferocity of persecution as pursued by Endicott. Whittier in his poem, "Cassandra Southwick," has given us the colour of this event but, for poetic purposes, has made the woman young. In point of fact, however, Lawrence and Cassandra Southwick were an aged couple, members of the Salem church. Besides the son Josiah, already referred to, they had a younger boy and girl named Daniel and Provided. The father and mother were first arrested in 1657 for harbouring two Quakers, and although her husband was soon released Cassandra was imprisoned for seven weeks and fined forty shillings because there was found on her person a Quaker tract. Later, the three elder Southwicks were again arrested and sent to Boston to serve as an example. Here, in the February of 1657 they were whipped without form of trial, imprisoned eleven days and their cattle seized and sold to pay a fine of £4 13 s. for six weeks' absence from worship on the Lord's day. The letter which they sent from their prison in Boston

to Endicott and the others at Salem is worthy
of being reproduced in full because it breathes
the very spirit of that peace for which the
Quakers ideally stood.

" This to the Magistrates at Court in Salem.
" Friends,
" Whereas it was your pleasure to commit
us, whose names are underwritten, to the house
of correction in Boston, altho' the Lord, the
righteous Judge of heaven and earth, is our
witness, that we had done nothing worthy of
stripes or of bonds; and we being committed
by your court to be dealt withal as the law
provides for foreign Quakers, as ye please to
term us; and having some of us suffered your
law and pleasures, now that which we do expect is, that whereas we have suffered your
law, so now to be set free by the same law, as
your manner is with strangers, and not to put
us in upon the account of one law, and execute
another law upon us, of which according to
your own manner, we were never convicted as
the law expresses. If you had sent us upon
the account of your new law, we should have
expected the jaylor's order to have been on
that account, which that it was not, appears
by the warrant which we have, and the punish-

ment which we bare, as four of us were
whipp'd, among whom was one who had formerly been whipp'd so now also according to
your former law.

" Friends, let it not be a small thing in your
eyes, the exposing as much as in you lies, our
families to ruine. It's not unknown to you
the season and the time of year for those who
live of husbandry, and what their cattle and
families may be exposed unto; and also such
as live on trade; we know if the spirit of
Christ did dwell and rule in you these things
would take impression on your spirits. What
our lives and conversation have been in that
place is well known; and what we now suffer
for is much of false reports, and ungrounded
jealousies of heresie and sedition. These
things lie upon us to lay before you. And, for
our parts, we have true peace and rest in the
Lord in all our sufferings, and are made willing in the power and strength of God, freely
to offer up our lives in this cause of God for
which we suffer: Yea and we do find (through
grace) the enlargements of God in our imprisoned state, to whom alone we commit ourselves
and families, for the disposing of us according
to his infinite wisdom and pleasure, in whose
love is our rest and life.

" From the House of Bondage in Boston
wherein we are made captives by the wills of
men, although made free by the Son, John 8,
36. In which we quietly rest, this 16th of the
5th month, 1658.

" LAWRENCE ⎫
" CASSANDRA ⎬SOUTHWICK,
" JOSIAH ⎭
" SAMUEL SHATTOCK,
" JOSHUA BUFFUM."

When Lawrence and Cassandra Southwick
were rearrested after banishment for not having gone away promptly, the old people pite-
ously pleaded " that they had no otherwhere
to go." But they were none the less commanded to get out quickly under pain of death.
They went to Shelter Island, where they died
within a few days of each other as a result of
flogging and starvation. And, inconceivable as
it seems, the *sale as slaves* of the younger children, Daniel and Provided, was actually authorized by law to satisfy a debt accumulated
from fines for their non-attendance at church!
Thus were free-born English subjects dealt
with for cherishing a faith subversive of a
theocracy.

In all honesty, however, it should be said

that not all the Quakers, by any means, were as mild and inoffensive as the Southwicks. Even the gentle-spirited Roger Williams was at one time so sorely tried in patience by them that he allowed himself to write: " They are insufferably proud and contemptuous. I have, therefore, publicly declared myself that a due and moderate restraint and punishment of these incivilities, though pretending conscience, is so far from persecution, properly so called, that it is a duty and command of God unto all mankind, first in Families, and thence unto all mankind Societies."

What did they do? Everything which they thought might tend to batter down the intolerant spirit of Puritanism. A favourite method of protest was for Quaker women to break bottles over the head of a preacher " as a sign of his emptiness." John Norton was more than once thus affronted while engaged in the solemn delivery of the Thursday lecture in Boston. This could scarcely have been pleasant, of course, either to the preacher or his people. But a little tact, above all a sense of humour, would have smoothed the sharpness of the controversy. *Only,* these qualities were precisely the ones which the Puritans and the Quakers both conspicuously lacked.

Against the Puritan persistency, therefore,
there was ranged the exceeding contumacy of
the Quakers. And if the war had been left to
fight itself out, the Quakers, because they had
a great principle on their side, would probably
have won the day, revolting and bloody as must
have been the battles. Happily, however, three
or four influences coöperated to put an end to
this unseemly conflict.

One of the sufferers from persecution having gone to England and gained access to
Charles II, brought back from that monarch
a peremptory command that the death penalty
against the Quakers should be no more in-
flicted and that those who were under judgment or in prison should be sent to England
for trial. Sir Richard Saltonstall, too, — who
had returned to England some time before, and
was watching with great interest, though at a
distance, the course of events in and about Boston, — perceived that the intolerance of Wilson
and Cotton would work great harm to the colony, and to these two teachers of the Boston
First Church he had addressed a manly letter
of remonstrance. Most important of all for
the Quakers, John Norton, who of all the clergy
had exercised the most baleful influence in the
direction of intolerance, died in 1663, suddenly

Sir Richard Saltonstall

BOS
PUI
LIBR

and of apoplexy, and the friends of the Quakers, after the fashion of the day, pronounced his sudden taking off a punishment sent by the Lord.

Already John Norton had been nearly frightened to death in England by the Quakers. The narrow-minded but well-meaning priest had been sent with Simon Bradstreet to present an address to the just-crowned Charles and find out what his attitude towards the colonies was to be. Norton had accepted this mission with reluctance, for he knew perfectly well that, in the eye of the English law, the executions he had pushed against the Quakers were homicide. But, after long vacillation, " the Lord so encouraged and strengthened his heart " that he ventured to sail. From the king and his prime minister he and his companion soon found they had nothing to fear, but they were none the less uncomfortable in London, the reason whereof may be gleaned from this anecdote related by Sewel:

" Now the deputies of New England came to London, and endeavoured to clear themselves as much as possible, but especially priest Norton, who bowed no less reverently before the archbishop, than before the king. . . . They would fain have altogether excused themselves; and priest Norton thought it sufficient to say that he did not assist in the bloody trial nor had advised to it.

"But John Copeland, whose ear was cut off at Boston, charged the contrary upon him: and G. Fox the elder, got occasion to speak with them in the presence of some of his friends and asked Simon Bradstreet, one of the New England magistrates, ' whether he had not a hand in putting to death those they nicknamed Quakers '? He not being able to deny this confessed he had. Then G. Fox asked him and his associates that were present, ' whether they would acknowledge themselves to be subjects to the law of England? and if they did by what law they had put his friends to death? ' They answered ' They were subject to the laws of England and they had put his friends to death by the same law as the Jesuits were put to death in England.' Hereupon G. Fox asked, ' whether they did believe that those, his friends whom they had put to death, were Jesuits or jesuistically affected? ' They said ' Nay.' ' Then ' replied G. Fox, ' ye have murdered them; for since ye put them to death by the law that Jesuits are put to death here in England, it plainly appears you have put them to death arbitrarily, without any law.' ''

Fox might have turned the tables, it is clear, upon the magistrate and the minister, but he had no desire to do that. Though many royalists urged him to prosecute relentlessly these New England persecutors of his followers, he said he preferred to leave them '' to the Lord to whom vengeance belonged.'' So Bradstreet and John Norton came back to their homes in safety though they passed a very bad quarter of a year in London.

The election in 1673 of Leverett as governor sounded, however, the death-knell to persecution. For though he had been trained under Cotton's preaching, he was personally opposed to violent methods of suppressing dissenting sects, and, during his administration, the Baptists, the Quakers and all the rest worshipped their God undisturbed by any legal interference. Long and bitter had been the struggle, but now, at last, there was assured to those in Massachusetts a boon for which men have ever been content to yield up their life in dungeons, on the scaffold and at the stake, — that very noble and precious thing we call '' freedom to worship God.''

VIII

WHAT the Journal of Madame Knight is to
those who are studying tavern and transportation conditions in the New England of two
centuries ago,[1] the Letters of John Dunton are
to us when we are concerned with Boston in
the latter part of the seventeenth century.
That time was peculiarly barren of description
at the hands of visitors, upon whom the city
made an impression rather favourable as a
whole. Sewall's Diary is of inestimable value,
of course, but he was a part of all that he described and so could not bring an unbiased
mind to bear upon his subject. And many of
the visitors who wrote about us took a hostile
tone and so presented material by no means
trustworthy.

Sometimes, to be sure, there was good reason for the harshness of the picture drawn.
When Jasper Dankers and Peter Sluyter, for

[1] See "Among Old New England Inns."

138

instance, gained the impressions which have
since been published by the Long Island Historical Society, they were strangers, unable to
speak English, and " as Jesuits who had come
here for no good " were of course regarded
with suspicion. Some of the things which
Dunton saw through rather rose-coloured
glasses, they seem to have found not at all
prepossessing. But their understatements of
the country's attractions are generally less to
be credited than his slight overstatement.
What they wrote is interesting, though, and
some few passages from their pens may well
enough be quoted before we proceed to enjoy
Dunton's racy discourse.

Our Jesuit friends shared in a fast day at
one of the Boston churches and they were not
in the least edified. " In the first place a minister made a prayer in the pulpit of full two
hours in length; after which an old minister
delivered a sermon an hour long, and after
that a prayer was made and some verses sung
out of the psalm. In the afternoon three or
four hours were consumed with nothing except
prayers, three ministers relieving each other
alternately: when one was tired another went
up into the pulpit. The inhabitants are all
Independent in matter of religion, if it can be

called religion; many of them perhaps more for the purposes of enjoying the benefit of its privileges than for any regard to truth and godliness. . . . All their religion consists in observing Sunday by not working or going into the taverns on that day; but the houses are worse than the taverns. . . . There is a penalty for cursing and swearing such as they please to impose, the witnesses thereof being at liberty to insist upon it. Nevertheless, you discover little difference between this and other places. Drinking and fighting occur there not less than elsewhere.''

One of the most curious items is their picture of Harvard College. Apparently the institution was not then very flourishing (June, 1680), for they found only ten students and no professor! On entering the College building they discovered '' eight or ten young fellows sitting about, smoking tobacco, with the smoke of which the room was so full that you could hardly see; and the whole house smelt so strong of it that when I was going upstairs, I said, this is certainly a tavern. . . . They could hardly speak a word of Latin so that my comrade could not converse with them. They took us to the library where there was nothing particular. We looked over it a little.''

Dunton's experience at Harvard we shall find to be quite a different one though his visit there was only six years later than that of the missionaries. A very red-blooded gentleman was this London bookseller and journalist, who, after Monmouth's insurrection, came to New England to sell a consignment of books and so retrieve his depressed fortunes. Dunton had been intended for the ministry, but developing some tendencies of the gay Lothario stripe he became, instead, apprenticed to a bookseller and, succeeding in this line of work, soon set up a shop for himself. On August 3, 1682, he married the daughter of Dr. Samuel Annesley, a distinguished non-conformist minister. One sister of this lady became the mother of John Wesley and another the wife of Defoe. She herself must have been a remarkable person for she held the affection of her flighty husband the while she enabled him to keep his credit good and to be of financial aid to several dependent relatives.

She had a piquant dash of Bohemianism, too, and this adds to her charm for us, as for her devoted spouse. She and John were always Iris and Philaret to each other and instead of having a house and living staidly in it they settled down, when their honeymoon

days were over, in the Black Raven, on Prince's
street, London, where they lived for two years
without a single care. " Look which way we
would the world was always smiling on us,"
wrote Dunton of this time of their lives. " The
piety and good-humour of Iris made our lives
one continued courtship." But our bookseller
had been " born under a rambling planet "
and so, when opportunity came to him, he
armed himself with a stock of his wares, took
along plenty of ink and white paper and went
forth to sell books, — and make them. In his
letters home he was, from the start, very deliberate and naive writing his wife from Cowes
all about her leave-taking with him, adding as
explanation that " 'tis necessary to render
the History of my Rambles perfect, which I
design to print."

During the voyage Dunton enjoyed a sea-
sickness which he so vividly describes as to
induce similar suffering on the part of his
readers. But when the New World was
reached he recovered speedily and began diligently to write back to Iris and his friends all
he did, saw, read or squeezed out of others in
the course of his stay in the town. The first
letter descriptive of Boston was addressed to
his London printer, sixty letters to Iris having

been immediately dispatched previous to the inditing of this one. To Larkin he declares that he will in this New England letter " 1. Give an account of my reception at Boston. 2. The character of my Boston Landlord, his wife and daughter: 3. Give you an account of my being admitted into the freedom of the City: 4. I shall describe next the town of Boston, it being the Metropolis of New England; and say something of the government, Law and Customs thereof. 5. I shall relate the Visits I made, the Remarkable friendships I contracted, and shall conclude with the character of Madam Brick as the Flower of Boston, and some other Ladyes. And I'll omit nothing that happened (if remarkable) during my stay here. And in all this I will not copy from other, as is usual with most Travellers, but relate my own Observations." After which preface Dunton goes on with characteristic verbosity to tell his little tale. Opposite to the Town House he found " in Capital Letters:

LODGINGS TO BE LET WITH A CONVENIENT WAREHOUSE

" I found 'twas convenient for my purpose and so we soon made a bargain. My Landlord,

Mr. Richard Wilkins, like good old Jacob, is a good plain man. He was formerly a bookseller in Limerick, and fled hither on the account of conscience . . . and is now a member of Mr. Willard's church.''

Having unloaded his books, opened his shop and presented letters which he bore to the Deputy Governor, William Stoughton, and to Joseph Dudley [Governor from 1702-1715] Dunton was made a freeman of the town through the good offices of Francis Burroughs. In a book at the City Clerk's office may still be found the document of this last transaction which is so interesting that I herewith reproduce it:

'' Witnesse these presents, that I, Francis Burrowes, of Bostone, Merchant, doe bind my-selfe, my Executors and Administrators to Edward Willis, Treasurer of the Towne of Bostone, in the sume of forty pounds in mony, that John Dunton booke-seller, nor any of his familie, shall not be chargeable to this towne duringe his or any of there abode therein. Witnesse my hand the 16th of February, 1685.

'' That is, sd Burrowes binds himselfe as above to sd Willis and his successors in the

office of Treasurer, omitted in the due place
above. (Signed)   FRANCIS BURROUGHS.
"JOHN DUNTON."

This formality over, Dunton was in a position to enjoy himself. Which he did by
promptly accepting an invitation to "dine
with the Governour and Magistrates of Boston; the Place of Entertainment was the
Town-Hall, and the Feast Rich and Noble: As
I enter'd the Room where the Dinner was, the
Governour in Person [Bradstreet], the Deputy
Governour, Major Dudley, and the other Magistrates, did me the Honour to give me a particular welcome to Boston, and to wish me success in my undertaking." One wishes that
Dunton had dwelt upon this dinner instead of
proceeding to tell us, guide-book fashion, about
the latitude and longitude of the city, and the
manner in which it had been settled. But we
would not for a great deal be without his description of the houses:
  "The Houses are for the most part raised
on the Sea-banks, and wharfed out with great
industry and cost; many of them standing
upon piles, close together, on each side the
streets, as in London, and furnished with many
fair Shops; where all sorts of commodities are

sold. Their streets are many and large, paved with Pebbles; the Materials of their Houses are Brick, Stone, Lime, handsomely contrived, and when any New Houses are built, they are made conformable to our New Buildings in London since the fire. Mr. Shrimpton has a very stately house there, with a Brass Kettle atop, to shew his Father was not ashamed of his Original [he had been a brazier]: Mr. John Usher (to the honour of our Trade) is judg'd to be worth above £20,000, and hath one of the best Houses in Boston; They have Three Fair and Large Meeting-Houses or Churches, [the First Church, which stood on the south side of what is now State street on Washington street; the second church or North Meeting-House which stood at the head of North square; and the Third or Old South Church] commodiously built in several parts of the Town, which yet are hardly sufficient to receive the Inhabitants, and strangers that come in from all Parts.

" Their Town-House [which stood from 1657 to 1711 on the site of the present Old State House] is built upon Pillars in the middle of the Town, where their merchants meet and confer every day. In the Chambers above they keep their Monthly Courts. The South-side of the Town is adorned with Gardens and

SIMON BRADSTREET

BOSTON
PUBLIC
LIBRARY

Orchards. The Town is rich and very populous, much frequented by strangers. Here is
the dwelling of Mr. Bradstreet, Esq. their
present Gouvernour. On the North-west and
North-east two constant Fairs are kept, for
daily Traffick thereunto. On the South there
is a small but pleasant Common, where the
Gallants a little before sunset walk with their
Marmalet Madams, as we do in Moorfield &c
till the Nine-a Clock Bell rings them home;
after which the Constables walk their Rounds
to see good order kept, and to take up loose
people. In the high-street towards the Common, there are very fair Buildings, some of
which are of stone.''

Dunton was a kindly and a liberal person,
so he can speak with very little patience of the
religious persecutions which he found going on
all about him. '' The Quakers here have been
a suffering Generation,'' he writes, '' and
there's hardly any of the Yea and Nay Per-
suasion but will give you a severe account of
it; for the Bostonians, though their forefathers fled hither to enjoy liberty of conscience, are very unwilling any should enjoy it
but themselves: But they are now grown more
moderate. The Government, both Civil and
Ecclesiastical is in the hands of the Independ-

ents and Presbyterians, or at least of those that pretend to be such."

Thanks to Dunton, we have an outsider's glimpse of a church collection among the Puritans. " On Sundays in the After-noon, after Sermon is ended, the People in the Galleries come down and march two a Brest, up one Isle and down the other, until they come before the Desk, for Pulpit they have none: Before the Desk is a long Pew, where the Elders and Deacons sit, one of them with a Money-box in his hand, into which the People, as they pass put their Offerings, some a shilling, some two shillings, and some half a Crown or five shillings, according to the Ability or Liberality of the Person giving. This I look upon to be a Praise-worthy Practice. This money is distributed to supply the Necessities of the Poor, according to their several wants, for they have no Beggars there. Every Church (for so they call their particular Congregations) have one Pastor, one Teacher, Ruling Elders and Deacons."

Borrowing adroitly from Josselyn's Two Voyages Dunton now describes what he calls " their Laws: This Colony is a Body Corporate, Politick in Fact, by the Name of, The Governeur and Company of the Massachusetts

Bay in New-England. Their Constitution is,
That there shall be one governour and Deputy-
Governour, and eighteen Assistants of the
same Company, from time to time. That the
Governour and Deputy Governour, who for
this year are Esq Bradstreet and Esq Stoughton, Assistants and all other officers, to be
chosen from among the Freemen the last
Wednesday in Easter Term, yearly, in the
General Court. The Governour to take his
corporal oath to be True and Faithful to the
Government, and to give the same Oath to the
other Officers. They are to hold a Court once
a month, and any seven to be a sufficient Quo-
rum. They are to have four General Courts
kept in Term-Time, and once General and solemn Assembly, to make Laws and Ordinances;
Provided, They be not contrary or repugnant
to the Laws and Statutes of the Realm of England. In Anno 1646, They drew up a Body of
their Laws for the benefit of the People.
Every Town sends two Burgesses to their
Great and Solem General Court.

" Their Laws for Reformation of Manners
are very severe," he now goes on to say, " yet
but little regarded by the People, so at least
to make 'em better or cause 'em to mend their
manners. For being drunk, they either Whip

or impose a Fine of Five shillings: And yet
notwithstanding this Law, there are several of
them so addicted to it, that they begin to doubt
whether it be a Sin or no; and seldom go to
Bed without Muddy Brains. For Cursing and
Swearing they bore through the Tongue with
a hot Iron. For kissing a woman in the Street,
though but in way of Civil Salute,[1] Whipping
or a Fine. . . . For adultry they are put to
Death, and so for Witchcraft; For that they
are a great many Witches in this Country the
late Tryals of 20 New England Witches is a
sufficient Proof. . . . An English Woman suffering an Indian to have carnal knowledge of
her had an Indian cut out exactly in red cloth,
and sewed upon her right Arm, and enjoyned
to wear it Twelve Months. Scolds they gag,
and set them at their own Doors, for certain
hours together, for all comers and goers to
gaze at. Stealing is punished with Restoring four-fold, if able; if not, they are sold
for some years, and so are poor Debtors. I
have not heard of many Criminals of this
sort. . . . For I say again you must make
a Distinction: For amongst all this Dross,
there runs here and there a vein of pure Gold:
And though the Generality are what I have

[1] See " Among Old New England Inns," p. 22.

describ'd 'em, yet is there as sincere a Pious and truly Religious People among them, as is any where in the Whole World to be found.

" The next thing I have to do is to proceed to give you some account of the Visits I made: For having gotten a Warehouse and my Books ready for sale, (for you know mine was a Learned Venture) 'twas my Business next to seek out the Buyers: So I made my first Visit to that Reverend and Learned Divine, Mr. Increase Mather: He's the Present Rector of Harvard College: He is deservedly called, The Metropolitan Clergy-Man of the Kingdom. And the next to him in Fame (whom I likewise visited at the same time) is his son, Mr. Cotton Mather, an Excellent Preacher, a great Writer; He has very lately finish'd the Church-History of New England, which I'm going to print; And which is more than all, He Lives the Doctrine he Preaches. After an hour spent in his company (which I took for Heaven) he shew'd me his Study: And I do think he has one of the best (for a Private Library) that I ever knew. . . . I am sure it was the best sight I had in Boston.

" Early the next morning (before the Sun could shew his Face) I went to wait upon Mr. Willard: He's the Minister of the South Meet-

ing in Boston: He's a Man of Profound No-
tions: Can say what he will, and prove what
he says: I darken his Merits if I call him less
than a Walking Library." Among the other
clergymen visited by Mr. Dunton that day
when he rose so early was Joshua Moody, hon-
ourably distinguished by his opposition to the
witchcraft delusion and extolled by Dunton, a
little further on, for a sermon which he
preached upon the hanging of James Morgan
for murder.

The booksellers of the town are now described, together with Samuel Green, the
printer, George Monk, landlord of the Blue
Anchor, — which, standing as it did on the site
of the present Globe building, was a very convenient refuge for Dunton when the felicity of
family life at the Wilkins' began to pall, — and
Dr. Bullivant in whom were combined the pro-
fessions of apothecary and physician. Bullivant was a good deal of a character. It is of
him that Hutchinson says: " Among the more
liberal was one Bullivant, an apothecary who
had been a justice of the peace under Andros.
Lord Bellamont, going from the lecture to his
house, with a great crowd round him, passed
by Bullivant standing at his shop door loiter-
ing. ' Doctor,' says his lordship with an audi-

ble voice, ' you have lost a precious sermon
to-day.' Bullivant whispered to one of his
companions who stood by him, ' If I could have
got as much by being there as his lordship will,
I would have been there too.' " Bullivant was
a Church of England man and his lordship —
ought to have been.

We are now come, in Dunton's discursive
letter to Larkin, to the portion devoted to his
" Female Friends in Boston." Highly entertaining reading this! One of these friends was
a maiden, another was the wife of a rival bookseller and the third and most significant, referred to interchangeably as " Madam Brick "
and " the flower of Boston " was a widow.
" I shall Speak first of the Damsel, [Comfort
Wilkins, his landlord's daughter]. . . . She
was a little Transported with the Zeal of Vol-
untary Virginity as knowing there's few Practice it. But tho' an old (or Superannuated)
Maid, in Boston, is thought such a curse as
nothing can exceed it, and looked on as a Dis-
mal Spectacle, yet she by her Good Nature,
Gravity and strict Vertue, convinces all that
'tis not her Necessity but her Choice that keeps
her a Virgin. She's now about Twenty Six
years (the Age which we call a Thornback) yet
she never disguises her self by the Gayetys of

a Youthful Dress, and talks as little as she thinks of Love: She goes to no Balls or Dancing Match, as they do who go (to such Fairs) in order to meet with Chapmen. . . . Her Looks, her Speech, her whole behaviour are so very chaste, that but once going to kiss her I thought she had blush'd to death.'' [One wonders if Dunton ever *did* kiss her; we know that he talked to her by the hour of '' Platonick Love.'']

Mrs. Green, though married, seems to have been quite as modest as this incomparable maiden. The talk of that time was not always delicate and this the printer's wife set herself to reform. Dunton tells us that she '' was so severely scrupulous that, there being an invitation of several Persons to a Gentleman's House in Boston and some that were invited resolving to be very merry, one of the company made this Objection ' that Mrs. Green woul'd be there which woul'd spoil their Mirth.' ''

Of the Flower of Boston Dunton makes the rather terrifying statement that her '' Head has been cut off yet she lives and walks.'' This, being interpreted, means that the lady's husband was dead and that she devoted her life to keeping his memory green. '' Yet she did not think her self oblig'd to such Starch'd-

ness of Carriage," comments Dunton tersely,
" as is usual among the Bostonians, who value
themselves thereby so much that they are ready
to say to all others, Stand off, I am holier than
thou."

Not all the women in the Boston of that day
were in a class with Cæsar's wife, however.
Dunton records that he had " several Acquaintance with Persons of a far different character:
For all sorts came to my Ware house to buy
Books, according to their several Inclinations.
There was Mrs. Ab—l, (a Person of Quality):
A well-wisher to the Mathematics: A young
Proficient, but willing to learn, and therefore
came to Enquire for the School of Venus; She
was one of the first that pos'd me, in asking
for a Book I cou'd not help her to; I told her
however, I had the School of Vertue; but that
was a Book she had no occasion for. . . . Yet
bad as she is, for her Father's sake, I hope
she'll live to repent. The next I shall mention
is Mrs. D—, who has a bad face and a worse
tongue; and has the report of a Witch; whether
she be one or no, I know not, but she has ig-
norance and malice enough to make her one:
And indeed she has done very odd things, but
hitherto such as are rather strange than hurt-
ful; yea, some of them are pretty and pleas-

ing, but such as I think cann't be done without
the help of the Devil: As for instance: She'll
take 9 sticks, and lay 'em across, and by mum-
bling a few words, make 'em all stand up an
End like a pair of Nine-Pins; but she had best
have a care, for they that use the Devil's help
to make sport, may quickly come to do mischief.
I have been told by some that she has actually
indented with the Devil; and that he is to do
what she would have him for a time, and afterwards he is to have her Soul in Exchange:
What pains poor Wretches take to make sure
of Hell!'' This naive description of a
'' witch,'' hot from the pen of a contemporary,
is most interesting and worth bearing in mind
when we are studying the phenomenon of witchcraft, as seen by the persecuting Mathers.

Of women who shop without knowing what
they want the Boston of that day evidently had
its due share. Dunton amusingly describes one
of them: '' Doll- S-der's life is a perpetual
Contradiction; and she is made up of ' I will '
and ' I will not.' ' Reach me that Book, yet
let it alone too; but let me see't however: and
yet 'tis no great matter neither; ' was her constant Dialect in my Ware house: She's very
fantastical but cann't be called Irresolute; for
an Irresolute Person is always beginning, and

she never makes an End. She writes and blots
out again, whilst the other deliberates what to
write: I know two negatives make an affirma-
tive but what her aye and no together make
I know not. Her head is just like a Squirrel's
Cage and her Mind the Squirrel that whirls it
round.'' One of his single women customers
Dunton characterizes as '' Vox et preterea
nihil,'' adding that it is certainly '' some bodies
happiness that she is yet unmarried, for she
wou'd make a Husband wish that she were
dumb, or he were deaf. . . . She us'd to come
to my Warehouse, not to buy Books, (for she
talk'd so much she had no time to read) but
that others might hear her.''

And now, as if to balance the entertainment
offered by the first part of this letter Dunton
reproduces, almost in full, the three sermons
preached at the unfortunate James Morgan
before his execution! This event had just
taken place in Boston and was remarkable for
being the first of its kind to occur there in three
years. The two Mathers and Joshua Moody
officiated as preachers, the crowd present at the
New Church being such that '' the Gallery
crack'd, and so they were forced to remove to
Mr. Willard's.'' After the execution, to which
Dunton '' rid with Mr. Cotton Mather,'' our

indefatigable friend, in the company of Mrs. Green, Madam Brick, Comfort Wilkins and two or three other acquaintances of both sexes, "took a Ramble to a place call'd Governour's Island, about a mile from Boston, to see a whole Hog roasted. We all went in a Boat; and having treated the Fair Sex, returned in the Evening."

To just this period belongs the holding of the first Church of England service in Boston and it is interesting to know that Dunton was present. The parson was Robert Ratcliffe who "the next Sunday after he landed, preached in the Town-house and read Common-Prayer in his Surplice, which was so great a Novelty to the Bostonians, that he had a very large Audience, myself among others." Dunton also bore his part in the Training Day exercises on the Common. "Tis their custom here for all that can bear arms, to go out on a Training Day: But I thought a pike was best for a young Souldier, and so I carry'd a Pike; . . . Between you and I, Reader, there was another reason for it too, and that was I knew not how to shoot off a Musquet. Twas the first time I was ever in arms.

"Being come into the Field the Captain call'd us all into Close Order, in order to go

to Prayer, and then Pray'd himself: And when
our Exercise was done, the Captain likewise
concluded with Prayer. I have heard that Gus-
tavus Adolphus, the warlike King of Sweden,
wou'd before the beginning of a Battel, kneel
down devoutly at the head of his Army, and
pray to God (the Giver of Victories) to give
them Success against their Enemies, which
commonly was the Event; and that he was as
Careful also to return thanks to God for the
Victory. But solemn Prayer in the Field upon
a Day of Training, I never knew but in New
England, where it seems it is a common Custom. About three of the Clock both our Exercise and Prayers being over, We had a very
Noble Dinner, to which all the Clergy were
invited."

The influence of the " rambling planet "
under which Dunton had been born, continuing
as potent in New England as in old, our friend
made many little journeys to places of interest
near Boston, diligently writing back to his cor-
respondents on the other side all that befell
him on these occasions. His visit to the community " that at first was called New Town
but is now made a University and called Cambridge, there being a colledge erected there by
one Mr. John Harvard, who gave £700 for the

Erecting of it in the year 1638," is most entertainingly described. " I was invited hither by
Mr. Cotton [son of the Reverend John Cotton
and librarian of the College] by whom I was
very handsomely Treated and shewn all that
was remarkable in it. He discoursed with me
about my venture of Books; and by this means
I sold many of my Books to the Colledge."
The book talk which then went on between these
two is pleasantly hinted at. Dunton, when
asked who were " his great authors," spoke of
" Jeremy Taylor, Mr. John Bunyan, who tho'
a man of but very ordinary Education, yet was
as well known for an Author through'out England as any, . . . Robert Boyle, Sir Matthew
Hale, Cowley and Dryden." In return for
which Cotton instanced as distinguished contemporary authors of New England the " Famous Mr. Elliot " and the inevitable Mathers.

Eliot, who was now a very old man, Dunton
soon went to see " alone that I might have
nothing to hinder me in conversing with him.
When I came he receiv'd me with all the Ten-
derness and respect imaginable, and had me up
into his Study; and then he enquir'd of me
with all the Expressions of Love and Kindness
that cou'd be how my Father-in-Law, the Reverend Doctor Annesly did? . . . And then

speaking to me, said, ' Well, Young Man, how
goes the Work of Christ on in England? ' I
then told him of the Troubles that were there,
and how like Popery was to be set up again.
' No,' said he, ' it never will be, it never shall:
They may indeed attempt it; they have Towering Thoughts, as their Brethren the Babel-
Builders had of old, but they shall never be able
to bring their wicked Intentions to pass; . . .''
And this he spake with good Assurance.
' But,' says he, ' do the People of God keep up
their Meetings still? Is the Gospel preach'd?
Does the work of Conversion go forward? '
. . . I told him that tho' the Gaols were full
of Dissenters, yet the Meetings were as numerous, and as much throng'd as ever. And I
had heard my Father say, That more Members
had been added to the Church the last year than
in some years before.

" Mr. Elliot was very well pleas'd at what
I had told, and said, ' It was a Token for Good,
that God had not forsaken his People.' . . .
After which he presented me with 12 Bibles in
the Indian Language, and gave me a charge to
present one of 'em to my father Dr. Annesly;
he also gave me Twelve Speeches of Converted
Indians, publish'd by himself, to give to my
Friends in England: After which, he made me

stay and dine with him, by which means I had the opportunity of hearing him Pray, and expound the Scriptures with his Family. After Dinner, he told me that both for my own, but especially for my Father's sake, whom he said he admir'd above most Men in England, if his Countenance and Recommendation cou'd be of any Service to me, I sho'd not want it: And I have already found the good Effects of it.''

So favourably, indeed, were Dunton's books received that he was almost persuaded to take up his permanent residence in Boston. But while debating the matter, he was suddenly seized with a great desire to ramble back to London and once again behold his beloved Iris. So, leaving his good landlord Wilkins to collect the remittances still due him, he sailed for England, where he arrived early in August, 1686. His whole stay in America covered, therefore, but four months. One of his first acts, after being restored to the arms of his faithful wife, was to send his regards to Comfort Wilkins, with whom he had so often discoursed upon Platonic love, and his '' service in a more particular manner to the Widow Brick.'' Already, he had let it be known that only the excellent health enjoyed by Iris prevented him from making actual love to this '' flower of Boston.''

His subsequent career was a bit checkered. A " ramble to Holland, where he lived four months," and up the Rhine, where he stayed, as he himself says, " until he had satisfied his curiosity and spent all his money," occupied the next two years. Then he took a shop opposite London's Poultry Counter which he opened the day the Prince of Orange entered the city. Here he sold books with varying success for ten years, publishing, the while, several semi-political pamphlets. The blow of his life came in May, 1697, in the death of Iris. But within twelvemonths he had married another woman, — for her fortune, — and the last years of his life were full of squalid quarrels with this lady and with her mother.

Dunton's always-flowery style of composition seems to have grown more marked as time went on, and the Spectator found his effusions good matter for ridicule. One kind friend tried to tell him this. " If you have essays or letters that are valuable, call them essays and letters in short plain language," this common-sense person counselled, " and if you have anything writ by men of sense and on subjects of importance, it may sell without your name to it."

But Dunton was now sixty and could not give up the old way. To the last his projects had the catchword of Athenian appended to them. He died in obscurity in 1733, aged 74. If he had never come to Boston his name would long ago have been forgotten. Even as it is his " Letters " are almost unobtainable. For since the Prince Society of Boston reprinted a very limited edition, forty years ago, the volume has been growing every year more and more rare. To-day only collectors can boast of its possession.

IX

THE DYNASTY OF THE MATHERS

DUNTON's letters abound, as we have seen, in references to the Mathers, Increase and Cotton; and the same thing is true of all the literature of the period. Brooks Adams has cuttingly observed in his remarkable volume, "The Emancipation of Massachusetts," that one weak point in the otherwise strong position of the early Massachusetts clergy was that the spirit of their age did not permit them to make their order hereditary. With the Mathers, however, the priesthood was hereditary, and they constituted a veritable dynasty in the government of Boston. The story of their lives offers a remarkable illustration of power — theological and otherwise — transmitted through at least four generations.

When " the shining light " was extinguished by death, late in 1652, he left a widow who became, before long, the second wife of the Reverend Richard Mather, minister of Dorchester.

This Mather had already a theologically minded son named Increase, who had been born in Dorchester in June, 1639, and who, after preaching his first sermon on his birthday, in 1657, sailed for England and pursued post-graduate studies in Trinity College there. Then he preached for one winter in Devonshire and, in 1659, became chaplain to the garrison of Guernsey. But the Restoration was now at hand and, finding that he must " either conform to the Revived Superstitions in the Church of England or leave the Island," he gave up his charge and, in June, 1661, sailed for home. The following winter he passed preaching alternately for his father and " to the New Church in the North-part of Boston." In the course of that year the charms of Mrs. Mather's daughter, Maria Cotton, impressed themselves upon him and,

" On March 6, 1662, he Came into the Married State; Espousing the only Daughter, of the celebrated Mr. John Cotton; in honor of whom he did . . . call his First-born son by the Name of COTTON."

Two years after his marriage Increase Mather was ordained pastor of the North Church in Boston and for some twenty years he appears to have performed with notable suc-

INCREASE MATHER

BOSTON PUBLIC LIBRARY

cess the duties of this important parish. At the same time, he exercised — beneficently on the whole — his great power in the temporal affairs of the colony. For he had good sense and sound judgment, — exactly the qualities, it may be remarked, which his more brilliant son conspicuously lacked.

One of the most attractive traits in the younger Mather's character is his appreciation of his father. Barrett Wendell, who has written a highly readable Life of Cotton Mather, observes dryly that the persecutor of the witches " never observed any other law of God quite so faithfully as the Fifth Commandment." And there seems to have been excellent reason for this. Increase Mather devotedly loved his precocious young son and upon him he lavished a passionate affection which the lad repaid in reverence which was almost worship. The motto of Cotton Mather's life seems indeed to have been, My Father can do no Wrong.

The schoolmaster whose privilege it became to plant the seeds of learning in the mind of this hope of the Mathers was Ezekiel Cheever, whose life Sewall has written for us in the following concise paragraph:

" He was born January 25, 1614. Came over

to N. E. 1637, to Boston: To New Haven 1638.
Married in the Fall and began to teach School;
which work he was constant in till now. First,
at New-Haven, then at Ipswich; then at
Charlestown; then at Boston, whither he came
1670. So that he has laboured in that Calling
Skilfully, diligently, constantly, Religiously,
Seventy years. A rare instance of Piety,
Health, Strength, Serviceableness. The Well-
fare of the Province was much upon his spirit.
He abominated Perriwigs.''

That Cheever was in truth an excellent
teacher may be accepted from the fact that
he had Cotton Mather ready at twelve to enter
Harvard College. And this, too, in spite of the
fact that one fault of the lad was '' idleness.''
Warning his son against this fault, Cotton
Mather wrote, the '' thing that occasioned me
very much idle time was the Distance of my
Father's Habitation from the School; which
caused him out of compassion for my Tender
and Weakly constitution to keep me at home
in the Winter. However, I then much employed myself in Church History; and when
the Summer arrived I so plied my business,
that thro' the Blessing of God upon my endeavours, at the Age of little more than eleven
years I had composed many Latin exercises,

both in prose and verse, and could speak Latin
so readily, that I could write notes of sermons
of the English preacher in it. I had conversed
with Cato, Corderius, Terence, Tully, Ovid and
Virgil. I had made Epistles and Themes; pre-
senting my first Theme to my Master, without
his requiring or expecting as yet any such
thing of me; whereupon he complimented me
Laudabilis Diligentia tua [Your diligence deserves praise]. I had gone through a great
part of the New Testament in Greek, I had read
considerably in Socrates and Homer, and I had
made some entrance in my Hebrew grammar.
And I think before I came to fourteen, I composed Hebrew exercises and Ran thro' the
other Sciences, that Academical Students ordi-
narily fall upon.''

In a later chapter we shall discuss at some
length the rules and regulations, the studies
and the social life which, all together, constituted a highly important formative influence
in the life of this and the other Puritan youth
who went to Harvard. Suffice it, therefore, in
this place to say that Cotton Mather was put
through the mill duly and was able in 1678 to
present himself for the bachelor's degree, being
at that time the youngest who had ever applied for it. This fact it was, which added to

his illustrious ancestry, inspired President
Oakes to single him out at Commencemcent for
the following eulogy delivered in sounding
Latin: " The next youth is named Cotton
Mather. What a name! Or rather, dear
friends, I should have said ' what names.' Of
his reverend father, the most watchful of
guardians, the most distinguished Fellow of
the College I will say nothing, for I dare not
praise him to his face. But should this youth
bring back among us the piety, the learning,
the sound sense, the prudence, the elegant accomplishment and the gravity of his very reverend grandfathers, John Cotton and Richard
Mather, he will have done his highest duty. I
have no slight hope that in this youth there
shall live again, in fact as well as in name,
Cotton and Mather."

Can you wonder that a boy of sixteen, thus
conspicuously praised at the very entrance
upon serious life, felt himself to be a person of
considerable importance in his community, a
man born to sustain a theological dynasty?
Of course the ministry was the profession for
which he was destined, but, for some seven
years after matriculation, he followed the calling of a tutor because he was afflicted with a
tendency to stammer. Then he began the study

of medicine. Soon after this he was advised
to practise speaking with " dilated delibera-
tion," which he did so successfully as completely to overcome the impediment which had
bothered him and, possessing already every
educational qualification as a preacher, he was
thus able (in May, 1685) to become the associate of his father in the charge of the church
in North Square. Before accepting this trust
he had kept many days of fasting and prayer,
for he had long desired remotely to emulate
that Rabbi mentioned in the Talmud whose face
was black by reason of his fasting. The fasts
observed by Cotton Mather throughout his life
were so frequent that his son observes of him
in his funeral sermon " that he thought himself
starved unless he fasted once a month! "

Such then was the Mather to whom the celebrated Eliot had extended, at the age of twenty-
two, the fellowship of the churches! Ten days
after coming into this high estate the young
parson was present at a " private Fast " in
the home of Samuel Sewall, an occasion which
happily supplies us with an authentic glimpse
of the manners of the times. For Sewall
writes: " The Magistrates . . . with their
wives here. Mr. Eliot prayed, Mr. Willard
preached. I am afraid of thy judgments. —

Text Mather gave. Mr. Allen prayed; cessation half an hour. Mr. Cotton Mather prayed; Mr. Mather preached, Ps. 79. 9. Mr. Moodey prayed about an hour and half; Sung the 79th Psalm from the 8th to the End; distributed some Biskets & Beer, Cider, Wine. The Lord hear in Heaven his dwelling place."

But of course a young minister of that day — as of this — must very soon, if only in self-defence, take unto himself a wife. Cotton Mather was already matrimonially minded: he had begun to ask " the guidance and blessing of God in what concerns the change of my condition in the world from Single to married, *whereunto I have now many invitations.*" These last words we must not take as an evidence of Leap Year activity in his parish, but rather as meaning that the young parson desired to enter into the state of matrimony but had not as yet met *the* girl whose charms should draw him thither. His attitude of mind at this stage is singularly like that of the pure young woman of our own time whose heart is still untouched, — and it is in striking contrast to the pronounced dislike with which young men of to-day regard marriage *per se.*

The girl was now sure to arrive, and so it came about that the year 1686 — troublous

BOSTON PUBLIC LIBRARY

HOUSE OF COTTON MATHER, WHICH STOOD AT WHAT IS NOW 298 HANOVER STREET

enough to New England, because Edward Randolph and Joseph Dudley had succeeded in
wresting away the Charter — was a decidedly
happy one for Cotton Mather. His wooing was
very godly, as it was bound to be, but it re-
sulted in his bringing home as a wife Abigail,
daughter of the Honourable Colonel Phillips
of Charlestown. On his wedding day he got
up early to ponder; but in spite of his ponder-
ing he reached Charlestown ahead of time and
had to put in an hour or so in the garden with
his Bible while Abigail was being arrayed in
her wedding finery. Two Sundays afterwards
he preached at his own church in Boston on
Divine Delights. This was the very Sunday
when Mr. Willard " prayed not for the Governour."

The implications of this just-quoted entry in
Sewall's invaluable Diary are enormous. Now
that we have married off Cotton Mather, let
us turn aside briefly to consider them. From
the settlement of the Colony it had been governed under a royal charter granted, as we
have seen, to the governor and Company of
Massachusetts Bay in 1629. Under this none
but church members had been freemen, and as
these freemen elected all political officers and
developed their own system of law it is clear

that the government was much more nearly a theocracy than a dependency of the crown. Tacitly, England had agreed to this state of affairs, but this was only because she had been too busy with Civil Wars and internal dissensions to do anything else. For the sovereign did not forget by any means that New England was theoretically the private property of the crown by virtue of its discovery at the hands of the Cabots, who had been fitted out with crown money. What rights the Colonists had to the land came, it was argued, from the Charter; at best, therefore, their positions could be compared only to that of tenants on a private estate. From the very beginning, however, the Charter had been contested by some gentlemen who maintained that it had been given originally in violation of previous royal grants to them. Among these contestants was one Gorges, a name we readily recognize as potential in more way than one.

By the time Charles II ascended the throne New England had become so prosperous that the opponents of the Charter could not let the matter longer alone, and there appeared in Boston as their agent, Edward Randolph, " the evil genius of New England," with a letter requiring the governor and Assistants of Mas-

sachusetts at once to send representatives to
England, there to answer the claims of those
who contested their rights. The contest thus
begun lasted until 1684, a period of nearly nine
years, during which Randolph made no less
than eight voyages to New England, the colonists sending back to London meanwhile innumerable long-drawn petitions.

But the blow fell at last and on June 18,
1684, the Court of Chancery decreed that the
Charter should be vacated. In the Colony itself there had appeared, by this time, a party
which favoured submission to royal authority.
This party had been built up chiefly by the
exertions of Randolph and at its head was
Joseph Dudley, a son of the Colony's second
governor. He, as '' president of New England,'' was now named to succeed Simon Bradstreet, the last governor elected by the people
of the colony, — and the last survivor, as well,
of the magistrates, who, nearly sixty years
before, had founded the government.

It was a goodly heritage for which Randolph
and his tools had fought. From the day that
Winthrop landed, the Puritan State of his ideal
had risen steadily, and Boston, its chief town,
was now a thriving and well-built settlement.
Moreover, it was distinctly an English town,

for the migration had been unmixed, and, varied as were the religious beliefs of its inhabitants, they agreed perfectly in their love of English names for their streets, English flowers for their gardens, English furniture for their rooms and English architecture for their homes. But they had few books, no amusements, and no intellectual interest except religion. "The people of Boston," as Henry Cabot Lodge remarks in his excellent study of that city's rise and development, "practically went from work to religion and from religion to work without anything to break the monotony except trouble with England and wars with the savages. . . . And now the charter, under which they had enjoyed power and exercised independence was taken from them."

If we read Sewall's account of those days in the spring of 1686 with this great impending change in mind the brief entries become dramatic in the extreme. He tells us how the Rose frigate arrived in Nantasket on the 14th of May; how Randolph came to town by eight in the morning and took coach for Roxbury, where Dudley lived; and how, with other magistrates, he himself was summoned to see the judgment against the charter with the great seal of England affixed. He tells how, on the following Sunday, Randolph came to the Old South Church, where Mr. Willard, in his prayer, made no mention of governor or government; but spoke as if all were changing or changed. He tells how, the next day the General Court assembled, and how Joseph Dudley, temporarily made President of New England, exhibited the condemnation of the Charter and his own commission, how the old magistrates began to make some formal answer and how Dudley refused to treat with them as a court. There is a note of very real pathos in Sewall's picture of that sorrowful group of old magistrates, who, when Dudley was gone, decided that there was " no room " for a protest: " The foundations being gone what can the righteous do? "

So, for seven months, Joseph Dudley was President of the Provisional Government of New England, and during those months the birthdays of the king and queen were celebrated by the royalists in Boston, and to Episcopalians was granted the right to hold services in the east end of the Town House. The Puritan Pepys, as Sewall has well been called, duly notes these developments, telling us that on Sunday, May 30, he sang "the 141 Psalm . . . exceedingly suited to the day. Wherein there is to be worship according to the Church of England, as 'tis called, in the Town House, by countenance of Authority." In August Sewall has grave doubts as to whether he can conscientiously serve in the militia under a flag in which the cross, cut out by Endicott, has been replaced; and three months later he answers his own question by resigning as captain of the South Company. A few Saturdays before this the queen's birthday had been celebrated with drums, bonfires and huzzas, thereby causing Mr. Willard to express, next day, "great grief in's Prayer for the Profanation of the Sabbath last night."

Then, on Sunday, December 19, while Sewall was reading to his family an exposition of Habakkuk, he heard a great gun or two, which made him think Sir Edmund Andros might be come. Such proved to be the case. The first governor sent out from England had arrived "in a Scarlet Coat laced." That day Joseph Dudley went to listen to Mr. Willard preach, and had the chagrin of hearing that personage say, "he was fully persuaded and confident God would not forget the Faith of those who came first to New England."

Between sermons the President went down the harbour to welcome Sir Edmund. The

SIR EDMUND ANDROS

BOSTON
PUBLIC
LIBRARY

next afternoon the king's appointee landed in state, and was escorted to the Town House by eight militia companies. Here a commission was read, declaring his power to suspend councillors and to appoint others, — and vesting the legislative power in him and his Council thus appointed. Then he took the oath of allegiance and stood by, with his hat on, while eight councillors were sworn. The same day he demanded accommodation in one of the meeting-houses for the services of the Church of England!

Andros was a gentleman of good family, had served with distinction in the army, had married a lady of rank and for three years had very successfully ruled as governor of New York. When James came to the throne he quite naturally turned to him as a person well fitted, by his previous American experience — as well as by his well-known personal devotion to the Stuarts — to preside acceptably over the New England colonies. But, New York was not Boston then any more than to-day and, as ill luck would have it, Andros from the very start, made mistakes which soon caused him to be one of the best-hated men Massachusetts had ever known. Scarcely had he set foot in the town when he proceeded, as we have seen, to assail

the religious sensibilities of the Puritans. All
forms and ceremonies, symbols and signs were
to them marks of the Beast, and it was a cruel
shock, after what they had suffered to get away
from the Church of England, to have a priest
in a surplice conducting in their Town House
a service hateful to them, to see men buried
according to the prayer-book and to learn that
marriages, which they had made a purely civil
contract, must henceforth be solemnized by the
rites of the church. Even worse was the enforced celebration of royal anniversaries and
the reappearance of old sports upon certain
holidays.

Samuel Sewall was the type of a class of
well-to-do Puritans, who were, on the whole,
inclined to be submissive to the new government, but he shows himself to have been hurt
in a tender spot by many of the things Andros
did. His Diary may well enough be held to
reflect the deep feeling of many. As early as
November, 1685, he sees the change coming
and records that " the Ministers Come to the
Court and complain against a Dancing Master
who seeks to set up here and hath mixt dances,
and his time of Meeting is Lecture-Day; and
'tis reported he should say that by one Play
he could teach more Divinity than Mr. Willard

or the Old Testament. . . . Mr. Mather [In-
crease] struck at the Root, speaking against
mixt Dances.'' Early in September, 1686, we
read, '' Mr. Shrimpton . . . and others come
in a Coach from Roxbury about 9 aclock or
past, singing as they come, being inflamed with
Drink: At Justice Morgan's they stop and
drink Healths, curse, swear, talk profanely and
baudily to the great disturbance of the Town
and grief of good people. Such high-handed
wickedness has hardly been heard of before in
Boston.''

With ill-concealed exultation the old diarist
notes that the people, for the most part, refused
to observe Christmas and the other imported
holidays, but kept the shops open, brought firewood into the town and generally went on with
their business as under the old régime. But
some annoyances they could not avoid. On the
'' Sabbath Feb. 6, 1686-7,'' he writes, '' Between half hour after eleven and half hour
after twelve at Noon many Scores of great
guns fired at the Castle and Tower suppose
upon account of the King's entering on the
third year of his Reign. . . . This day the
Lord's Super was administered at the middle
and North Church; the rattling of the Guns
during almost all the time gave them great

disturbance. 'Twas never so in Boston before.'' Again he says on '' February 15
1686-7, Jos. Maylem carries a Cock at his back
with a bell in's hand, in the Main Street; several followed him blindfold, and under pretence of striking him or's cock, with great Cart-
whips strike passengers and make great disturbance.'' By countenancing such practices
as these did Andros inflame every possible
prejudice against the crown he fain would
represent.

But the horse-play of Shrove Tuesday, with
its suggestions to the Puritans of Papacy and
the hated days of Laud, was only a forerunner
of what Andros really purposed: i. e. a Church
in which the service of his king and country
should be fittingly carried on! Pending the
erection of such an edifice Sir Edmund determined that, regardless of the wishes of the pop-
ulace, he would have his prayer-book service
read in one of the three meeting-houses of the
town and on '' Wednesday March 23 '' Sewall
tells us, '' the Govr sends Mr. Randolph for
ye keys to our Meetingh. yt may say Prayers
there. Mr. Eliot, Frary, Oliver, Savage Davis
and self wait on his Excellency; shew that ye
Land and House is ours, and that we can't
consent to part with it to such use; exhibit an

extract of Mrs. Norton's Deed [this lady was
the widow of the Reverend John Norton, had
owned the land upon which the church was
built [1] and had given the same in trust for ever
" for the erecting of a house for their assem-
bling themselves together publiquely to worship God.''] and How 'twas built by particular persons as Hull, Oliver £100 a piece &c.''
All this appears to have been of non-avail, however, for three days later, the Diary sadly records: " The Govr has service in ye South
Meetinghouse; Goodm. Needham (the Sex-
ton) tho' had resolv'd to ye Contrary, was
prevail'd upon to Ring ye Bell and open ye
door at ye Governour's Comand, one Smith
and Hill, Joiner and Shoemaker, being very
busy about it. Mr. Jno. Usher was there,
whether at ye very begining, or no, I can't
tell.''

Yet a year later even Sewall has so far
capitulated as to be willing to attend part of
a Church of England service in this same
church. The occasion, to be sure, was one to
make a tender-hearted man forget enmities for
the nonce, for it was the " Funeral of ye Lady
Andros, I having been invited by ye Clark of
ye South-Company. Between 7 and 8 Lychrs

[1] See " Romance of Old New England Churches.''

[torches] illuminating ye cloudy air The Corps was carried into the Herse drawn by six Horses. The Souldiers making a Guard from ye Governour's House down ye Prison Lane to ye South-M. House, there taken out and carried in at ye western dore and set in ye Alley before ye pulpit with six Mourning women by it. House made light with candles and Torches; was a great noise and clamor to keep people out of ye House, yt might not rush in too soon. I went home, where about nine a clock I heard ye Bell toll again for ye Funeral. It seems Mr. Ratcliff's Text was, Cry, all flesh is Grass.'' Three years later an Episcopal church, the King's Chapel, was built on the spot where it now stands. But by this time Sir Edmund Andros had paid the penalty of the affront he had put upon the Puritans by forcing them to lend their cherished meeting-house for a service utterly obnoxious to them.

Besides the church affront two others even more vital were offered by this choice of the English crown. One of these was his assumption of the power of taxation without their consent; the other was the laying down of the principle that all titles to lands had been vacated along with the charter and that whoever wanted a sound title must get his claim confirmed by Sir Edmund, — and pay for it. In short, as Cotton Mather said, " all was done that might be expected from a Kirk, Except the Bloody Part. But that was coming on." He and his father honestly believed, as did many other good people of New England that their heads were in danger! Increase Mather accordingly opposed Andros in every possible way beseeching God the while to " send Reviving News out of England." As if in answer to this prayer James II issued in April, 1687, his Declaration of Indulgence which, though designed, of course, to relieve the Catholics, was very grateful to Dissenters as well assuring them, as it did, of entire freedom to meet and serve God in their own way.

So full of joy were the ministers of New England that they wished to hold a public thanksgiving and when Sir Edmund forbade this, with threats of military force, they drew up, on the motion of Increase Mather, an address of thanks to the king. This it was thought best to intrust to some " well qualified person " who " might by the Help of such Protestant Dissenters as the King began, upon Political Views, to cast a fair Aspect upon, Obtain some Relief to the Growing Distresses of the Country: and Mr. Mather was the Per-

son that was pitch'd upon.'' Since 1685 this
busy minister had been president of Harvard
College as well as one of the first citizens of
Boston. Randolph hated him violently and was
determined to prevent his embarkation, if possible. So, when his church had released him
and the college had bidden him God Speed he
had to slip off, in disguise, in order to avoid
arrest! After being concealed at what was
afterwards the Pratt House in Chelsea he was
carried by boat, on a night early in April, 1688,
to the ship, President, lying outside the bay.
Safely aboard he sailed away to England,
charged with the enormous task of persuading
a Catholic king to restore, of his own free will,
the vacated charter of Massachusetts.

The Mathers feared that it was James's purpose to set up the Roman Catholic religion in
America, and Increase Mather was secretly
determined, therefore, to bring back into power
the theocratic democracy of the fathers. As a
means to this end he hoped to obtain for the
College, whose head he had the honour to be,
a royal charter by which it should be perma-
nently secured to the Calvinists who had
founded and cherished it.

King James received him graciously enough,
but answered his requests only in fair-sounding

THE PRATT HOUSE, CHELSEA

BOSTON PUBLIC LIBRARY

promises. He could, indeed, do little else for his own seat was far from secure; and, in less than a year from the time Increase Mather sailed from Boston William and Mary were proclaimed rulers of England and its territories. Sewall, who had gone to join Mather in London, gives us a vivid account of these rapid and far-reaching changes.

In Boston several very important steps were taken even before the accession of William and Mary was established as a fact. For on April 4, 1689, there came over a young man named John Winslow, bearing with him a copy of the Declaration issued by the Prince of Orange upon his landing in England. Sir Edmund Andros would not listen to Winslow and angrily committed him to prison "for bringing traitorous and treasonable libels and papers of news." But the people of Massachusetts were willing to take their chance on William's turning out the king he had proclaimed himself to be and, on April 18, Boston rose in arms and seized the chief magistrates.

This was perhaps the most astounding incident in the whole history of Boston. There does not appear to have been any plan to seize the reins of government or to rise up in arms. Yet it was just this which was done. "I knew not anything of what was intended until it was begun," writes an eye-witness, " yet being at the north end of the town where I saw boys running along the streets with clubs in their hands, encouraging one another to fight, I began to mistrust what was intended; and, hasting towards the Town Dock I soon saw men running for their arms, but before I got to the Red Lion I was told that Captain George and the Master of the Frigate [upon which Andros had tried to escape] were seized and secured in Mr. Colman's house, at the North End; and when I came to the Town Dock I understood that Bullivant and some others of them were laid hold of, and then, immediately the drums began to beat and the people hastened and ran, some with and some for arms. Young Dudley and Colonel Lidget with some difficulty attained to the Fort."

The fort, in which Andros had promptly intrenched himself, was at the summit of Fort Hill, on the site of what is now Fort Hill Square. This hill was formerly one of the three great hills of " Treamount " (Copp's Hill and Beacon Hill being the two others) and ascended sharply from the foot of what is now Milk street. From this safe place Andros sent forth messengers, requesting the four minis-

ters and one or two other persons of importance in the town to come to him for consultation. But they refused on the ground that they
did not think such action safe.

For, " by this time," as our eye-witness continues, " all the persons who they [the revo-
lutionists] concluded not to be for their side
were seized and secured. . . . All the companies were soon rallied together at the Town
House, where assembled Captain Winthrop,
Shrimpton, Page and many other substantial
men to consult matters: in which time the old
Governor [Bradstreet] came among them at
whose appearance there was a great shout by
the soldiers."

The self-restraint exercised both by the people and by Andros on this occasion seem to me
very remarkable. Both sides were full of desire to fight, but neither was quite sure just
how things stood in England and so let wisdom
be the better part of valour. In the Assembly
the following paper was drawn up and sent to
Andros:

" At the Town House in Boston,
" April 18, 1689.
" To Sir Edmund Andros,
" Sir: Ourselves and many others, the in-

habitants of this town and the places adjacent,
being surprised with the people's sudden taking up of arms; in the first motion, whereof
we were wholly ignorant, being driven by the
present accident, are necessitated to acquaint
your Excellency that for the quieting and securing of the people inhabiting in this country
from the imminent dangers they many ways lie
open and disposed to, and tendering your own
safety, we judge it necessary you forthwith
surrender and deliver up the Government and
Fortifications to be preserved and disposed according to order and direction from the Crown
of England, which suddenly is expected may
arrive; promising all security from violence
to yourself or any of your gentlemen or souldiers in person and estate; otherwise we are
assured they will endeavour the taking of the
Fortification by storm, if any opposition be
made: —

SIMON BRADSTREET,
JOHN RICHARDS,
ELISHA COOKE,
JS. ADDINGTON,
JOHN FOSTER,
PETER SERGEANT,
DAVID WATERHOUSE,
ADAM WINTHROP,

J. NELSON,
WAIT WINTHROP,
WILLIAM STOUGHTON,
THOMAS DANFORTH,
SAMUEL SHRIMPTON,
WILLIAM BROWNE,
BARTHOLO. GEDNEY.''

At first Andros refused to do what was here demanded, but, after a little reflection, he complied and Captain Fairweather, with his soldiers proceeded to take peaceable possession of the fort. The deposed governor with his friends was then marched with scant ceremony to the Town House, from the balcony of which William's Declaration had already been read to the assembled crowd. Upon the demand of the country people, who had come armed into the town, he was bound and straightway sent back as a prisoner to the fort he had just surrendered. The people, too, were all for resuming the vacated charter, but it was finally decided that the old officers of the government of 1686 should assume a sort of conservative control until more news should be received from England. The day following this arrangement a ship arrived proclaiming that William and Mary were indeed king and queen. The writers of the time pronounce this " the most joyful news ever before received in Boston." Certainly the Puritans were unwontedly gay in celebrating it, " civil and military officers, merchants and principal gentlemen of the Town and Country, being on horseback, the regiment of the Town and many companies of horses and foot from the Country appearing in arms; a grand entertainment was prepared in the Town-house and *wine was served out to the soldiers!*"

All that summer and the following autumn Sir Edmund Andros, Joseph Dudley and " the rest of his crew," as Cotton Mather expressively put it, were kept prisoners. Some attempts at escape were made by the chief captive, and at one time he even got as far as Rhode Island before being retaken. On one previous occasion, he had passed two guards in the disguise of woman's clothing, and if he had taken as much care about his boots, in preparing for flight, as with the rest of his make-up, he would undoubtedly have secured his liberty. The Provisional Government did not keep him confined because it wanted to however, only because it did not know what else to do with him. We can be sure the whole town gave a deep sigh of relief when an order from the king was received, the following February, that the prisoners should be sent to England.

Meanwhile Increase Mather in England had been rapidly making friends with the new sovereign. At first it even looked as if he would be able to obtain the first charter again, but while the matter was hanging fire, the enemies

SIR WILLIAM PHIPS

BOSTON
PUBLIC
LIBRARY

of the old system busied themselves against it. Yet if Mather failed to reinstate the old charter, he did succeed in separating New England from the other colonies and in securing for it a charter much more liberal than was granted to any other colony. And while he could not prevent the provision of a royal governor equipped with a veto power, he was adroit enough to have the territories of Nova Scotia, Maine and Plymouth annexed to Massachusetts and to gain a confirmation for all the grants made by the General Court. Also he was able practically to select the new governor. After four years of unremitting effort, therefore, he sailed in March, 1692, for New England pretty well satisfied with himself.

The new governor was Sir William Phips and his lieutenant-governor was William Stoughton, who had been bred for the church and who possessed just enough bigotry to make him very acceptable to the clergy. The news of the men whom the elder Mather had caused to be put into office was so glorious to the son, who had been watching and working at home, that he broke into a shout of triumph when he heard it: "The time has come. The set time has come. I am now to receive an answer of so many prayers. All the counsellor's of the

province are of my father's nomination; and
my father-in-law with several related unto me,
and several brethren of my own church are
among them. The governor of the province is
not my enemy but one whom I baptized;
namely Sir William Phips, one of my own
flock and one of my dearest friends.''

A most romantic figure was this new governor. Born in the woods of Maine, one of a
family of twenty-six children, he had early
been left to pick up, as best he could, his living
and his scanty education. At the age of
twenty-two he came to Boston in pursuit of
the fortune he had determined should be his
and, while working at his trade of carpenter,
attracted the attention of a prosperous widow.
This lady had the advantage of him both in
years and in estate, but the marriage which
soon followed proved a fairly happy one, —
and it certainly helped Phips to launch out
into the profession of ship-builder, through
which he afterwards came to renown. On one
of his voyages he heard of a Spanish treasure-
ship which had been sunk in the waters of the
Spanish main and, fired with ambition to raise
from the deep the untold wealth the ship was
supposed to contain, he went to London and,
young and unknown though he was, managed

so to plead his cause that (in 1684) James II gave him an eighteen-gun ship and ninety-five men with which to make his fortune — and the king's. For two years he cruised in the West Indies without any very striking success, but he did obtain, during this time, knowledge of the precise spot where the treasure-ship had foundered, nearly half a century before, and when he returned to England he gave such a good account of this to the Duke of Albermarle and other courtiers that he managed to obtain from them another vessel, on shares. This time he succeeded in his expedition.

One wonders if Stevenson had not freshly read the story of Phips's adventures when he wrote his incomparable Treasure Island. Certainly in this case history fairly rivals fiction. For Phips's men mutinied, one poor fellow went mad at the mere thought of the wealth which was to be his if only he would do his duty, there was a lot of fighting, much diplomacy of a sort and through it all the cleverness of a born sea dog. But Phips accomplished his purpose. From the sunken galleon he raised bullion to the value of £300,000 together with many precious stones. After the shares had been distributed according to contract there was about £20,000 for his own share. Armed

with this, a gold cup that the Duke of Albermarle had caused to be fashioned for his wife,
and reinforced by the rank of knight, the
Maine carpenter was able to sail in triumph
back to his native New England. The time
when he thus arrived was that of Andros,
and the office bestowed upon the doughty sailor
by James II had been "High Sheriff of New
England." But since Phips knew nothing of
law and could not write plainly, he was not a
very great success as a sheriff. He did better
as head of the expedition sent out in 1690
against Port Royal. But he failed in that
against Quebec and so happened to be back in
England and " out of a job " just at the time
Increase Mather wanted a promising person to
be first governor of the royal Province of
Massachusetts.

Sir William Phips particularly recommended himself to the Mathers because they
saw in him one whom the people would respect
as self-made, and who would respect them as
ministers of the Gospel. Increase Mather had
preached the sermon, away back in 1674, which
caused Phips to feel himself a sinner and seek
for enrolment among the righteous of the
state; Increase Mather also had now named
him for the office which crowned his worldly

Cotton Mather

BOSTON PUBLIC LIBRARY

ambition. Why, then, might not Increase
Mather expect, through Sir William Phips and
a new charter, which gave the governor more
power than he had ever had under the former
one, to bring back the good old days of the
theocracy? Unhappily for his hopes an unexpected influence now entered into the life of
the people. And it was because Cotton Mather
was so intimate a part of this that the Mather
dynasty finally fell.

The great tragedy of witchcraft! This and
the part Cotton Mather played in it did for the
theocracy, I repeat, what no mortal power
could undo. Long before the time of the great
outbreak at Salem, which constituted the most
marked event of Phips's administration, there
had occurred in Boston the somewhat notorious affair of the Goodwin children. To go
deeply into the subject of witchcraft would not
be fitting in this volume, especially as I have
elsewhere [1] advanced what seems to me as good
a theory as any concerning the delusion. Moreover, certain phases of the whole matter are
now beginning to be pretty well understood
under the name of hypnotism, suggestion and
the like. But they were not at all understood
in Cotton Mather's time, and to blame him for

---

[1] See " Romance of Old New England Roof-Trees."

not possessing scientific knowledge to which
we, two centuries later, have scarcely found
the key seems as unfair as it is unnecessary.
He had to pay the price, however, of the witchcraft trials which he incessantly urged on.
And the process by which he paid it is certainly our concern.

Let us therefore look into the affair of the
children who were his special care. We may
perhaps get the facts most clearly in mind by
quoting from Governor Hutchinson's account,
reproduced by Mr. Poole in the Memorial History of Boston.

" In 1687 or 1688 began a more alarming instance than any that had preceded it. Four of
the children of John Goodwin, a grave man and
good liver at the north part of Boston, were
generally believed to be bewitched. I have
often heard persons who were in the neigh-
bourhood speak of the great consternation it
occasioned. The children were all remarkable
for ingenuity of temper, had been religiously
educated, were thought to be without guile.
The eldest was a girl of thirteen or fourteen
years. She had charged a laundress with taking away some of the family linen. The
mother of the laundress was one of the wild
Irish, of bad character, and gave the girl harsh

language; soon after which she fell into fits which were said to have something diabolical in them. One of her sisters and two brothers followed her example, and, it is said, were tormented in the same part of their bodies at the same time, although kept in separate apartments and ignorant of one another's complaints. . . . Sometimes they would be deaf, then dumb, then blind; and sometimes all these disorders together would come upon them. Their tongues would be drawn down their throats, then pulled out upon their chins. Their jaws, necks, shoulders, elbows and all other joints would appear to be dislocated, and they would make the most piteous outcries of burnings, of being cut with knives, beat, etc., and the marks of wounds were afterwards to be seen.

" The ministers of Boston and Charlestown kept a day of fasting and prayer at the troubled house; after which the youngest child made no more complaints. The others persevered and the magistrates then interposed, and the old woman was apprehended; but upon examination would neither confess nor deny, and appeared to be disordered in her senses. Upon the report of physicians that she was *compos mentis,* she was executed, declaring at her death the children should not be relieved."

This case derives its peculiar interest from the fact that Cotton Mather wrote a book about it and then engaged in numerous controversies in defence of statements which were made therein. He also preached upon the subject more than was either wise or good when one considers that all delusions grow by what they feed upon. Such words as these seem clearly reprehensible from a " man of God: " " Consider the misery of them whom witchcraft may be let loose upon. . . . O what a direful thing it is to be prickt with pins and stabbed with knives all over, and to be fill'd all over with broken bones." In a credulous community the mere circulation of suggestions like these served almost literally to pour oil upon the fire.

So by the time Sir William Phips landed in the chief city of his province the prisons were filled to overflowing with those suspected of witchcraft and those who had given information on the subject. One of his first acts, therefore, — and there is little reason to doubt that it was suggested by the Mathers, — was to appoint a special court of Oyer and Terminer to try the witches. Of this court William Stough-

WILLIAM STOUGHTON

BOSTON
PUBLIC
LIBRARY

ton, the bigoted Deputy Governor, was made
chief justice; and Samuel Sewall was appointed one of his associates. When their
stomachs for the horrible work upon which
they had enlisted failed them they applied to
the Boston ministers for advice. Cotton
Mather " earnestly recommended that the proceedings should be vigorously carried on." It
is for this recommendation that he is execrated
to-day. But I do not see why we should doubt
the honesty of his purpose in giving this harsh
counsel. Witchcraft was to him a terrible
reality and the active presence of the devil in
the world a thing in which he implicitly believed. More than once in his various writings
he adduces as evidence of the devil's activity
the fact that steeples of churches are more
often struck by lightning than are any other
edifices!

Soon no one was safe from accusation, even
Mr. Willard, the pastor of the Old South, being
threatened and Lady Phips herself named.
Possibly it was this bringing of the thing
home which made the governor put an abrupt
stop to proceedings that had already begun to
menace the well-being of the entire community.
Very likely, too, he had come to fear, that he
might be called to account in England. At any

rate the court so unceremoniously instituted by him was summarily dismissed and a general pardon issued to all those who had been convicted or accused. And though a few infatuated individuals continued to urge prosecutions juries refused to bring in the verdict of guilty, — and Judge Samuel Sewall stood up manfully (in 1696) at the old South Church while his confession of having done wrong in admitting " spectral evidence " at the witchcraft trials was read aloud by one of the clergymen. Stoughton, when he heard of this, declared that he had no such confession to make having acted according to the best light God had given him. Nor did Cotton Mather feel at this time any consciousness of wrong-doing. Seventeen years later, however, when his public influence was on the wane and the power of the Church, for which he had had such hopes, was also notably diminished he wrote in his Diary: " I entreated the Lord that I might understand the meaning of the Descent from the Invisible World which, nineteen years ago, produced a sermon from me, a good part of which is now published." The sermon in question was the one which had done so much to incite the witch trials. Evidently Cotton Mather had at last come to doubt its inspiration.

Witchcraft, however, was by no means the worst of poor Sir William Phips's troubles. He had to carry on French and Indian wars not all of which turned out well, the new charter was not nearly so much liked as the Mathers had hoped it might be, and, — what was of more importance than anything else, — the governor had a hasty temper and was inclined to resort to the strength of his fists when matters proved especially trying to him. Early in his administration, he had an altercation with the collector of the port of Boston which culminated in a hand-to-hand fight. And, in January, 1693, a little difficulty between him and the captain of the Nonesuch frigate brought upon the officer a caning in the streets of Boston and upon Sir William Phips a summons to return to England to explain his undignified conduct. He obeyed the summons, passed through his trial without any very great difficulty and was permitted to turn his energy into lines for which he was better fitted than for government. Then he suddenly died at the early age of forty-five.

With him died all hope of ever restoring the power of the theocracy. For though Lieutenant-Governor Stoughton, one of the old Puritan stock, remained at the head of the government until 1699 flood-tide in the affairs of the Mathers had passed for all time. That they did not recognize this fact makes their subsequent history only the more pitiable.

X

To discuss in any detail the history of Harvard College would be, of course, quite outside the province of a book on Colonial Boston. But, as an institution of which Increase Mather, one of Boston's most noted divines, was for a number of years president, as an enterprise to which Cotton Mather longed throughout his later life to give himself as head, and as a school in which almost all the men who made deep marks upon Boston's early history were educated, Harvard has, undeniably, a certain claim upon our attention. This, too, quite apart from the fact that it memorializes an early Puritan minister to whom we owe it to ourselves here to pay at least a passing tribute.

Only seven years after the arrival of Governor Winthrop with the first charter of the colony the General Court voted (1636) '' four hundred pounds towards a school or college.''

Two years later, John Harvard, a young graduate of Emmanuel College, Cambridge, who
had emigrated to Charlestown, died, and bequeathed one-half of his whole property and
his entire library to the proposed institution.
His estate amounted to £779 17s. 2d., which
shows he must have been among the most
wealthy of the early settlers, — and his library
consisted of three hundred and twenty volumes.
Of this goodly collection of books but one sur-
vives to-day, — Downame's " Christian War-
fare," — all the others having been destroyed
in the fire of 1764. At the time of his death
Harvard was assistant minister to Rev. Z.
Symmes in the first church at Charlestown.
He was buried in the old Charlestown burying-
ground and to his memory the alumni of Harvard University there erected September 26,
1828, what was then regarded as a very impressive granite monument.

The munificence of the Rev. John Harvard
inspired further enthusiasm in the magistrates
and made the common people, also, very
anxious to give their mites towards the new
institution of learning. There is, indeed, something very touching in these early gifts, which
reflect the simplicity of the necessities in that
period as well as the earnest desire of the

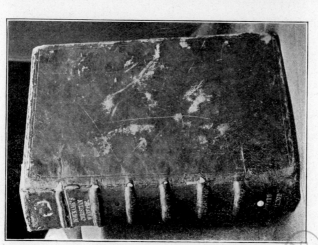

COVER AND TITLE-PAGE OF JOHN HARVARD'S BOOK

BOSTON
PUBLIC
LIBRARY

colonists to help on the good work of education. One man bequeathed a number of sheep, another a quantity of cotton cloth worth nine shillings, another a pewter flagon worth ten shillings and not a few their household treasures amounting to perhaps a pound or so when sold.

In 1642 a Board of Overseers, consisting of the Governor and Deputy Governor, all the magistrates and the teaching elders of the six adjoining towns was established. In 1650, a charter was granted by the General Court, empowering a corporation, consisting of the President, the treasurer, five fellows and the overseers to perpetuate themselves and govern the affairs of the college. The first president was Henry Dunster, whose pathetic end has already been referred to in the chapter on the religious persecutions. Dunster deserves always to be recalled, however, when Harvard in the making is being discussed for he contributed, at a time of its utmost need, one hundred acres of land towards the support of the college and for many years served the institution unweariedly for scarcely any recompense. How the college rewarded him we have seen.

But if they treated their presidents differently two hundred and fifty years ago they also maintained quite a different attitude, from to-day, towards their students. In the college records are preserved several documents which throw interesting side-lights upon the academic life of that early period. None of these is more illuminating than " Dunster's Rules " printed in President Josiah Quincy's " History of Harvard University," but quite worth reprint-ing here because that volume is now so rare.

The original rules were in Latin and all con-tinued in force at least until the revision of 1734 when a few were made less harsh. In translation they read:

" The Laws, Liberties and Orders of Har-vard College, Confirmed by the Overseers and President of the College in the years 1642, 1643, 1644, 1645, and 1646, and Published to the Scholars for the Perpetual Preservation of their Welfare and Government."

" 1. When any scholar is able to read Tully, or such like classical Latin author, extempore, and make and speak true Latin in verse and prose suo (ut aiunt) Marte, and decline per-fectly the paradigms of nouns and verbs in the Greek tongue, then may he be admitted into the college, nor shall any claim admission be-fore such qualifications.

" 2. Everyone shall consider the main end
of his life and studies, to know God and Jesus
Christ, which is eternal life; John xvii., 3.

" 3. Seeing the Lord giveth wisdom, everyone shall seriously, by prayer in secret, seek
wisdom of Him; Proverbs ii., 2, 3, etc.

" 4. Everyone shall so exercise himself in
reading the Scriptures twice a day, that they
be ready to give an account of their proficiency
therein, both in theoretical observations of
language and logic, and in practical and spiritual truths, as their tutor shall require, according to their several abilities respectively, seeing the entrance of the word giveth light, etc.;
Psalm cxix., 130.

" 5. In the public church assembly they shall
carefully shun all gestures that show any contempt or neglect of God's ordinances, and be
ready to give an account to their tutors of their
profiting, and to use the helps of storing themselves with knowledge, as their tutors shall
direct them. And all sophisters and bachelors
(until themselves make common place) shall
publicly repeat sermons in the hall, whenever
they are called forth.

" 6. They shall eschew all profanation of
God's holy name, attributes, word, ordinances
and times of worship; and study, with rever-

ence and love, carefully to retain God and His truth in their minds.

" 7. They shall honour as their parents, magistrates, elders, tutors and aged persons, by being silent in their presence (except they be called on to answer), not gainsaying; showing all those laudable expressions of honour and reverence in their presence that are in use, as bowing before them, standing uncovered, or the like.

" 8. They shall be slow to speak, and eschew not only oaths, lies and uncertain rumours, but likewise all idle, foolish, bitter scoffing, frothy, wanton words and offensive gestures.

" 9. None shall pragmatically intrude or intermeddle in other men's affairs.

" 10. During their residence they shall studiously redeem their time, observe the general hours appointed for all the scholars, and the special hour for their own lecture, and then diligently attend the lectures, without any disturbance by word or gesture; and, if of anything they doubt, they shall inquire of their fellows, or in case of non-resolution, modestly of their tutors.

" 11. None shall, under any pretence whatsoever, frequent the company and society of such men as lead an ungirt and dissolute life.

Neither shall any, without the license of the overseers of the college, be of the artillery or trainband. Nor shall any, without the license of the overseers of the college, his tutor's leave, or, in his absence, the call of parents or guardians, go out to another town.

" 12. No scholar shall buy, sell or exchange anything, to the value of sixpence, without the allowance of his parents, guardians or tutors; and whosoever is found to have sold or bought any such things without acquainting their tutors or parents, shall forfeit the value of the commodity, or the restoring of it, according to the discretion of the president.

" 13. The scholars shall never use their mother tongue, except that in public exercises of oratory, or such like, they be called to make them in English.

" 14. If any scholar, being in good health, shall be absent from prayers or lectures, except in case of urgent necessity, or by the leave of his tutor, he shall be liable to admonition (or such punishment as the president shall think meet), if he offend above once a week.

" 15. Every scholar shall be called by his surname only, till he be invested with his first degree, except he be a fellow commoner or knight's eldest son, or of superior nobility.

" 16. No scholar shall, under any pretence
of recreation or other cause whatever (unless
foreshowed and allowed by the president or
his tutor), be absent from his studies or appointed exercises, above an hour at morning
never, half an hour at afternoon never, an
hour and a half at dinner, and so long at
supper.

" 17. If any scholar shall transgress any of
the laws of God, or the House out of perverse-
ness, or apparent negligence, after twice admonition, he shall be liable, if not adultus, to
correction; if adultus, his name shall be given
up to the overseers of the college, that he may
be publicly dealt with after the desert of his
fault; but in greater offences such gradual
proceeding shall not be exercised.

" 18. Every scholar, that on proof is found
able to read the original of the Old and New
Testament into the Latin tongue and to resolve
them logically, withal being of honest life and
conversation, and at any public act hath the
approbation of the overseers and master of the
college, may be invested with his first degree.

" 19. Every scholar that giveth up in writing a synopsis or summary of logic, natural
and moral philosophy, arithmetic, geometry,
and astronomy, and is ready to defend his

theses or positions, withal skilled in the orig-
inals as aforesaid, and still continues honest
and studious, at any public act after trial, he
shall be capable of the second degree, of Master of Arts.''

By orders of the overseers in 1650, it was
provided among other things that '' no scholar
whatever, without the fore-acquaintance and
leave of the president and his tutor, shall be
present at any of the public civil meetings, or
concourse of people, as courts of justice, elections, fairs, or at military exercise, in the time
or hours of the college exercise, public or private. Neither shall any scholar exercise himself in any military band, unless of known
gravity, and of approved sober and virtuous
conversation, and that with the leave of the
president and his tutor.

'' No scholar shall take tobacco, unless permitted by the president, with the consent of
their parents or guardians, and on good reason
first given by a physician, and then in a sober
and private manner.''

At a meeting of the corporation in 1659, it
was voted that, '' whereas there are great complaints of the exorbitant practices of some students of this college, by their abusive words
and actions to the watch of this town,'' the

Cambridge town watch were authorized to exercise their powers within the precincts of the college. It was provided, however, that none " of the said watchmen should lay violent hands on any of the students being found within the precinct of the college yards, otherwise than so that they may secure them until they may inform the president or some of the fellows." It was also voted that " in case any student of this college shall be found absent from his lodging after nine o'clock at night, he shall be responsible for and to all complaints of disorder in this kind, that, by testimony of the watch or others shall appear to be done by any student of the college, and shall be adjudged guilty of the said crime, unless he can purge himself by sufficient witness." In 1682, the civil authority " was formally recognized as the last resort for enforcing, in extreme cases," college discipline.

In October, 1656, the president and fellows were empowered by statute " to punish all misdemeanours of the youth in their society, either by fines, or whipping in the hall openly, as the nature of the offence shall require, not exceeding ten shillings, or ten stripes for one offence." The tutors " chastised at discretion, and on very solemn occasions the overseers

were called together, either to authorize or to
witness the execution of the severer punish-
ments.'' An old diary tells of the punishment,
in 1674, of one who had been guilty of '' speaking blasphemous words.'' The sentence of the
overseers was read twice in the library. Then,
'' the offender having kneeled, the president
prayed, and then publicly whipped, before all
the scholars,'' the blasphemer. '' The solemnities were closed by another prayer from the
president.''

Although this public flogging by the president gradually fell into disuse, it was not formally abolished until 1734 when the right of
punishing undergraduates by '' boxing '' was
'' expressly reserved to the president, professors, and tutors.'' In 1755, the doing away
with this form of punishment was considered;
but no decisive action was taken, although the
practice was gradually given up.

The system of imposing fines for infractions
of the rules continued. Here is the schedule.

'' List of pecuniary mulcts:

'' Absence from prayers, 2d; tardiness at
prayers, 1d; absence from professor's public
lecture, 4d; tardiness at professor's public
lecture, 2d; profanation of Lord's Day, not
exceeding 3s; absence from public worship,

9d; tardiness at public worship, 3d; ill behaviour at public worship, not exceeding 1s 6d;
going to meeting before bell-ringing, 6d; neglecting to repeat the sermon, 9d; irreverent
behaviour at prayers, or public divinity lectures, 1s 6d; absence from chambers, etc., not
exceeding 6d; not declaiming, not exceeding
1s 6d; not giving up a declamation, not exceeding 1s 6d; absence from recitation, not exceeding 1s 6d; neglecting analyzing, not exceeding
3s; bachelors neglecting disputations, not exceeding 1s 6d; respondents neglecting disputations, from 1s 6d to 3s; undergraduates out
of town without leave, not exceeding 2s 6d;
undergraduates tarrying out of town without
leave, not exceeding, per diem, 1s 3d; undergraduates tarrying out of town one week without leave, not exceeding 10s; undergraduates
tarrying out of town one month without leave,
not exceeding £2 10s; lodging strangers without leave, not exceeding 1s 6d; entertaining
persons of ill character, not exceeding 1s 6d;
going out of college without proper garb, not
exceeding 6d; frequenting taverns, not exceeding 1s 6d; profane cursing, not exceeding 2s
6d; graduates playing cards, not exceeding 5s;
undergraduates playing cards, not exceeding

2s 6d; undergraduates playing any game for
money, not exceeding 1s 6d; selling and ex-
changing without leave, not exceeding 1s 6d;
lying, not exceeding 1s 6d; opening door by
pick-locks, not exceeding 5s; drunkenness, not
exceeding 1s 6d; liquors prohibited under penalty, not exceeding 1s 6d; second offence, not
exceeding 3s; keeping prohibited liquors, not
exceeding 1s 6d; sending for prohibited
liquors, not exceeding 6d; fetching prohibited
liquors, not exceeding 1s 6d; going upon the
top of the college, 1s 6d; cutting off the lead,
1s 6d; concealing the transgression of the 19th
law, 1s 6d; tumultuous noises, 1s 6d; second
offence, 3s; refusing to give evidence, 3s;
rudeness at meals, 1s; butler and cook to keep
utensils clean, not exceeding 5s; not lodging
at their chambers, not exceeding 1s 6d; sending freshmen in studying time, 9d; keeping
guns, and going on skating, 1s; firing guns or
pistols in college yard, 2s 6d; fighting or hurt-
ing any person, not exceeding 1s 6d."

It is noteworthy that " undergraduates playing cards " (whether merely " for pins " or
" for money ") were punished by a fine of 2s
6d; but that " lying " — an offence of which
very few students are now guilty, and for

which suspension, if not expulsion, is now considered a mild punishment — made the liar liable only to a fine of 1s 6d.

Naturally students were little disturbed by these fines. They proved so annoying to parents, however, that in 1761 a committee was appointed to consider some other method of punishing offenders. Although mulcts were not entirely abolished, a system was adopted which resembled somewhat the present methods of enforcing discipline by " admonition," " probation," " suspension," " dismissal," or " expulsion."

In addition to the formal rules, a system of " Ancient Customs of Harvard College, Established by the Government of It," grew up, was recognized by the authorities and soon had all the force of law. As these had to do chiefly with the conduct of freshmen, and as it was to the interest of all the " seniors " that these customs should be observed, doubtless they were more scrupulously lived up to than President Dunster's rules. Here is a copy of these customs as they appear in the official records:

" 1. No freshman shall wear his hat in the college yard, unless it rains, hails, or snows, provided he be on foot, and have not both hands full.

" 2. No undergraduate shall wear his hat in the college yard, when any of the governors of the college are there; and no bachelor shall wear his hat when the president is there.

" 3. Freshmen are to consider all the other classes as their seniors.

" 4. No freshmen shall speak to a senior with his hat on; or have it on in a senior's chamber, or in his own if a senior be there.

" 5. All the undergraduates shall treat those in the government of the college with respect and deference; particularly they shall not be seated without leave in their presence; they shall be uncovered when they speak to them or are spoken to by them.

" 6. All freshmen (except those employed by the immediate government of the college) shall be obliged to go on any errand (except such as shall be judged improper by some one in the government of the college) for any of his seniors, graduates or undergraduates, at any time, except in studying hours, or after nine o'clock in the evening.

" 7. A senior sophister has authority to take a freshman from a sophomore, a middle bachelor from a junior sophister, a master from a senior sophister, and any governor of the college from a master.

" 8. Every freshman before he goes for the person who takes him away (unless it be one in the government of the college), shall return and inform the person from whom he is taken.

" 9. No freshman, when sent on an errand, shall make any unnecessary delay, neglect to make due return, or go away till dismissed by the person who sent him.

" 10. No freshman shall be detained by a senior when not actually employed on some suitable errand.

" 11. No freshman shall be obliged to observe any order of a senior to come to him, or go on any errand for him, unless he be wanted immediately.

" 12. No freshman, when sent on an errand, shall tell who he is going for, unless he be asked; nor be obliged to tell what he is going for, unless asked by a governor of the college.

" 13. When any person knocks at a freshman's door, except in studying time, he shall immediately open the door, without inquiring who is there.

" 14. No scholar shall call up or down, to or from, any chamber in the college.

" 15. No scholar shall play football or any other game in the college yard, or throw anything across the yard.

"16. The freshmen shall furnish bats, balls and footballs for the use of the students, to be kept at the buttery.

" 17. Every freshman shall pay the butler for putting up his name in the buttery.

" 18. Strict attention shall be paid by all the students to the common rules of cleanliness, decency and politeness.

" The sophomores shall publish these customs to the freshmen in the chapel, whenever ordered by any in the government of the college; at which time the freshmen are enjoined to keep their places in their seats, and attend with decency to the reading."

About 1772, after the overseers had repeatedly recommended abolishing the custom of allowing the upper classes to send freshmen on errands, the president and fellows voted that " after deliberate consideration and weighing all circumstances, they are not able to project any plan in the room of this long and ancient custom, that will not be attended with equal, if not greater inconveniences." Indeed, in 1786, " the retaining men or boys to perform the services for which freshmen had been heretofore employed " was declared to be a growing evil, and was prohibited by the corporation.

In extenuation of the Dunster rules it should

be borne in mind, of course, that Harvard, instead of being the university for young men which we now know, was then little more than a " seminary " for boys. It was indeed the puerility of the students which made it difficult, for a long time, to get a man of first class powers to act as president at Cambridge. Increase Mather, of whose dallying with the office we shall hear much a few pages further on, finally said frankly, when pushed to it, that he had no mind whatever to " leave preaching to 1,500 souls . . . only to expound to 40 or 50 children, few of them capable of edification by such exercises."

Dunster, however, gladly consecrated fourteen years of his life to the upbuilding of the college. In this task he had the devoted co-operation of his wife, a woman of such parts as to entitle her to respectful notice on her own account. For Elizabeth Dunster was, by her first marriage, Elizabeth Glover, wife of Rev. Joseph Glover, — rector of the church at Sutton in Surrey, England, — who in 1638 resigned as minister and came to found the first printing-press ever known in New England. During the voyage over Rev. Joseph Glover passed away, and his wife was therefore confronted with the necessity of setting up her press alone. Her husband had already arranged with Stephen Daye of London to have a share in the undertaking, and it is his imprint — S. D. — which all the early productions of the press bear. But President Dunster gave accommodation in his own house to the plant and very likely had a good deal to do with its early output. It is even conceivable that between planning out his rigid " Rules " he relaxed by " holding copy " for the fair widow to whose heart he soon laid siege.

Certainly he would have assisted with unction in turning out the famous " Freeman's Oath " given on the broadside which was the very first issue of the press. This oath, printed in 1639, splendidly reflects the sturdy character of the early colonists and is indeed just as pertinent to-day as it was then. One of the most stirring sights I have ever seen is its administration each spring, at Faneuil Hall, Boston, on the occasion of the New Voters Festival. It reads in part: " I do solemnly bind myself in the sight of God, when I shall be called to give my voice touching any such matter of this state, in which Free-men are to deal, I will give my vote and suffrage as I shall judge in mine own conscience may best conduce and tend to the public weal of the body, without respect of persons, or favour of any man.''

After Dunster had been driven out, Chauncey, Hoar, and Oakes were successively presidents of the college, but there is little of interest to us, in the conduct of the institution, until the election in 1685 of Increase Mather as its head. Mather took the place with the understanding that he should not reside at Cambridge, and should be permitted to continue, at the same time, his work as pastor of the second church in Boston. He was still president when sent on his mission to England, and in July, 1688, in an interview with James II he brought his long-continued efforts to secure a royal charter for the college to what he thought to be a head. For he then asked the king directly to grant a charter for a non-conformist institution. Yet when the new charter really materialized, was signed by Sir William Phips and went back to England for ratification, the king vetoed it (July, 1696) for the reason that it provided no visiting board. Still Mather was not in the least discouraged; opportunity for another appointment to England seemed thus provided.

The object of the preacher-president in all this matter of the new charter — which it is

MASSACHUSETTS HALL, HARVARD UNIVERSITY, BUILT DURING THE PRESIDENCY

OF JOHN LEVERETT

BOSTON PUBLIC LIBRARY

not worth our while here to follow in detail —
was to make the college at Cambridge distinctly the stamping-ground of his own particular brand of dissent. The king, however,
had an eye to the recognition of episcopacy
at Cambridge, and so would not grant the kind
of charter for which Mather yearned. Moreover, during the absence abroad of the president, certain lay members, who were not en-
slaved to him, gained power on the board. In
spite of all that he could do, therefore, Mather
gradually lost his hold upon the college.

The occasion but not the cause of his enforced resignation was his refusal to live in
Cambridge. For several years the legislature
had been steadily passing resolutions requiring
the president to go into residence, but these
Mather, for the most part, blandly ignored.
Then, in 1698, they voted the president the liberal salary, for that age, of two hundred
pounds annually and appointed a committee to
wait upon him. Judge Sewall describes the
ensuing interview: "Mr. President expostu-
lated with Mr. Speaker . . . about the votes
being altered from 250. . . . We urged his
going all we could; I told him of his birth and
education here; that he look'd at work rather
than wages, all met in desiring him. . . . [He]

Objected want of a house, bill for corporation
not pass'd . . . must needs preach once every
week, which he preferred before the gold and
silver of the West Indies. I told him would
preach twice a day to the students. He said
that [exposition] was nothing like preaching.''

The real reason why Mather fought off settling in Cambridge was however his lingering
hope that he might still get the English mission he so ardently desired. But the Massachusetts Assembly was about at the end of its
patience, and on July 10, 1700, they voted
Mather two hundred and twenty pounds a
year, at the same time appointing a committee
to obtain from him a categorical answer. This
time the president apparently complied with
the request of the authorities, and after a
'' suitable place . . . for his reception and entertainment '' had been prepared at the public
expense, he moved to Cambridge. By the last
of October he was back in town again, however,
professing to Stoughton that Cambridge did
not suit his health and suggesting that another
president be found.

To his great surprise the General Court
'' took him up '' and resolved that '' foras-
much as the Constitution requires that the
President reside at Cambridge, which is now

altered by his removal from thence, and to the
intent that a present necessary oversight be
taken of the College, . . . in case of Mr. Mather's refusal absence, sickness or death, that
Mr. Samuel Willard be Vice-President.''
Stimulated by this Increase Mather managed
to sustain residence in Cambridge for three
months more. Then, in a characteristic note
to Stoughton, who was then acting governor,
he expressed his determination to '' return to
Boston the next week and no more to reside
in Cambridge; for it is not reasonable to desire me to be (as out of respect to the public
interest I have been six months within this
twelve) any longer absent from my family.
. . . I do therefore earnestly desire that the
General Court would . . . think of another
president.'' '' *But*,'' warns our reluctantly
retiring official, '' it would be fatal to the interest of religion, if a person disaffected to the
order of the Gospel, professed and practiced
in these churches, should preside over this society.''

This letter proved Mather's undoing, for
when he made it clear to the Court that he
could '' with no conveniency any longer reside
at Cambridge and take care of the College
there,'' a committee was promptly appointed

" to wait upon the Rev. Samuel Willard and
to desire him to accept the care and charge of
the said College and to reside in Cambridge
in order thereunto." The outcome of the
whole matter was that Mather, who for years
would neither reside nor resign, was succeeded
at length by Mr. Samuel Willard, who promised to stay at the college two days and nights
a week. This appointing was made on September 6, 1701, by the General Court Council
of which Sewall was a member. That worthy
had, therefore, to pay the price of the decision.
The manner of this is amusingly told in his
Diary:

" 1701, Oct. 20. Mr. Cotton Mather came
to Mr. Wilkins's shop and there talked very
sharply against me as if I had used his father
worse than a neger; spake so loud that people
in the street might hear him. . . . I had read
in the morn Mr. Dod's saying; Sanctified af-
flictions are good promotions. I found it now
a cordial.

" Oct. 6. I sent Mr. Increase Mather a
hanch of good venison; I hope in that I did
not treat him as a negro.

" Oct. 22, 1701. I, with Major Walley and
Capt. Saml. Checkly, speak with Mr. Cotton
Mather at Mr. Wilkins's. . . . I told him of

his book of the Law of Kindness for the
Tongue, whether this were corresponding with
that. Whether correspondent with Christ's
rule: He said, having spoken to me before
there was no need to speak to me again; and
so justified his reviling me behind my back.
Charg'd the council with lying, hypocrisy,
tricks and I know not what all . . . and then
show'd my share which was in my speech in
council; viz. If Mr. Mather should goe to Cambridge again to reside there with a resolution
not to read the Scriptures and expound in the
Hall: I fear the example of it will do more
hurt than his going thither will doe good. This
speech I owned. . . . I ask'd him if I should
supose he had done something amiss in his
church as an officer; whether it would be well
for me to exclaim against him in the street for
it." Samuel Sewall, a mere layman, thus re-
buking the impeccable Mathers must certainly
have been a spectacle for gods and men!

The truth is, however, that, in this matter
of the college, Cotton Mather put himself, on
this occasion and again on a later one, hope-
lessly in the wrong. For the thing did not end
with the defeat of his father for president.
He himself soon began to look with covetous
eyes on the executive chair at Cambridge. And

when, after the death of Willard in 1707, John
Leverett, the right-hand man of Governor Joseph Dudley, was elected to the office, the wrath
of the younger Mather knew no bounds. The
fact that thirty-nine ministers, presumably as
interested in the welfare of the college as even
he could be, had enthusiastically endorsed
Dudley's choice of Leverett, counted for nothing as against his wounded pride.

Sewall describes with unction Dudley's inau-
guration of his friend: "The govr. prepar'd
a Latin speech for instalment of the president.
Then took the president by the hand and led
him down into the hall. . . . The govr. sat
with his back against a noble fire. . . . Then
the govr. read his speech . . . and mov'd the
books in token of their delivery. Then president made a short Latin speech, importing the
difficulties discouraging and yet he did accept:
. . . Clos'd with the hymn to the Trinity. Had
a very good dinner upon 3 or 4 tables. . . .
Got home very well. Laus Deo."

The Mathers were now thoroughly beaten,
but they could not seem to understand that a
man might honestly fail in appreciation of
them, and they proceeded to charge Dudley
with all manner of bribery, hypocrisy and cor-
ruption. Their letters to the governor at this

GOVERNOR JOSEPH DUDLEY

time seem to me so pitiful an exhibition of
narrowness that I will not reproduce them.
For I still feel that both father and son were
sincere, and that to bury them beneath such
adjectives as " dastardly " and " venomous "
— after the manner of many writers — is not
to reproduce faithfully this interesting contention. Dudley, however, was an able man, even
if his political career had not, in every particular, been above reproach. And this time
he happened to be right. So we cannot do better than close our chapter with his admirably
dignified answer to the accusations of the
Mathers, a reply which is also, as it seems to
me, a deserved rebuke to the claims of the theocracy as regards the college.

" GENTLEMEN, Yours of the 20th instant received; and the contents, both as to the matter
and manner, astonish me to the last degree.
I must think you have extremely forgot your
own station, as well as my character; otherwise it had been impossible to have made such
an open breach upon all the laws of decency,
honour, justice and Christianity, as you have
done in treating me with an air of superiority
and contempt, which would have been greatly
culpable towards a Christian of lowest order,

and is insufferably rude toward one whom divine Providence has honoured with the character of your governour. . . .

" Why, gentlemen, have you been so long silent? and suffered sin to lie upon me years after years? You cannot pretend any new information as to the main of your charge; for you have privately given your tongues a loose upon these heads, I am well assured, when you thought you could serve yourselves by exposing me. Surely murder, robberies and other such flaming immoralities were as reprovable then as now. . . .

" Really, gentlemen, conscience and religion are things too solemn, venerable or sacred, to be played with, or made a covering for actions so disagreeable to the gospel, as these your endeavours to expose me and my most faithful services to contempt; nay, to unhinge the government. . . .

" I desire you will keep your station, and let fifty or sixty good ministers, your equals in the province, have a share in the government of the college, and advise thereabouts as well as yourselves, and I hope all will be well. . . .   I am your humble servant,

" J. DUDLEY.

" To the Reverend Doctors Mathers."

XI

THE BOSTON OF FRANKLIN'S BOYHOOD

THE Boston over which the Mathers reluctantly relinquished ascendency was, in its outward aspect, pretty much that which Franklin has described for all time in his matchless Autobiography. Their reign had covered a period of many changes. When Increase Mather had been at the height of his power the taxable polls of the town numbered a little less than nine hundred and the estates were valued (in 1680) at about £23,877. By 1722 there were more than eighteen thousand inhabitants in Boston.

To be sure this estimate of the earlier date followed closely two pretty serious fires. That of November, 1676, was thus described by a contemporary writer: "It pleased God to alarm the town of Boston, and in them the whole country, by a sad fire, accidentally kindled by the carelessness of an apprentice that sat up too late over night, as was conceived [the lad was rising before daylight to go to his work and fell asleep while dressing, the result being that his candle set the house on fire]; the fire continued three or four hours in which time it burned down to the ground forty-six dwelling houses, besides other buildings, together with a meeting-house of considerable bigness." This meeting-house of " considerable bigness " was the Second Church, the church of the Mathers, the first sermon in which had been preached in June, 1650. Rebuilt on its old site immediately after this fire, the edifice stood at the head of North Square until the British soldiers, in 1775, pulled it down for firewood. Mr. Mather's dwelling was destroyed in the same fire which deprived him of his parish church, " but not an hundred of his books from above a thousand " were lost. The town did not yet possess any fire-engine, but this great conflagration hastened the acquiring of one, and, two years later, Boston had its first organized fire company.

Then, on August 7, 1680, there came another " terrible fire," which raged about twelve hours. Capt. John Hull, who kept a Diary, records that this fire began " about midnight in an alehouse, which by sunrise consumed the body of the trading part of the Towne; from

BENJAMIN FRANKLIN

BOSTON PUBLIC LIBRARY

the Mill creek to Mr. Oliver's house, not one house nor warehouse left; and went from my warehouse to Mrs. Leveret's hence to Mr. Hez. Usher's, thence to Mrs. Thacher's thence to Thomas Fitch's.'' Another contemporary manuscript account adds that ''the number of houses burnt was 77 and of ware houses 35.'' This fire was believed to have been of incendiary origin, and one Peter Lorphelin, who was suspected of having set it, was sent to jail and then '' sentenced to stand two hours in the Pillory, have both ears cut off, give bond of £500 (with two sureties), pay charges of prosecution, fees of Court, and to stand committed till the sentence be performed.''

After this fire the burnt district was rebuilt with such rapidity that lumber could not be had fast enough for the purpose and an attempt was made to prohibit, temporarily, its exportation. One of the buildings then erected survived until 1860 and was long known as the Old Feather store. It stood in Dock (now Adams) Square so close, in early days, to tide-water that the prows of vessels moored in the dock almost touched it. The frame was of hewn oak and the outside walls were finished in rough-cast cement, with broken glass so firmly imbedded in it that time produced no

effect. The date 1680 was placed upon the
principal gable of the westerly front. For
many years the store on the ground floor was
used for the sale of feathers, though, from the
building's peculiar shape, it was quite as often
called The Old Cocked Hat as The Old Feather
Store.

The menace of fire had come to be a very
serious one in a town having so many wooden
buildings. Accordingly in the June, 1693,
term of the General Court there was passed
an " Act for building of stone or brick in the
town of Boston and preventing fire." It was
here ordained that " hence forth no dwelling
house, shop, warehouse, barn, stable, or any
other housing of more than eight feet in length
or breadth, and seven feet in height, shall be
erected and set up in Boston but of stone or
brick and covered with slate or tyle," except
in particular cases and then not without license
from the proper authorities. Six years later
the possible exceptions were greatly curtailed.

Yet in October, 1711, there was another
shocking fire which " reduced Cornhill into
miserable ruins and made its impression into
King's street [now State street], into Queen's
street [now Court street] and a great part of
Pudding-lane [Devonshire street]. Among

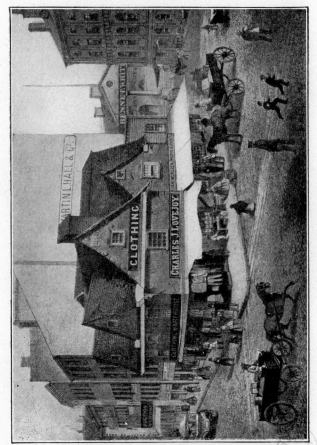

THE OLD FEATHER STORE

BOSTON PUBLIC LIBRARY

these ruins were two spacious Edifices, which
until now, made a most considerable figure,
because of the public relations to our greatest
solemnities in which they had stood from the
days of our Fathers. The one was the Town-
house; the other the Old Meeting-house. The
number of houses, and some of them very spacious buildings, which went into the fire with
these, is computed near about a hundred.''
Those not burned out in the fire contributed
about seven hundred pounds through the
churches of Boston to the families that had
suffered loss. The immediate effect of this
conflagration was the appointment of ten officers called Fire wards in the various parts
of the town who were '' to have a proper badge
assigned to distinguish them in their office,
namely a staff of five feet in length, coloured
red, and headed with a bright brass spire of
six inches long.'' These functionaries had full
power to command all persons at fires, to pull
down or blow up houses and to protect goods.

Among the small boys interested, as boys
have ever been, in the havoc wrought by this
fire of 1711, there would very likely have been
found the five-year-old son of Josiah Franklin,
tallow-chandler. Franklin had been a dyer in
England but, upon reaching Boston, had set

up in the business of chandlery and soap boil-- ing. In 1691 he had built — near the south meeting-house — on what is now Milk street, a dwelling for his family, and there on Sunday, January 17, 1706, his child Benjamin was born. Soon afterwards, Josiah Franklin removed to a house at the corner of Hanover and Union streets where he lived the rest of his life. Here he hung out, as a sign of his trade, the blue ball, about the size of a cocoanut, which now reposes in the old State House, Boston.

Although there were so many children swarming in that little house on Hanover street, with its parlour and dining room close behind the shop, it was not a bit too crowded. Franklin in his Autobiography records that he well remembers " thirteen sitting at one time at his father's table who all grew up to be men and women and married." There were many visitors, too, in the living-room back of the shop, because Josiah Franklin had sturdy common sense and so was sought out by " lead-ing people who consulted him for his opinion in the affairs of the town or the church he belonged to and showed a good deal of respect for his judgment and advise."

The life led by the Franklins we may well enough take to be a type of that lived in hun-

FRANKLIN'S BIRTHPLACE

BOSTON PUBLIC LIBRARY

dreds of self-respecting families of that day.
There was a great deal of work, a great deal
of church-going and considerable hardship of
a healthy kind. But there were pleasures, too,
chief among them being that of hospitality:
" My father," Franklin tells us, " liked to
have at his table, as often as he could, some
sensible friend or neighbour to converse with,
and always took care to start some ingenious
or useful topic for discourse, which might tend
to improve the minds of his children. By this
means he turned our attention to what was
good, just and prudent in the conduct of life;
and little or no notice was ever taken of what
related to the victuals on the table, . . . so
that I was brought up in such a perfect inat-
tention to those matters as to be quite indif-
ferent what kind of food was set before me,
and so unobservant of it to this day, that if
I am asked I can scarce tell a few hours after
dinner what I dined upon." We can the more
readily, after reading this, accept as authentic
an anecdote told by the grandson of Franklin
to the effect that, one day, after the winter's
provision of salt fish had been prepared, Benjamin observed, " I think, father, if you were
to say grace over the whole cask once for all,
it would be a vast saving of time."

Josiah Franklin, like every other good
Christian of his day, wished to give at least
one son to the order of the sacred ministry,
and Benjamin, being his tenth child, was singled out for this distinction. The boy was,
therefore, sent at the age of eight to the grammar school, where in less than a year he had
risen gradually from the middle of the class
in which he entered to the head of the class
above. But business at the sign of the blue
ball was now less brisk than heretofore and
Father Franklin began reluctantly to confess
that he could see no chance of providing a college training for the boy. A commercial education would bring quicker returns than that
provided by the grammar school. Accordingly, the lad was placed in an institution especially designed for the teaching of writing
and arithmetic. Here Franklin " acquired
fair writing pretty soon " but failed in arithmetic. So, since the family fortunes would not
permit of his being a clergyman and failure
in arithmetic made it impossible for him to be
a clerk, Benjamin was " taken home at ten to
assist in the business." This occupation he
utterly loathed and, in truth, cutting candle-
wicks and filling candle-molds with tallow must

have been sad drudgery to this imaginative book-loving lad of twelve.

Besides, he longed to run away to sea. Born and bred in a seafaring town, and accustomed from earliest childhood to rowing and sailing, nothing delighted him so much as adventures smacking of the salt water. One Franklin boy already had run away to sea, however, and been cut off, as a result, from the family home and hearth. Josiah Franklin determined that, if he could help it, he would not lose his youngest son in the same way. Accordingly, when he found that nothing would make the lad reconciled to soap-making, he set about fitting him to another calling.

After a round had been made of the various shops, it was settled that Ben be apprenticed as a printer to his elder brother James, who had then (1717) just returned from learning this trade in London. With this idea Benjamin fell in the more readily by reason of his already great fondness for books.

" From a child," he tells us in the Autobiography, " I was fond of reading, and all the little money that came into my hands was ever laid out in books. Pleased with the ' Pilgrim's Progress,' my first collection was of John Bunyan's works in separate little vol-

umes. I afterward sold them to enable me to
buy R. Burton's historical collections. They
were small chapmen's books, and cheap, forty
or fifty in all. . . . Plutarch's ' Lives ' there
was, in which I read abundantly, and I still
think that time spent to great advantage.

" This bookish inclination at last determined my father to make me a printer. . . .
I stood out some time, but at last was persuaded, and signed the indentures when I was
yet but twelve years old. I was to serve as an
apprentice till I was twenty-one years of age,
only I was to be allowed journeyman's wages
during the last year. In a little time I made
great proficiency in the business, and became
a useful hand to my brother.

" I now had access to better books. An acquaintance with the apprentices of booksellers
enabled me sometimes to borrow a small one,
which I was careful to return soon and clean.
Often I sat up in my room reading the greatest
part of the night, when the book was borrowed
in the evening and to be returned early in the
morning, lest it should be missed or wanted.

" And after some time an ingenious trades-
man, Mr. Matthew Adams, who had a pretty
collection of books, and who frequented our
printing-house, took notice of me, invited me

to his library, and very kindly lent me such books as I chose to read. I now took a fancy to poetry and made some little pieces. My brother, thinking it might turn to account, encouraged me, and put me on composing occasional ballads. One was called ' The Lighthouse Tragedy,' and contained an account of the drowning of Capt. Worthilake with his two daughters. The other was a sailor's song on the taking of Teach (or Blackbeard) the pirate. They were wretched stuff, in the Grub-Street-ballad style; and, when they were printed, he sent me about the town to sell them. The first sold wonderfully, the event being recent, having made a great noise. This flattered my vanity; but my father discouraged me by ridiculing my performances, and telling me verse-makers were generally beggars. So I escaped being a poet, most probably a very bad one."

But he taught himself to write excellent English prose by modelling his style upon that of Addison and Steele.

" About this time I met with an odd volume of the *Spectator*. It was the third. I had never before seen any of them. I bought it, read it over and over, and was much delighted with it. I thought the writing excellent, and wished, if possible, to imitate it. With this

view I took some of the papers, and, making
short hints of the sentiment in each sentence,
laid them by a few days, and then, without
looking at the book, tried to complete the papers again by expressing each hinted sentiment
at length, and as fully as it had been expressed
before, in any suitable words that should come
to hand.

" Then I compared my *Spectator* with the
original, discovered some of my faults, and
corrected them. But I found I wanted a stock
of words, or a readiness in recollecting and
using them, which I thought I should have acquired before that time if I had gone on making verses, since the continual occasion for
words of the same import, to suit the measure,
or of different sound for the rhyme, would
have laid me under a constant necessity of
searching for variety, and also have tended to
fix that variety in my mind and make me master of it. Therefore I took some of the tales
and turned them into verse; and, after a time,
when I had pretty well forgotten the prose,
turned them back again. I also sometimes
jumbled my collection of hints into confusion,
and after some weeks endeavoured to reduce
them into the best order, before I began to
form the full sentences and complete the paper.

This was to teach me method in the arrangement of thoughts.

"By comparing my work afterward with the original, I discovered many faults and amended them; but I sometimes had the pleasure of fancying that, in certain particulars of small import, I had been lucky enough to improve the method or the language, and this encouraged me to think that I might possibly in time come to be a tolerable English writer, of which I was extremely ambitious. My time for these exercises and for reading was at night after work or before it began in the morning, or on Sundays, when I contrived to be in the printing-house alone, evading as much as I could the common attendance on public worship, which my father used to exact of me when I was under his care, and which, indeed, I still thought a duty, though I could not, as it seemed to me, afford time to practise it."

Additional time — and additional money, too — for the indulgence of his love of books came to Franklin about this time through his adoption of a vegetarian diet. Meat had always been rather disagreeable to him, so he proposed to his brother that he should give him weekly half the money paid for his board, and let him board himself. His brother agreeing, he had opportunity, while the others were at meals, to be alone in the printing-house with his books.

"Despatching presently my light repast, which often was no more than a biscuit or a slice of bread," he writes, "a handful of raisins or a tart from the pastry-cook, and a glass of water, I had the rest of the time for study, in which I made the greater progress from that greater clearness of head and quicker apprehension which usually attend temperance in eating and drinking."

Sixteen years before that Sunday morning when the baby Benjamin was born the first American newspaper had been printed in Boston. It was a sheet of four pages, seven inches by eleven, with two columns on a page, and at the top of the first page the words, "*Publick Occurrences, both Foreign and Domestic*," printed in large letters. It was designed to be published once a month, or oftener, "if any glut of occurrences happened."

By reason of an unfortunate allusion in the first number to a political misunderstanding between those in high authority, *Publick Occurrences* died, immediately after its initial issue. No successor appeared until 1704, when John Campbell, postmaster of Boston, a dull, ignorant Scottish bookseller, began to put out a weekly sheet called the Boston *News-Letter,* which was for many years the only newspaper in America.

Newspapers went free of postage in those days. It was quite natural, therefore, that the publishing privilege should fall into the hands of postmasters. Usually when a postmaster lost his office he sold out his newspaper to his successor; but when John Campbell ceased to preside over the Boston mails, he refused to dispose of his paper, a fact which induced his successor, William Brocker, to set up, in December, 1719, a sheet of his own, the Boston *Gazette.* This paper James Franklin was employed to print.

Postmasters in those days were, of course, appointed from England, and before Brocker had been in office many months he found himself in turn superseded. James Franklin, however, having incurred some expense for the sake of printing the *Gazette* and being enamoured of publishing, determined that he would now start a paper of his own. It thus came about that on August 7, 1721, appeared the first number of the *New England Courant.*

The papers previously published in the colony had been either very dull or very pious.

But this journal, from the beginning, showed
the trenchant pen and free mind which appears
to have been a Franklin habit. The Mathers
did not at all approve of it, and the boy Benjamin probably had no need to stop at their
door when he " carried the papers through the
streets to the customers," after having set up
the type with his own hands and printed the
sheets from the old press now in the possession of the Bostonian Society.

The fortunes of this paper, and of Franklin
while connected with it, have been better told
by the person chiefly concerned than I could
ever tell them. Hear him then: " My brother
had some ingenious men among his friends,
who amused themselves by writing little pieces
for this paper, which gained it credit and made
it more in demand, and these gentlemen often
visited us. Hearing their conversations, and
their accounts of the approbation their papers
were received with, I was excited to try my
hand among them; but, being still a boy, and
suspecting that my brother would object to
printing anything of mine in his paper if he
knew it to be mine, I contrived to disguise my
hand, and, writing an anonymous paper, I put
it at night under the door of the printing-house.

" It was found in the morning, and commu-

nicated to his writing friends when they called
in as usual. They read it, commented on it in
my hearing, and I had the exquisite pleasure
of finding it met with their approbation, and
that, in their different guesses at the author,
none were named but men of some character
among us for learning and ingenuity. I suppose now that I was rather lucky in my judges,
and that perhaps they were not really so very
good ones as I then esteemed them.

" Encouraged, however, by this, I wrote and
conveyed in the same way to the press several
more papers which were equally approved;
and I kept my secret till my small fund of sense
for such performances was pretty well exhausted, and then I discovered it, when I began
to be considered a little more by my brother's
acquaintance, and in a manner that did not
quite please him, as he thought — probably
with reason — that it tended to make me too
vain. And perhaps this might be one occasion
of the differences that we began to have about
this time.

" Though a brother, he considered himself
as my master and me as his apprentice, and
accordingly expected the same services from
me as he would from another, while I thought
he demeaned me too much in some things he

required of me, who from a brother expected more indulgence. Our disputes were often brought before our father, and I fancy I was either generally in the right or else a better pleader, because the judgment was generally in my favour. But my brother was passionate, and had often beaten me, which I took extremely amiss; and, thinking my apprenticeship was very tedious, I was continually wishing for some opportunity of shortening it, which at length offered in a manner unexpected. (I fancy his harsh and tyrannical treatment of me might be a means of impressing me with that aversion to arbitrary power that has stuck to me through my whole life.)

" One of the pieces in our newspaper on some political point, which I have now forgotten, gave offence to the Assembly. He was taken up, censured, and imprisoned for a month, by the speaker's warrant, I suppose, because he would not discover his author. I, too, was taken up and examined before the council; but, though I did not give them any satisfaction, they contented themselves with admonishing me, and dismissed me perhaps as an apprentice who was bound to keep his master's secrets.

" During my brother's confinement, which I

resented a good deal, notwithstanding our
private differences, I had the management of
the paper; and I made bold to give our rulers
some rubs in it, which my brother took very
kindly, while others began to consider me in
an unfavourable light, as a young genius that
had a turn for libelling and satire. My
brother's discharge was accompanied with an
order from the House (a very odd one) that
' JAMES FRANKLIN SHOULD NO LONGER PRINT
THE PAPER CALLED THE " NEW ENGLAND COU-
RANT," EXCEPT IT BE FIRST SUPERVISED BY THE
SECRETARY OF THIS PROVINCE.'

" There was a consultation held in our
printing-house among his friends what he
should do in this case. Some proposed to
evade the order by changing the name of the
paper; but my brother seeing inconveniences
in that, it was finally concluded on, as a better
way, to let it be printed for the future under
the name of Benjamin Franklin. And, to
avoid the censure of the Assembly that might
fall on him as still printing it by his apprentice, the contrivance was that my old indenture
should be returned to me, with a full discharge
on the back of it, to be shown on occasion; but,
to secure to him the benefit of my service, I
was to sign new indentures for the remainder

of the term, which were to be kept private. A very flimsy scheme it was. However, it was immediately executed, and the paper went on accordingly under my name for several months.''

The next number of the *Courant* announced that '' the late Publisher of this Paper, finding so many Inconveniences would arise by his carrying the Manuscripts and publick News to be supervis'd by the Secretary as to render his carrying it on unprofitable, has intirely dropt the Undertaking.''

Possibly the display of his own name in big type as publisher of a newspaper bred in Benjamin something more of self-importance than he had hitherto had. In any case, he and his brother got on very badly after this. There were knocks and cuffs and general unbrotherly treatment, which Benjamin, as a high-spirited lad, soon found unendurable. These blows had the effect, too, of inspiring in the younger Franklin a determination to be tricky, — just as his brother had been with the authorities. So '' a fresh difference arising between us two I took upon me to assert my freedom, presuming that he would not venture to produce the new indentures. It was not fair in me to take this advantage, and this I therefore reckon one of the first errata of my life; but the unfairness of it weighed little with me when under the impressions of resentment for the blows his passion too often urged him to bestow upon me, though he was otherwise not an ill-natured man. Perhaps I was too saucy and provoking.

" When he found I would leave him, he took care to prevent my getting employment in any other printing-house of the town, by going round and speaking to every master, who accordingly refused to give me work. I then thought of going to New York as the nearest place where there was a printer. . . . My friend Collins, therefore, undertook to manage a little for me. He agreed with the captain of a New York sloop for my passage. So I sold some of my books to raise a little money, was taken on board privately, and, as we had a fair wind, in three days I found myself in New York, near three hundred miles from home, a boy of but seventeen, without the least recommendation to or knowledge of any person in the place, and with very little money in my pocket."

Franklin had now left for ever the Boston of his boyhood. Not many times in his life, indeed, did he return there. But, when a famous man, he wrote, to be placed over the graves of

his parents in the old Granary burying ground,
this epitaph which touchingly connects, for all
time, his talents with the city of his birth:

Josiah Franklin
and
Abiah, his wife,
Lie here interred.
They lived lovingly together in wedlock
Fifty-five years.
And without an estate or any gainful employ-
ment,
By constant labour and honest industry,
Maintained a large family comfortably,
And brought up thirteen children and seven
grandchildren reputably.
From this instance, reader,
Be encouraged to diligence in thy calling,
And distrust not Providence.
He was a pious and prudent man;
She a discreet and virtuous woman.
Their youngest son,
In filial regard to their memory,
Places this stone.

SAMUEL SEWALL

BOSTON PUBLIC LIBRARY

XII

A PURITAN PEPYS

WHAT the Diary of Samuel Pepys is to seventeenth century England the Diary of Samuel Sewall is to the Boston of the Puritan era. This invaluable contribution to New England literature covers more than fifty-five years of old Boston life and covers it, too, at a time when that life was putting itself into form. It is therefore a rich mine of history, a veritable storehouse of old ways and social customs. The man who wrote it was a part of all that he met and he was, besides, a red-blooded healthy-minded human being in an age which too many people think wholly given over to disagreeable asceticism. We cannot do better, then, than follow for a chapter Sewall's varied career as he himself traces it for us in the vivid pages of his mental and spiritual day-book.

At the outset we must do the old judge the justice to believe that, — to him, — New England was a colony with a mission. In a speech made in 1723 after Lieutenant-Governor Dummer had taken the oath of office he said: " The people you have to do with are a part of the Israel of God and you may expect to have of the prudence and patience of Moses communicated to you for your conduct. It is evident that our Almighty Saviour counselled the first planters to remove hither and settle here; and they dutifully followed his advice; and therefore he will never leave nor forsake them nor theirs." All his life long Sewall strove to help the Lord do the work he felt to be marked out for the Puritans. We must bear this in mind when the judge of the witches seems narrow to us. But he does not often so seem for he was a generous-minded man, temperamentally and physically easy-going in spite of his Puritan training. The Reverend N. H. Chamberlain, who has written most entertainingly of " Sewall and the World He Lived In " attributes the endearing qualities of his hero to the fact that he was much more Saxon than Dane, and came from the English South Land where the sun is warmer than in the North, the gardens and orchards fuller.

Moreover, none of the Sewalls had suffered from persecution. Samuel's great-grandfather, beyond whom the family cannot be

traced, made a fortune as a linen-draper at
Coventry and was several times elected mayor.
His life was then an eminently successful one.
The mayor's eldest son, however, was a Puritan of such strong convictions that he sent
Sewall's father, Henry, to New England. But
the climate of Newbury, where Henry Sewall
took up land, did not agree with the family and
they returned to the mother country. Thus it
happened that Samuel Sewall was born in
Bishopstoke, Hampshire, England, in 1647 and
spent the impressionable years of his young
life in a background where orchards flourished
mightily, where cock-fighting was a favourite
sport and where roast beef and attendant good
things exercised a potent formative influence.

When the boy Samuel was nine the family
returned to America. His account of their
landing at Boston is given thus naïvely: " We
were about eight weeks at sea where we had
nothing to see but water and sky; so that I
began to fear that I should never get to shore
again; only I thought the captains and the
mariners would not have ventured themselves,
if they had not hopes of getting to land again.
On the Lord's Day my mother kept aboard;
but I went ashore; the boat grounded and I
was carried out in arms, July 6, 1661.''

The future Diarist was educated at his
father's house in Newbury by a private tutor
and at Harvard College, from which he was
graduated in 1671. Three years later he took
his master's degree, an occasion which he described thus in a letter written to his son,
Joseph, when he (Sewall) was a grown man:
" In 1674 I took my second degree and Mrs.
Hannah Hull, my dear wife, your honoured
mother was invited by Doctor Hoar and his
lady (her kinsfolk) to be with them awhile at
Cambridge. She saw me when I took my degree and set her affection on me, though I
knew nothing of it until after our marriage
which was February 28, 1675-76. Governor
Bradstreet married us." Sewall's thesis on
this interesting commencement day was a
Latin discourse on original sin!

For of course the young man was ministeri-
ally minded and, at this stage of his career,
bade fair to follow the profession of most Harvard men of the day. Very likely, too, he
would have kept on with his preaching but for
the fact that, after a supplementary year or
two at Cambridge, it was made easy for him
to enter the business and the family of John
Hull, the New England mint-master. Hull was
now old and Sewall seems to have been en-

trusted, almost at once, with the correspondence appertaining to the merchant branch of his profession. Ere long the Diarist is importing and exporting on his own account.

First, though, came his marriage with the bouncing Hannah Hull, a lady whose weight played a more important part in her charms, than has been the case with any other heroine of romance. Hawthorne is chiefly responsible for this, of course, for he has described in fascinating fashion the marriage of Sewall to this, his first wife. But if Sewall *did* get his wife's weight in pine-tree shillings when he got her he had not stipulated for this or any other dowry. "The mint-master was especially pleased with his new son-in-law because he had courted Miss Betsy *out of pure love*," we are told, "and had said nothing at all about her portion." It is good for us to remember this passage when we read the story of Judge Sewall's later courtships.

About a year after his marriage Sewall joined the Old South Church and having fulfilled this pre-requisite to citizenship, he was (in 1678) made a freeman. In 1681 he was appointed master of the public printing-press, an office which he held for some three years printing public and religious documents, and especially the Assembly's Catechism, five hundred copies of which he gave away to the children of his relations. Sewall had now gone to live at Cotton Hill, on Tremont street, almost opposite King's Chapel burying ground, on property which once belonged to Sir Harry Vane. In the colony records we find (1684) : — " In answer of the petition of Sam' Sewall Esq, humbly showing that his house of wood in Boston, at the hill where the Revd John Cotton former dwelt, which house is considerably distant from other building and standeth very bleak, he humbly desiring the favour of this court to grant him liberty to build a small porch of wood, about seven foot square, to break off the wind from the fore door of said house, the court grants his request."

A pleasant glimpse of the social life of the period is gained from an entry made in the Diary the spring following the building of this porch: " June 20, Carried my wife to Dorchester to eat Cherries and Raspberries, chiefly to ride and take the air; the time my wife and Mrs. Flint spent in the orchard I spent in Mr. Flint's study reading Calvin on the Psalms." The following January he tells us that the cold was so extreme that the " harbour is frozen up and to the Castle, so cold that the sacramental bread is frozen pretty bad and rattles sadly as broken into the plates.''

From November, 1688, to November, 1689, Sewall was abroad combining with the business of helping Increase Mather make terms with the King's government the pleasure of renewing family friendships in the land of his birth. There was naturally a good deal of sermon-hearing mingled with these occupations and we find one excellent description of the fashion in which the Lord's supper was administered in England at the church of that Dr. Annesley of whom we have already heard as Dunton's father-in-law. '' The Dr. went all over the meeting first, to see who was there, then spake something of the sermon, then read the words of institution, then prayed and eat and drunk himself, then gave to every one with his own hand, dropping pertinent expressions. In our pew said, ' Now our Spikenard should give its smell; ' and said to me ' Remember the death of Christ.' The wine was in quart glass bottles. The deacon followed the Doctor and when his cup was empty filled it again; as at our pew all had drunk but I, he filled the cup and then gave it to me; said as he gave it — must be ready in new obedience and stick at nothing for Christ.''

To Cambridge and to Oxford, the colleges where many of the Puritan preachers had been educated, Sewall made pious pilgrimages with Mather and between whiles he ate and drank with his numerous relatives. At " Cousin Jane Holt's " he had " good bacon, veal and parsnips, very good shoulder of mutton and a fowl roasted, good currant suet pudding and the fairest dish of apples I have eat in England."

But he was very glad to get back to Boston for that city was now his dear home and he was one of its most useful citizens. In 1683 he is a deputy to the General Court from Westfield, as his father-in-law, John Hull, had been before him — it being then possible for a man to be elected from a town other than that in which he lived — and he belonged to the Boston Fire Department and to the Police and Watch. In business he was prospering mightily and so was able May 23, 1693, to lay the corner-stone of his new house, next Cotton Hill, " with stones gotten out of the Common." Two years later we find the house completed and Governor Bradstreet " drinking a glass or two of wine, eating some fruit and taking a pipe or two of tobacco " under its substantial

THE DEANE WINTHROP HOUSE, WINTHROP

BOSTON
PUBLIC
LIBRARY

roof. " Wished me joy of the house and desired our prayers," comments the Diary.

Picnics and weddings were favourite diversions with Sewall. The Diary records one fes-
tivity of the former class held Oct. 1, 1697, the
refreshments for which consisted of " first,
honey, butter curds and cream. For dinner
very good roast lamb, turkey, fowls and apple
pie. After dinner sung the 121 Psalm. A
glass of spirits my wife sent stood upon a joint
stool which Simon W. jogging it fell down and
broke all to shivers. I said it was a lively
emblem of our fragility and mortality."

Not long after this our Diarist attended the
wedding of Atherton Haugh, his ward, and
Mercy Winthrop, daughter of Deane Winthrop,
at the latter's house which still stands in the
town bearing his name. " Sang a Psalm together," writes Sewall in describing the occasion. " I set St. David's tune." None of the
many duties which Sewall discharged was better done than that which had to do with settling
his young people in life. On several occasions
we find the Diary saying: " Prayed for good
matches for my children as they grow up; that
they may be equally yoked." It was the Puritan habit to marry, not once, but several times,

if death came to separate. Instances of old
maids were very rare and those of old bachelors
even more so. (Stoughton stands almost alone
among Puritan worthies as a man who never
took unto himself a wife.) The elders on the
man's side seem to have had a custom of sending a suitable present to the lady's parent as
a sign that Barkis was "willin'." If the
match was to be refused the present was very
likely returned. This custom may be held to
explain the following rather blind letter of
Sewall's:

"BOSTON, Jan. 13, 1701.

"MADAM: — The inclosed piece of silver, by
its bowing, humble form bespeaks your favour
for a certain young man in town. The name
(Real) the motto (plus ultra) seem to plead
its suitableness for a present of this nature.
Neither need you accept against the quantity;
for you have the means in your own hands;
and by your generous acceptance you may
make both it and the giver great. Madam, I am
"Your affect. friend,
"S. S."

When the Puritans first came to New England they ordered (1646), in a reaction against

House of Richard Bellingham, Chelsea, Mass.

BOSTON PUBLIC LIBRARY

the Church of England, that only magistrates
or one appointed by the authorities should join
parties in holy wedlock. Under this law Governor Richard Bellingham, the last survivor of
the patentees named in the charter, performed
a marriage service for himself and his new
bride: — " His last wife was ready to be contracted to a friend of his who lodged in his
house and by his consent had proceeded so far
with her when, on the sudden, the governor
treated with her and obtained her for himself.
He was fifty and the lady twenty *and Bellingham also solemnized the marriage himself.*"
By Sewall's time, however, the ministers, as
we have seen, were performing the marriage
ceremony.

One rather curious courtship custom which
obtained at this time was that of addressing
fervid petitions to a near woman-relative of
the girl a man wished for his wife, praying
that this sister or mother would intercede with
the " divine mistress." Drake in his " Roxbury " gives such a letter sent by Paul Dudley,
son of the royal governor, to Mrs. Davenport,
sister of his " dearest Lucy ":

" DEAR MADAM: — It is impossible but that
you must take notice of that most affectionate

Respect and Dutiful Passion I Bear to your
most charming and amiable Sister, and you as
easily guess at my Design in it which I Blush at
the thought of. But the just honour and Regard I have and ought to have to Colonel Wain-
wright, [the girl's father] and his Lady in this
affair, forbids my pursuing it any further till I
have mentioned it to them; for Which Reason
it is that I am now going Hither (though with a
trembling and heavy heart) and carry with me
a letter from the Governor to your Father that
he would allow me to wait upon my Sweetest
fairest Dearest Lucy. But unless my Dearest
Davenport will assist and make An Interest
for me I Can't Hope for Success. I Confess
I have no grounds to ask or expect such a
favour from you, unless it Be by reminding you
of the many obligations you have already laid
me Under, and this is an argument which goes
a great way with Noble and Generous minds,
and I am sure if you did but know what I Un-
dergoe Both Day and Night, you would Pity
me at least. I must beg of you therefore if
you have any regard to my Health and Happiness, I might say to my life, you would show
your compassion and friendship to me in this
matter;* and Hereby lay such an obligation
upon me as shall not, cannot ever Be forgotten.

I Beg a thousand pardons of my Dame for this Freedom; and Pray her not to expose my folly to any one, tho' if she thinks it proper, or that it will Doe me any Service She may Read (to the mark * above) to my Divine Mistress; I know you have smiled all along and By this time are weary of my Scrawle. I'll have done therefore, and when I have asked the favour of you to present, as on my knees, my most Sincere, passionate, Dutifull and Constant Soul to My Charming Nymph, With whom I hope to find it upon my Return, of which I shall be most Impatient. Dear Madam, I once more beg pardon of you and pray you to think me in Earnest in what I write for every Word of it Comes from the Bottom of My Soul, and I hope Before I have done to Convince My Dearest Lucy of the truth of it tho' as yet She Believes nothing that I say to her. Madam, I am, with all affection and Respect, Your most obliged tho' now Distressful Humble Servant,

"PAUL DUDLEY."

"You may show all this letter if you think fit, Mrs. Davenport."

He married Lucy in 1703 and there are occasional references, in Sewall's Diary, to the fortunes of the couple.

This son of Governor Dudley it was, by the
bye, who entered Harvard at the tender age of
eleven and about whom his father thus wrote
the president: "April 26, 1686. I have
humbly to offer you a little sober well-disposed
son, who, though very young, if he may have
the favour of admittance I hope his learning
may be tolerable; and for him I will promise
that, by your and my care, his own Industry
and the blessing of God, his mother, the university, shall not be ashamed to allow him the
place of a son at seven years end. Appoint a
time when he may be examined."

Sewall's children all made good matches
(except Hannah, who was an invalid and never
married), the oldest son winning as a wife the
daughter of Governor Dudley. This alliance
made it very difficult for Sewall to be as sympathetic as he must otherwise have been when
the Mathers, with whom he was very intimate,
solicited his support in their memorable controversy with that official.

After the weddings of the poorer classes
there had been wont to be dancing at a nearby
ordinary or tavern, but the court early took
this abuse vigorously in hand and ordered
(May, 1651) that " whereas it is observed that
there are many abuses and disorders by dan-

cing in ordinaries whether mixed or unmixed,
upon marriage of some persons, this Court
doth order that henceforward there shall be
no dancing upon such occasion, or at any other
times in ordinaries, upon the pain of five shilling for every person that shall so dance in
ordinaries.'' Sewall especially hated dancing
and writes it down with glee in his Diary when
one Stepney, who had come over to teach this
accomplishment, had to run away because of
debt.

In his relations to Indians, negroes and the
witchcraft delusion Sewall showed himself considerably in advance of his time, however.
Reference has already been made to his brave
confession of error in the acceptance of '' spectral evidence,'' so we can here confine our attention to his attitude towards the two other
persecuted peoples. After King Philip's War,
which reached its crisis in May, 1676, the cause
of the Indians went down apace and it was
ordered '' that a guard be set against the entrance of the town of Boston (on the Neck)
and that no Indian be suffered to enter upon
any pretext, and without a guard and two musketeers and not to lodge in town.'' Indians
even approaching by land or water were liable
to arrest. But a few men, and Sewall was

among them, still persisted in their labours
for these people. Cotton Mather sets down the
fact that Judge Sewall built a meeting-house
at his own charge for one of the Indian congregations and " gave those Indians cause to
pray for him because ' he loveth our nation
for he hath built us a synagogue.' " This
meeting-house was in Sandwich, Barnstable
County, Cape Cod. Already Sewall had written as to ways of dealing with the race: " The
best thing we can do for our Indians is to
Anglicize them in all agreeable instances; in
that of language as well as others. They can
scarce retain their language without a tincture
of other savage inclinations. . . . I should
think it requisite that convenient tracts of land
should be set out to them; and that by plain
and natural boundaries as much as may be; as
lakes, rivers, mountains, rocks; upon which
for any man to encroach should be accounted
a crime. Except this be done, I fear their own
jealousies and the French Friars will persuade them, that the English as they increase
and think they want more room will never
leave till they have crowded them quite out
of all their lands. And it will be a vain attempt
for us to offer heaven to them, if they take up

prejudices against us as if we did grudge them a living upon their own earth."

To the negro also Sewall was a constant friend. He wrote a remarkable anti-slavery tract " On the Selling of Joseph," and he ranks first among those who strove to give the black man a chance at decent and respectable married life. The Diary of June 22, 1716, records " I essayed to prevent Indians and negroes being rated with horses and hogs but could not prevail." As a justice he gave some highly important decisions in cases where negroes had been wronged, one of them setting forth in truly stirring language that " the poorest boys and girls within this province, such as are of the lowest condition, whether they be English or Indians or Ethiopians, they have the same right to religion and life that the richest heirs have. And they who go about to deprive them of this right, they attempt the bombarding of Heaven; and the shells they throw shall fall down upon their own heads."

Sewall experienced, of course, that very thrilling thing, the birth of a new century. The Diary of January 2, 1701, records that " just about break of day Jacob Amsden and 3 other trumpeters gave a blast with the trum-

pets on the Common near Mr. Alford's. Then
went to the Green Chamber and sounded there
till about sunrise. Bell man said these verses
a little before break-a day which I printed and
gave them. The trumpeters cost me five pieces
of 8.'' These verses were from Sewall's own
pen; they were fittingly reread on Beacon Hill
by the Reverend Edward Everett Hale at midnight on the eve of our present century's dawn.
The first two are:

> "Once more! Our God vouchsafe to shine:
>   Tame thou the rigor of our clime.
>   Make haste with thy impartial light
>   And terminate this long dark night.

> "Let the transplanted English vine
>   Spread further still; still call it thine;
>   Prune it with skill: for yield it can
>   More fruit to thee the husbandman."

Nothing about the Diary is more significant
than some of its omissions. When '' news is
brought to us '' (September 17, 1714) of Queen
Anne's death the only comment Sewall makes
upon the sad countenance of him who bore the
tidings is, '' I was afraid Boston had burnt
again.'' Anne was a High Churchwoman and
had given aid and succour to the Church of
England to which Sewall had refused to sell

GREEN DRAGON TAVERN

BOSTON PUBLIC LIBRARY

land for a parish home. Though Sewall was
now sixty-two, he was on hand bright and
early, we may be sure, for that dinner held at
the Green Dragon tavern to proclaim George I
king of England and " Supreme Lord of the
Massachusetts."

Judge Sewall's wife Hannah died October
19, 1717. He mourned her deeply, but briefly.
It was expected with the rigour of a law in the
Puritan land that widows and widowers should
remarry. They all did it, and not to do it was
a social offence. Apparently they all helped
each other to do it, and for a man in Judge
Sewall's social station there was no chance of
escape, even though he was sixty-five. But he
appears to have bent his neck cheerfully
enough to the matrimonial yoke, for we find
the Diary recording:

" Feby. 6, 1718. This morning wandering in
my mind whether to live a single or married
life, I had a sweet and very affectionate meditation concerning the Lord Jesus. Nothing
was to be objected against *his* person, parentage, relations, estate, house, home. Why did
I not presently close with him. And I cried
mightily to God that he would help me so to
do."

" Feby. 10. I received a letter from Mr.

Winthrop having one enclosed to his mother
which I carry to her. She tells me Mr. Eyre
[Mrs. Winthrop's first husband] married her
May 20, 1680. Lived together about twenty
years.''

'' March 10. In Madame Usher's absence
Madam Henchman took occasion highly to commend Madame Winthrop, the Major-General's
widow [as a wife] March 14. Deacon Marion
comes to me, sits with me a great while in the
evening; after a great deal of discourse about
his courtship — he told me all the Olivers said
they wished I would court their aunt (Madam
Winthrop). I said 'twas not five months since
I buried my dear wife. Said little, but said
before 'twas hard to know whether best to
marry again or no; whom to marry. Dr.
Mather (Increase) sends me his Marah in a
letter in which is this expression, ' But your
honor will allow me now at length to offer you
my opinion that all the regards are not yet
paid which you owe unto the Widow, and which
are expected from you.' ''

This Marah was probably one of the elder
Mather's books, with the title, '' An Essay to
do Good unto the Widow,'' and the grave bad-
inage here of the Puritan divine at the expense
of the Puritan Judge is characteristic.

" March 19. Mr. Leverett, when he and I are alone, told me his wife and he had laid out Madam Brown for me and yet took occasion to say that Madam Winthrop had done very generously by the Major General's family in giving up her dower. I said if Madam Brown should leave her fair accommodations at Salem, she might be apt to repent it."

But soon, either because fate was unpropitious, or Sewall's discretion had the upper hand, he turned for comfort to the Widow Dennison, whose husband had died shortly before — " an autumnal matron," as Hawthorne would phrase it, but withal a business woman not wasting property on sentiment. Judge Sewall had written the late Dennison's will and attended his funeral, for we read:

" March 19. I write Mr. William Dennison's will, being desired by a messenger from Roxbury with minutes."

On March 26, Sewall, with other Puritan notables, attended Mr. Dennison's funeral at Roxbury, where his pastor, Mr. Walter, said: " He was a man of truth, and of trust, a man of prayer, integrity and piety."

" Gov. Dudley and I went next the mourners," the Judge records. " Went back to the house in a coach. At coming away I prayed

God to keep house with the widow." " Mr.
Danforth gives the widow Dennison a high
commendation for her piety, prudence, diligence, humility." " April 7. I prove Mr.
Dennison's will. Her brother, Edmund Wells,
brought the widow to town and gave me notice
before hand. I gave her 10s. to give her sister
Weld for her Indian Bible. Mr. Dorr took
occasion in her absence to say she was one of
the most dutiful wives in the world. Her
cousin, the widow Hayden, accidentally came
in with her. April 8. Mr. Boydell, when I
was at his office and signed the papers, smiling
said Mr. Dennison's will looked as if it was
written by me. I told him, ' Yes, but there was
not a tittle of it mine, but the form.' "

" June 3d. Go to Roxbury, talk with Mr.
Walter about Mrs. Dennison. He advises me
not to see her then, lest should surprise her
undressed [not dressed for callers]. Told him
I came on purpose; yet finally submitted to
his advice; he spake of her coming to town
on Thursday. June 5. Nobody came — I writ
to Mr. Walter. June 9. Note, Mrs. D. came in
the morning about nine o'clock, I took her up
into my chamber and discoursed thoroughly
with her. She desired me to procure another
and better nurse. [Sewall had represented

that he needed some one to look after him in
his old age.]

" I gave her the last two News Letters, —
told her I intended to visit her at her own
house next lecture day. She said 'twould be
talked of. I answered in such cases persons
must run the gauntlet. Gave her Mr. Whi-
ting's oration, for Abijah Walter who brought
her on horseback to town. I think little or no
notice was taken of it."

" June 17. Went to Roxbury Lecture. Visited Govr. Dudley, Mrs. Dennison; gave her
Dr. Mather's sermons very well bound; told
her we were in it *invited to a wedding*. She
gave me very good curds. July 2. I gave Mrs.
Dennison her oath to the inventory [of her husband's goods.] At night when all were gone to
bed, Cousin Moody went with me into the new
hall, read the history of Rebecca's Courtship
and prayed with me respecting my widowed
condition. July 16. Went and visited Mrs.
Dennison. Gave her King George's effiges in
copper; and an English crown of King Charles
II., 1677. Eat curds with her; I craved a blessing and returned thanks; came home after it."

" July 25. I go in a hackney coach to Roxbury. Call at Mr. Walter's who is not at home;
nor Gov. Dudley nor his lady. Visit Mrs. Den-

nison; she invites me to eat. I give her two
cases with a knife and fork in each; one, turtle
shell tackling; the other long with ivory han-
dles, squared, cost 4s. 6d.; pound of raisins
with proportional almonds. Visit her brother
and sister Weld."

"Aug. 6. Visited Mrs. Dennison, carried
her sister Weld, the widow and Mrs. Weld to
her brother, where we were courteously entertained. Brought Mr. Edmund Weld's wife
home with me in the coach; she is in much
darkness [concerning the outcome of his suit].
Gave Mrs. Dennison a psalm book neatly
bound in England with Turkey leather. 27th.
I ride and visit Mrs. Dennison, leave my horse
at the Grey Hound. She mentions her discouragements by reason of discourses she
heard; I prayed God to direct her and me."

In fact, Sewall visits this lady upon almost
every opportunity; but as his duty as circuit
judge took him away, Mrs. Dennison disap-
pears from the Diary while he is on his travels.
The next significant entry is Oct. 15: —

"Visit Mrs. Dennison on horseback; present her with a pair of shoe buckles cost 5s.
3d." "Nov. 1. My son from Brookline being
here, I took his horse and visited Mrs. Dennison. I told her 'twas time to finish our busi-

ness. Asked her what I should allow her. She
not speaking, I told her I was willing to give
her £250 pr. annum during her life, if it should
please God to take me out of the world before
her. She answered she had better keep as she
was than to give a certainty for an uncertainty.
She should pay dear for dwelling at Boston. I
desired her to make proposals but she made
none. I had thought of publishment next
Thursday. But now I seemed to be far from
it. May God who has the pity of a father,
direct and help me!' "

Her late husband, as Sewall well knew, had
left Mrs. Dennison a life interest in all his
estates. The trouble in this case seems to have
been that the lady declined to alienate any of
her interests by marriage. In fact, all through
his later courtships Sewall shines more as a
sharp business man than a lover with tact or
sentiment.

" Novr. 28, 1718. I went this day in the
coach [to Mrs. Dennison's], had a fire made
in the chamber where I stayed with her before.
I enquired how she had done these three or
four weeks. Afterwards, I told her our conversation had been such when I was with her
last that it seemed to be a direction in Providence not to proceed any further; she said

it must be what I pleased, or to that purpose."

Then there apparently proceeded one of those wrangles not peculiar to Puritan courtships, but in this case carried on with due Puritan decorum, which, as usual with persons in such relations, came to nothing, she holding her own. But the ending entry is delicious:

"She asked me if I would drink; I told her Yes. She gave me cider, apples, and a glass of wine; gathered together the little things I had given her and offered them to me; but I would take none of them. Told her I wished her well, should be glad to hear of her welfare. She seemed to say she would not take in hand a thing of this nature. Thanked me for what I had given her and desired my prayers. I gave Abijah Weld an Angel. Got home about 9 at night. My bowels yearn towards Mrs. Dennison; but I think God directs me in his Providence to desist."

We catch one more glimpse of the lady, Lord's Day, Nov. 30, when, in the evening, while Sewall was at family prayers: —

"She came in, preceded by her cousin Weld, saying she wished to speak to me in private. I was very much startled that she should come so far afoot in that exceeding cold season. She asked pardon if she had affronted me.

Seemed inclined the match should not break
off, since I had kept her company so long. I
fetched a tankard of cider and drank to her.
She desired that nobody might know of her
being here. I told her they should not. She
went away in the bitter cold, no moon being
up, to my great pain. I saluted her at parting."

The last glimpse of Mrs. Dennison in the
Diary is this: —

" Dec. 22. Mrs. Dorothy Dennison brings
an additional inventory. I gave her her oath;
asked her brother Brewer and her to dine with
me; she said she needed not to eat; caused
her to sit by the fire and went with her to the
door at her going away. She said nothing to
me nor her brother Brewer."

Mrs. Dennison remarried in 1720, Sewall
having already taken to wife Mrs. Tilly whom
he had formerly considered, and then set aside
because they could not agree upon the terms
of settlement. This lady died when they had
been married but a short time and then the
twice-widowed judge began — after an interval of only four months, this time — to pay
attentions to Mrs. Winthrop, a highly eligible
widow. The ardent fashion in which this lady
was pursued by the venerable justice I have

elsewhere [1] described. But the courtship came to nothing, because Sewall would not agree to set up a coach nor wear a periwig. He soon found another woman less exacting, however, and her he blithely took to be his third wife, thought he was now over seventy. She survived him, for he died Jan. 1, 1730. He sleeps in death in the Old Granary Burying Ground almost on the very spot where he long ago had his home.

[1] "Romance of Old New England Churches."

XIII

THE year in which Sewall died marked the
appointment of Jonathan Belcher as governor
of Massachusetts. He was the sixth governor
to be sent out by the crown and the third who
was a native of the province. But he succeeded in his office no better than the gentlemen who had preceded him, the wrangling
which had become a regular feature of legislative life here marring his administration as it
had done those of his predecessors. Belcher
was the son of a prosperous Boston merchant
and a graduate of Harvard College. He was
polished and sociable and had had the benefit of
extensive travel. But he found himself in an
impossible situation and the only thing for him
to do was to make as few enemies as possible
and wait for death or the king to remove him.
People who for two generations had been practically independent were not going to take

kindly to any appointee of a throne they were determined to find tyrannical.

Of course the opposition was by no means unanimous. Quite a few persons there were in Boston and its nearby towns to whom the old régime, with its subserviency to men like the Mathers, had been noxious in the extreme, and they naturally welcomed the change. But to most of those who in lineage, sentiment, and habit, represented the first planters the foisting upon New England of a royal governor, bound in loyalty to a far-off king, was an affront to be neither forgiven nor condoned. Though the holder of this office had been a man of superhuman breadth and of extraordinary generosity he would not have been acceptable to this portion of the inhabitants. William Phips had been indigenous to a degree found in no man elected by the people. But he suited neither the Mathers, who nominated him, nor the common people who hated the Mathers. Even the Earl of Bellomont, the " real lord " who succeeded Phips, got on better with the captious people who moulded public opinion in Boston than did this Maine carpenter.

For a time, indeed, it looked as if Bellomont were going to get on very well indeed. A vigorous man of sixty-three, fine looking, with

elegant manners and courtly ways, he had
little difficulty, at first, in making friends with
even the least friendly of the Bostonians.
Churchman though he was, he was not averse
to attendance at the Thursday lecture and this,
of course, made upon the stiff-necked Puritans
just the impression he had calculated that it
would.

The Assembly hired of Peter Sergeant for
him the Province House afterwards renowned
as the official home of the governors, and here
he entertained handsomely. By a curious co-
incidence his lady thus succeeded as mistress
of the handsome mansion Lady Phips, whom
Peter Sergeant had married for his third wife.
The builder, owner and first occupant of what
is perhaps the most interesting house in colonial history was a rich London merchant who
came to reside here in 1667 and died here February 8, 1714. Sergeant had held many offices
under the old charter government, was one of
the witchcraft judges and, when Andros had
been deposed, played an important part in
that proceeding. That he was a very rich man
one must conclude from the extreme elegance
of the homestead which he erected, nearly opposite the Old South Church, on a lot three
hundred feet deep with a frontage of nearly

a hundred feet on what was then called High street but which we now know as Washington street.

The house was square and of brick. It had three stories, with a gambrel roof and lofty cupola, the last-named adornment surmounted with the gilt-bronzed figure of an Indian with a drawn bow and arrow. Over the portico of the main entrance was an elaborate iron balustrade bearing the initials of the owner and the date " 16 P. S. 79." Large trees graced the court-yard, which was surrounded by an elegant fence set off by ornamented posts. A paved driveway led up to the massive steps of the palatial doorway. Two small out-buildings, which, in the official days served as porters' lodges, signified to passers-by that *this* house was indeed the dwelling-place of one who represented the majesty of England.

Hawthorne in his " Legends of the Province House " has repeopled for us this impressive old mansion and, at the risk of anticipating somewhat the arrival of governors not yet on the scene, I shall quote his description while suppressing, as far as possible, his allusions to the deplorable condition of the house at the time he himself visited it: " A wide door with double leaves led into the hall or entry on the

THE PROVINCE HOUSE

BOSTON
PUBLIC
LIBRARY

right of which was a spacious room, the apartment, I presume, in which the ancient governors held their levees with vice-regal pomp,
surrounded by the military men, the Counsel-
lors, the judges, and other officers of the
Crown, while all the loyalty of the Province
thronged to do them honour. . . . The most
venerable ornamental object is a chimney-
piece, set round with Dutch tiles of blue-figured
china, representing scenes from Scripture;
and, for aught I know, the lady of Pownall or
Bernard may have sat beside this fireplace and
told her children the story of each blue tile. . .

" The great staircase, however, may be
termed without much hyperbole, a feature of
grandeur and magnificence. It winds through
the midst of the house by flights of broad steps,
each flight terminating in a square landing-
place, whence the ascent is continued towards
the cupola. A carved balustrade . . . borders
the staircase with its quaintly twisting and
intertwining pillars, from top to bottom. Up
these stairs the military boots, or perchance
the gouty shoes of many a Governor have
trodden, as the wearers mounted to the cupola,
which afforded them so wide a view over the
metropolis and the surrounding country. The
cupola is an octagon with several windows, and

a door opening upon the roof. . . . Descending
. . . I paused in the garret to observe the pon-
derous white oak framework, so much more
massive than the frames of modern houses,
and thereby resembling an antique skeleton."

The cheerful task of recalling the courtly
functions of the Province House in its bright
days has been ably discharged by Edwin L.
Bynner who, writing in the Memorial History
of Boston on the "Topography of the Provincial Period" invokes "this old-time scene of
stately ceremonial, official pomp or social gay-
ety, of many a dinner rout or ball. Here dames
magnificent in damask or brocade, towering
head-dress and hoop petticoat — here cavaliers
in rival finery of velvet or satin, with gorgeous
waistcoats of solid gold brocade, with wigs of
every shape, — the tie, the full-bottomed, the
ramillies, the albermarle, — with glittering
swords dangling about their silken hose —
where, in fine, the wise, the witty, gay and
learned, the leaders in authority, in thought
and in fashion, the flower of old Provincial life,
trooped in full tide through the wainscoted
and tapestried rooms, and up the grand old
winding staircase with its carved balustrade
and its square landing-places, to do honour to
the hospitality of the martial Shute, the courtly

Burnet, the gallant Pownall, or the haughty Bernard.''

At the time of Bellomont's administration, however, the house had not yet become identified with any great amount of official grandeur. The Boston of that year (1699) impressed one traveller, indeed, as a very poor sort of place. This traveller's name was Edward Ward and he is worth some attention as a wit, even though we may need to discount a good deal of what he wrote about the chief town of New England: '' The Houses in some parts Joyn as in London,'' he says, '' the Buildings, like their women, being neat and handsome; their Streets, like the Hearts of the Male Inhabitants are paved with Pebble. In the Chief or High street there are stately Edifices, some of which have cost the owners two or three thousand pounds the raising; which, I think, plainly proves two old adages true, — viz that a Fool and his Money is soon parted, and Set a Beggar on Horseback he'll Ride to the Devil, — for the Fathers of these men were Tinkers and Peddlers. To the Glory of Religion and the Credit of the Town there are four Churches. . . . Every Stranger is invariably forc'd to take this Notice, That in Boston there are more religious zealouts than honest men. . . . The

inhabitants seem very religious showing many
outward and visible signs of an inward and
Spiritual Grace but though they wear in their
Faces the Innocence of Doves, you will find
them in their Dealings as subtile as Serpents.
Interest is Faith, Money their God, and Large
Possessions the only Heaven they covet. Election, Commencement and Training days are
their only Holy-Days. They keep no saints'
days nor will they allow the Apostles to be
saints; yet they assume that sacred dignity to
themselves, and say, in the title-page of their
Psalm-book, ' Printed for the edification of the
Saints in Old and New England.' ' '

A witty fellow certainly, this taverner and
poet whom Pope honoured with a low seat in
the Dunciad and who so cleverly hit off the
peculiarities of our Puritan forbears that we
have to quote him whether we will or no. In
connection with the law against kissing in public he tells a story which has since become
classic of a ship captain who, returning from
a long voyage, happened to meet his wife in
the street and, of course, kissed her. For this
he was fined ten shillings. " What a happiness," comments Ward, " do we enjoy in old
England, " that can not only kiss our own
wives but other men's too without the danger

of such a penalty." Ward regarded our women as highly kissable, observing that they had better complexions than the ladies of London. " But the men, — they are generally meagre and have got the hypocritical knack, like our English Jews, of screwing their faces into such puritanical postures that you would think they were always praying to themselves, or running melancholy mad about some mystery in the Revelations."

One of the chief objects that the king had in mind in appointing Lord Bellomont governor was the suppression of piracy, which had long been an appalling scourge on the whole American coast. The new incumbent did not disappoint his royal master, for he promptly arrested and caused to be sent to England for subsequent hanging the notorious Captain Kidd, who, from pirate hunting with Bellomont as silent partner, himself turned pirate and had to be given short shrift. While Kidd was in jail he proposed to Bellomont that he should be taken as a prisoner to Hispaniola in order that he might bring back to Massachusetts the ship of the Great Mogul, which he had unlawfully captured, and in the huge treasure of which Bellomont and his companions would own four-fifths *if* the prize were adjudged a lawful one. Bellomont refused this offer, for he well knew that the Great Mogul's ship ought not to have been attacked inasmuch as that personage was on friendly terms with England. It is to this " great refusal " of Bellomont that we owe the mystery that to this day enshrouds the whereabouts of Captain Kidd's treasure.

Bellomont died in New York — whither he had gone for a short visit — March 5, 1701, after a sojourn in Boston of a little over a year. The stern-faced Stoughton again filled the gap as the head of the government. And then, on July 11, 1702, there arrived in Boston harbour as governor that Joseph Dudley who, eleven years before, had been sent out of the country a prisoner in the " crew " of the hated Andros. Dudley has been more abused than any of the royal governors. Most historians speak of him as " the degenerate son of his father " but, as far as I can see, they mean by this only that he honoured the king instead of the theocracy and attended King's Chapel instead of the Old South Church. He had been born in Roxbury July 23, 1647, after his father had attained the age of seventy, and was duly educated for the ministry. But, preferring civil affairs to the church, he held various of-

fices and was sent to England in 1682, one of
those charged with the task of saving the old
charter. He soon saw that this could not be
done and so advised the surrender of that document, — counsel which, of course, caused him
to be called a traitor to his trust. But it served
to recommend him to the royal eye and brought
him the appointment of President of New England. How he was imprisoned, how he at-
tempted escape and how he was finally punished (?) in England we have already seen.
Dudley was in truth much too able a man to
be ignored. During the almost ten years of his
exile from America, he not only served as
deputy governor of the Isle of Wight but he
was also a member of Parliament. Most interesting of all he enjoyed the close friendship
of Sir Richard Steele, who acknowledged that
he '' owed many fine thoughts and the manner
of expressing them to his happy acquaintance
with Colonel Dudley; and that he had one
quality which he never knew any man possessed of but him, which was that he could talk
him down into tears when he had a mind to
it, by the command he had of fine thoughts and
words adapted to move the affections.'' Even
those who admired Dudley did not invariably
trust him, however. Sewall, whose son had

married the governor's daughter, records that
" the Governor often says that if anybody
would deal plainly with him he would kiss
them. But I (who did so) received many a
bite and many a hard word from him." Dudley, first among the royal governors, began
that fight for a regular salary which lasted
almost as long as did the office. For some time
he refused the money grants which were voted
to him but, when he found that he would get
nothing else, he at last gave way. Yet he was
so unpopular that there was hardly any year
when he received more than six hundred
pounds. When Queen Anne died he knew that
his power must come to an end. So he retired
from public office to his estate at West Roxbury, where he died in 1720, having bequeathed
fifty pounds to the Roxbury Free school for
the support of a Latin master. All his life he
had been a conspicuous friend of letters and,
in distributing commissions, he uniformly gave
the preference to graduates of the college for
which he had done so much.

To the year of Dudley's death belongs the
institution of what is perhaps Boston's most
unique educational enterprise, — " a Spinning
School for the instructions of the children of
this Town." There had arrived in Boston,

shortly before this, quite a number of Scotch-Irish persons from in and about Londonderry, bringing with them skill in spinning and a habit of consuming the then-little-known potato. The introduction of the potato had no immediate social effect but the coming of the linen wheel, a domestic implement which might be manipulated by a movement of the foot, was looked upon as a matter of great importance. Accordingly, a large building was erected on Long-Acre street (that part of Tremont street between Winter and School) for the express purpose of encouraging apprentices to the manufacture of linen. Spinning-wheels soon became the fad of the day and, at the commencement of the school " females of the town, rich and poor appeared on the Common with their wheels and vied with each other in the dexterity of using them. A larger concourse of people was perhaps never drawn together on any occasion before." By a curious kind of irony the General Court appropriated to the use of this spinning school the tax on carriages and other articles of luxury.

The Common, by the bye, had now come to be the cherished possession which Bostonians of to-day still esteem it. Purchased by Gov. Winthrop and others of William Blackstone in

1634 for thirty pounds, a law was enacted as early as 1640 for its protection and preservation. Originally it extended as far as the present Tremont Building, and an alms-house and the Granary as well as the Granary Burying Ground (established in 1660) were within its confines. It is certainly greatly to be regretted that the famous Paddock Elms, set out on the Common's edge in 1762 by Major Adino Paddock, the first coachmaker of the town, whose home was opposite the Burying-Ground, had to be removed in 1873, in order to make way for traction improvements!

The next governor after Dudley was Colonel Samuel Shute, in whose behalf friends of the Province, then in London, purchased the office from the king's appointee for one thousand pounds. Shute was a brother of the afterwards Lord Barrington and belonged to a dissenting family. It was, of course, expected by Ashhurst, Belcher and Dummer — when they obtained from Colonel Elisha Burgess the right to the governorship — that Shute would give them their money's worth and help them to down the rising Episcopal party in Boston. But their incumbent promptly showed that he was a king's man by voting an adjournment of the court over December 25, 1722. " The

Governor mentioned how ill it would appear to have votes passed on that day," records Sewall; and on further argument Colonel Shute " said he was of the Church of England."

This must have been a bitter fact for our old friend, the justice, to write down in his Diary, for none had struggled harder than he against the inevitable advance of Episcopacy. Of course the religion of England must surely, if slowly, make its way forward in an English province governed by officials sent out from England. Sewall was too sensible a man not to know this. But he would not raise his left little finger to help the matter on. His Diary abounds, as we have already seen, in references to the difficulties encountered by those who were trying to introduce into Boston the ways and the worship of the old country. When Lady Andros died he had none of his usual exclamations of pity for the sorrow of the bereaved husband, and when Andros tried to buy land for a church-home Sewall refused to sell him any.

But the governor got land just the same, for he appropriated a corner of the burial ground for his church. The Reverend Increase Mather, speaking of the matter in 1688 said: " Thus

they built an house at their own charge; but
can the Townsmen of Boston tell at whose
charge the land was purchased?'' This refers,
however, only to the land occupied by the original church. The selectmen of Boston docilely
granted, in 1747, the additional parcels needed
for the enlargement of the building then on the
spot.

Sufficiently unpretentious, certainly, was the
exterior of the early home of prayer-book service in Boston. It was of wood crowned by
a steeple, at the top of which soared a huge
'' cockerel.'' In the one cut which has come
down to us of the building, the height of this
scriptural bird rivals that of the nearby Beacon. This, however, is very likely attributable
to an error in perspective on the part of the
'' artist.'' Greenwood tells us that '' a large
and quite observable crown '' might be discerned just under this ambitious bird. The
interior of the church was much more attractive to the eye than was the case in the other
Boston meeting-houses. Though there were no
pews for several years, this defect had been
remedied, by 1694, as the result of a purse of
fifty-six pounds collected from the officers of
Sir Francis Wheeler's fleet, which had been in
the harbour shortly before. Further to offset

THE ORIGINAL KING'S CHAPEL AND THE KING'S CHAPEL OF TO-DAY

BOSTON PUBLIC LIBRARY

las was the chief opponent of the new theory and he printed in the paper of the Franklins his attacks upon those who urged it. Two years after the scourge Shute went to England on a visit from which he never returned, and Lieutenant Governor William Dummer took the chair, which, as the event proved, he was to occupy for nearly six years.

During this interim both Increase and Cotton Mather died, the one in 1723, the other five years later. The father had preached sixty-six years and had presided over Harvard College for twenty; the son was in the pulpit forty-seven years and was one of the overseers of the college. To bear him to his burying-place on Copp's Hill six of the first ministers of Boston gave their services, and the body was followed by all the principal officials, ministers, scholars and men of affairs, while the streets were thronged and the windows were filled " with sorrowful spectators." How expensive this funeral was I do not know, but when Thomas Salter died (in 1714) the bill was as follows:

	£	s.	d.
50 yds. of Plush	10	8	4
24 yds. silk crepe	2	16	0
9 3-8 black cloth	11	5	0
10 yards fustian	1	6	8

Francis Nicholson, Captain Hamilton, and the governors Dudley, Shute, Burnet, Belcher and Shirley. It was arranged that the royal governor and his deputy were always to be of the vestry. Joseph Dudley accordingly hung up his armorial bearings and took his place under the canopy and drapery of the state pew as soon as ever he came back to the land in which his father had been a distinguished Puritan. There is nothing to show that he did not do this conscientiously, however. Certainly it must have been much pleasanter here for a governor than in the bare meeting-houses where everything he might or might not do would be counted to his discredit.

During Colonel Shute's term of office the smallpox, which Boston had escaped for nearly twenty years, again visited the town (1721). Nearly six thousand people contracted the disease, of whom almost one thousand died. Inoculation was urged and Cotton Mather did really noble service in pushing its propaganda, soon converting to his belief in the efficacy of the practice Dr. Zabdiel Boylston, an eminent physician, and Benjamin Colman, first minister of the Brattle street Church and for nearly half a century (1701-1747) one of the famous preachers of the Province. Dr. William Doug-

lery was the first organ ever used in America.
The fashion in which the chapel acquired this
" instrument " (now in the possession of St.
John's parish, Portsmouth, New Hampshire) is
most interesting. It was originally the property of Mr. Thomas Brattle, one of the found-
ers of the old Brattle street church and a most
enthusiastic musician. He imported the organ
from London in 1713 and, at his death, left it
by will to the church with which his name is
associated, " if they shall accept thereof and
within a year after my disease procure a sober
person that can play skillfully thereon with a
loud noise." In the event of these conditions
not being complied with it was provided that
the organ should go to King's Chapel. The
Brattle street people failed to qualify and the
Episcopalians got the organ. It was used in
Boston until 1756 and then sold to St. Paul's
church in Newburyport, where it was in constant use for eighty years, after which it was
acquired for the State street Chapel of the
Portsmouth church, where it still gives forth
sweet sounds every Lord's day.

High up on the pulpit of King's Chapel stood
a quaint hour-glass richly mounted in brass
and suspended from the pillars, then as now,
were the escutcheons of Sir Edmund Andros,

its humble exterior the chapel had a " cushion
and Cloth for the Pulpit, two Cushions for the
Reading Desks, a carpet for the Allter all of
Crimson Damask, with silk fringe, one Large
Bible, two Large Common Prayer Books,
twelve Lesser Common Prayer Books, Linnin
for the Allter. Also two surplises." All these
were the gift of Queen Mary. There was besides a costly Communion service presented by
king and queen. Against the walls were " the
Decalougue viz., the ten Commandments, the
Lord's Prayer and the Creed drawne in England."

G. Dyer, the early warden of the chapel gave
also according to his means and wrote down
for posterity the manner of his generosity:
" To my labour for making the Wather cock
and Spindel, to Duing the Commandements
and allter rome and the Pulpet, to Duing the
Church and Winders, mor to Duing the Gal-
lary and the King's Armes, fortey pounds,
which I freely give." In 1710 the chapel was
rebuilt to twice its original size, to accommo-
date the rapidly growing congregation. As
now arranged the pulpit was on the north side,
directly opposite a pew occupied by the royal
governors and another given over to officers of
the British army and navy. In the western gal-

GOVERNOR WILLIAM BURNET

BOSTON PUBLIC LIBRARY

Wadding	0	6 9
Stay tape and buckram . . .	7	7 6
13 yds. shalloon	2	12 0
To making ye cloths	4	17 0
Fans and girdles	0	10 0
Gloves	10	9 6
Hatte, shoes, stockings . . .	3	15 0
50 1-2 yds. lutestring	25	5 0
Several rings	3	10 0
Also buttons, silk, cloggs . . .		
2 yards of cypress	3	10 0
To 33 gallons of wine @ 4s. 6d . .	7	8 6
To 12 ozs. spice @ 18d	0	18 0
To 1-4 cwt. sugar @ 7s	0	18 0
To opening ye Tomb		
To ringing ye Bells	3	10 0
To ye Pauls		
Doctor's and nurse's bills . . .	10	0 0

— the whole amounting to over £100.

Enter now as governor William Burnet, son
of the historian bishop. He arrived in Boston
July 13, 1728, and was escorted from the Neck
to the Bunch of Grapes Tavern by a large body
of enthusiastic citizens, among them the famous Mather Byles, who dropped into poetry
on this as on many a later occasion of state.
Burnet had in his train a tutor, a black laundress, a steward and a French cook. Upon the
latter, as will be easily understood, the Bostonians gazed with particular awe. But Burnet was merely preparing to live here as he

had lived in England and, later, in New York.
He was a true English gentleman, cultivated,
courteous, affable and inclined to be all things
to all men. Had he come in any other capacity
than that of royal governor he would have
found life in Boston exceedingly agreeable.
But one of his instructions was to push the
matter of salary, and as soon as this matter
was broached the people forgot that he was
personally a delightful man. As if to avert
any plea of poverty which the House might
advance, he referred in his first address, asking for a salary of £1,000, to the lavish fashion
in which he had been welcomed. But this quite
failed to make those whom he would have con-
ciliated agree to what he demanded. They had
planted themselves once and for all where the
war of the Revolution found them — on the
position that all " impositions, taxes and disbursements of money were to be made by their
own freewill, and not by dictation of king,
council or parliament." We must, as George
E. Ellis lucidly points out in his study of the
royal governors, honour their pluck and principle, while at the same time doing justice to
the " firm loyalty, the self-respect, the dignity
and persistency, with which Burnet stood to
his instructions, nobly rejecting as an attempt

at bribery, all the evasive ingenuity of the recusant House in offering him three times the sum as a present, while he was straitened by actual pecuniary need."

The dissension which followed after this question had been broached was harsh in the extreme and, in the midst of it, the governor, while driving from Cambridge to Boston in his carriage, was overturned on the causeway, cast into the water and so chilled as to be thrown into a fever from which he died on September 7, 1729. The Bostonians seem to have realized that chagrin and excitement probably played as much part in hastening his end as the ducking which was the immediate cause of it, and they buried him with great pomp at an expense of eleven hundred pounds.

The funeral was conducted after the English fashion and not in the slightly mitigated Puritan manner of Cotton Mather's interment. (Before Mather's day there had been wont to be no service whatever, the company coming together at the tolling of a bell, carrying the body solemnly to the grave and standing by until it was covered with earth and that, not in consecrated ground, but in some such enclosure by the roadside as one sees frequently to-day in sparsely settled country villages.)

Gloves and rings were given to the mourning
members of the General Court, and the ministers of King's Chapel, to three physicians, the
bearers, the president of Harvard College and
the women who laid out the body; while gloves
only were given to the under-bearers, the jus-
tices, the captains of the castle and of the man-
of-war in the harbour, to officers of the customs, professors and fellows of the college, and
the ministers of Boston who happened to attend the funeral. Wine in abundance was furnished to the Boston regiment. Apropos of
Governor Burnet's funeral Mr. Arthur Gil-
man states in his readable " Story of Boston "
that the distribution of rings was common on
such occasions, and until 1721 gloves and scarfs
were also given away. But in 1741 wine and
rum were forbidden to be distributed as scarfs
had been forbidden twenty years earlier.
(There had, however, been some advance since
the time of Charles II, when on the occasion
of the burying of a lord, as the oration was
being delivered " a large pot of wine stood
upon the coffin, out of which everyone drank
to the health of the deceased.")

Five years after Burnet's death the General
Court voted his orphan children three thousand
pounds.

And now we come to the appointment of Belcher, with whom this chapter opened. He was in London, on the Province's behalf, at the time when the news of Burnet's death arrived and, by the exercise of not a little diplomacy, he managed to get himself commissioned governor (January 8, 1730), and so was able to land in Boston from a warship in the autumn of that same year. He also was received with signs of rejoicing, accompanied by the inevitable sermon. To his credit, it should be said, that he alone, of the governors chosen by the king, seems to have stood faithful to his paternal religion. He gave the land for the Hollis Street Church, of which Rev. Mather Byles, Sr., was minister, and, for many years, lived conveniently near to this parish of which he was a patron. The house still standing in Cambridge, with which Belcher's name is associated, was an inheritance from his father and had passed out of his hands ten years before he became governor.

Apart from the salary matter, concerning which he of course strove with no more and no less success than his predecessors, Belcher's administration of eleven years was a very peaceable one. I have elsewhere [1] given an

[1] See "Among Old New England Inns."

account of the very interesting journey that
he and his Council made to Deerfield for the
purpose of settling a grievance of the Indians
in that section. The governor lost his wife
during his term of office and the News-Letter
of October 14, 1736, obligingly describes in detail the ensuing funeral:

" The Rev. Dr. Sewall made a very suitable
prayer. The coffin was covered with black velvet and richly adorned. The pall was supported by the Honourable Spencer Phipps
Esq., our Lieutenant-Governor; William Dummer Esq., formerly Lieutenant Governor and
Commander-in Chief of this province; Benjamin Lynde, Esq., Thomas Hutchinson, Esq.,
Edmund Quincy, Esq., and Adam Winthrop
Esq. His Excellency, with his children and
family followed the corpse all in deep mourning; next went the several relatives, according
to their respective degrees, who were followed
by a great many of the principal gentlewomen
in town; after whom went the gentlemen of
His Majesty's Council; the reverend ministers
of this and the neighbouring towns the reverend President and Fellows of Harvard College; a great number of officers both of the
civil and military order, with a number of other
gentlemen.

"His Excellency's coach, drawn by four horses, was covered with black cloth and adorned with escutcheons of the coats of arms both of his Excellency and of his deceased lady [She had been the daughter of Lieutenant Governor William Partridge of New Hampshire]. All the bells in town were tolled; and during the time of the procession the half minute guns begun, first at His Majesty's Castle William, which were followed by those on board His Majesty's ship 'Squirrel' and many other ships in the harbour their colors being all day raised to the heighth as usual on such occasions. The streets through which the funeral passed, the tops of the houses and windows on both sides, were crowded with innumerable spectators."

Belcher was removed from his post in Boston May 6, 1741, and, after an interval of four years, was made governor of New Jersey, where he was welcomed with open arms and did much to help Jonathan Edwards — in whose "Great Awakening" he had been deeply interested — put Princeton University on its feet. But he always retained his affection for his native place and he enjoined that his remains be brought to Cambridge and buried in the cemetery adjoining Christ Church, *in the same grave* with his cousin Judge Remington, who had been his ardent friend. He died August 31, 1757. He was succeeded in Boston by William Shirley, a man whose stay here was bound up with such an interesting romance that I have chosen to discuss his career along with the events traced in the next chapter. It must, however, be plain by now that Boston has advanced a long way from the prim town over which the Mathers held sway. Already it has become the scene and centre of a miniature court, with the state, the forms and the ceremonies appertaining thereto. Gold lace, ruffled cuffs, scarlet uniform and powdered wigs are by this time to be encountered everywhere on the street, and even when the governor went to the Thursday lecture he was richly attired and escorted by halberds. The bulk of the people to be sure are still thrifty mechanics, industrious and plain-living; but there are many persons of wealth, intelligence and culture, and these throng King's Chapel on Sunday. For the Brocade Age has dawned.

THE MATHER TOMB IN THE COPP'S HILL BURYING GROUND

BOSTON PUBLIC LIBRARY

XIV

A GENUINE COLONIAL ROMANCE

No single individual contributed more generously to King's Chapel than Sir Charles Harry Frankland, the hero of Boston's most charming colonial romance. Frankland's intimate friend Governor Shirley laid the cornerstone of the present building (in 1749) and both gentlemen seem to have felt keen interest that services here should flourish. This we must needs keep in mind about Frankland as we follow the outlines of his life-story. For it serves to prove, in a way, the contention of the Boston Puritans that loyalty to Church of England doctrines did not of necessity influence greatly in the middle of the eighteenth century the private life of those in high places.

When Jonathan Belcher was transferred from the governorship of Massachusetts to that of New Jersey and, by the death of John Jekyl, the office of collector of the port of Boston became at the same time vacant, the choice

of these royal favours was offered by the Duke
of Newcastle to the nephew of Sir Thomas
Frankland, then one of the Lords of the Admiralty. This nephew — who was also heir-
presumptive to the baronetcy and to the family
estates at Thirkleby and Mattersea — was,
however, a young man of only twenty-four at
this time and could boast no previous experience in colonial affairs, as could William Shirley, — a lawyer who had already lived seven
years in this country. The outcome of the
matter was therefore, that Shirley, whose wife
had strong influence at court, was made governor and Frankland came to New England as
collector of the port of Boston.

Both were well born, highly-bred Englishmen, Frankland resembling both in manners
and person the Earl of Chesterfield, whom he
had the happiness to count among his friends.
He had been born in Bengal, where his father
was a colonial officer, and to this fact his sympathetic biographer, the Reverend Elias Nason, attributes the trend of his talents towards
art and literature rather than towards politics
or trade. In Frankland's face, also, with its
noble cast of features and its expression of
peculiar melancholy may be discerned that
strain of introspection and self-analysis which

GOVERNOR WILLIAM SHIRLEY

BOSTON PUBLIC LIBRARY

not infrequently characterizes the Eastern-born children of English parents.

Both Frankland and Shirley were, of course, bound to count immensely in Boston society of that time. The important question of the day in the highest circles of the town was " How is this done at court? " And here were two handsome fellows who could tell with exactness just the procedure fitting on each and every state occasion. By the Amorys, Apthorps, Bollans, Hutchinsons, Prices, Auchmutys, Chardons, Wendells, and Olivers, who held the money, offices and power in the chief settlement of New England, they were therefore welcomed with the greatest enthusiasm. Nason, who has made a careful if limited study of the society which greeted them, tells us that it is hardly possible for us to conceive what distinction title, blood, escutcheon, and family conferred in that régime. " Those gentlemen and ladies who occupied the north, or court end of the town, who read the Spectator, Samuel Richardson's Pamela and the prayer-book, who had manors of a thousand acres in the country cultivated by slaves from Africa . . . were many of them allied to the first families in England and it was their chief ambition to keep up the ceremonies and customs of the aristocratic society which they represented. A baronet was then approached with greatest deference; a coach and four with an armorial bearing and liveried servants was a munition against indignity; the stamp of the crown upon a piece of paper, even, invested it with an association almost sacred. In those dignitaries, — who in brocade vest, goldlace coat, broad ruffled sleeves and small clothes; who, with three-cornered hat and powdered wig, side-arms and silver shoe buckles, promenaded Queen street and the Mall, spread themselves through the King's chapel, or discussed the measures of the Pelhams, Walpole and Pitt, at the Rose and Crown, — as much of aristocratic pride, as much of courtly consequence displayed itself, as in the frequenters of Hyde Park or Regent street."

An excellent contemporaneous description of life in Boston at just this period has come down to us in the manuscript of a Mr. Bennett, from which Horace E. Scudder quotes freely in the invaluable Memorial History: " There are several families in Boston that keep a coach and pair of horses, and some few drive with four horses; but for chaises and saddle-horses, considering the bulk of the place they outdo London. . . . Their roads, though they have

no turnpikes are exceedingly good in summer;
and it is safe travelling night or day for they
have no high-way robbers to interrupt them.
It is pleasant riding through the woods; and
the country is pleasantly interspersed with
farmhouses, cottages, and some few gentlemen's seats between the towns. When the
ladies drive out to take the air, it is generally
in a chaise or chair, and then but a single horse,
and they have a negro servant to drive them.
The gentlemen ride out here as in England,
some in chairs, and others on horseback, with
their negroes to attend them. They travel in
much the same manner on business as for
pleasure, and are attended in both by their
black equipages. . . .

" For their domestic amusements, every
afternoon, after drinking tea, the gentlemen
and ladies walk the Mall, and from thence ad-
journ to one another's house to spend the evening, — those that are not disposed to attend
the evening lecture; which they may do, if
they please, six nights in seven the year round.
What they call the Mall is a walk on a fine
green common adjoining to the south-west side
of the town. It is near half a mile over, with
two rows of young trees planted opposite to
each other, with a fine footway between in

imitation of St. James Park; and part of the
bay of the sea which encircles the town, taking
its course along the north-west side of the
Common, — by which it is bounded on the one
side and by the country on the other, — forms
a beautiful canal in view of the walk. . . . Notwithstanding plays and such like diversions
do not obtain here [the famous performance
of Otway's " Orphan " at the British Coffee
House, with its attendant theatrical riot, did
not occur until 1750] they don't seem to be
dispirited nor moped for want of them, for
both ladies and gentlemen dress and appear as
gay, in common, as courtiers in England on a
coronation or birthday. . . ."

It is this Boston that we see in the pictures
of Copley, himself a Bostonian by birth, and
described by Trumbull, when he visited him in
London, as an " elegant-looking man, dressed
in a fine maroon cloth with gilt buttons."

Small wonder that a young man who became
the pet of a Boston like this felt that he could
not marry, even though he must needs love, a
girl whom he had found scrubbing the floor of
a public house. The time of that historic first
encounter at the Fountain Inn in quaint old
Marblehead between these famous lovers was
the summer of 1742. Frankland's official du-

SIR HARRY FRANKLAND

BOSTON
PUBLIC
LIBRARY

ties had sent him riding down to Marblehead where the fortification, since named and to-day still known as Fort Sewall, was then just being built (at an expense of almost seven hundred pounds) for the defence of the harbour against French cruisers. On the way to the fort he stopped for a draught of cooling ale at the Inn where Agnes did odd jobs for a few shillings a month.

And lo! scrubbing the tavern floor there knelt before him a beautiful child-girl of six-teen, with black curling hair, shy dark eyes and a voice that proved to be of exquisite sweetness, when the maiden, glancing up, gave her good-day to the gallant's greeting. The girl's feet were bare, and this so moved Frank-land's compassion that he gently gave her a piece of gold with which to buy shoes and stockings. Then he rode thoughtfully away to conduct his business at the fort.

But he did not by any means forget that charming child just budding into winsome womanhood whom he had seen performing with patience and grace the duties that fell to her lot as the poor daughter of some honest hard-working fisher-folk of the town. When he happened to be again in Marblehead on busi-ness he inquired at once for her, and then, see-

ing her feet still without shoes and stockings,
asked a bit teasingly what she had done with
the money he gave her. Quite frankly she replied, blushing the while, that the shoes and
stockings were bought but that she kept them
to wear to meeting.

This reply and the sight for the second time
of the girl engaged in heavy work for which
her slender figure and delicate face showed her
to be wholly unfitted put it into Frankland's
head to take her away to Boston and educate
her for less menial employment. The consent
of the girl's parents to this proposal appears
to have been given with rather surprising readiness; but it is more than likely that Agnes
took the matter into her own hands, as many
a girl since has done, and that to *permit* her
to go was regarded as the wiser course.
Women matured early in those days, and a
strong reciprocal emotion, innocent though it
undoubtedly was in its nature, must have been
aroused in this girl's heart by the ardent admiration of the handsome gentleman from
Boston. Moreover the Reverend Dr. Edward
Holyoke, who had been the family pastor at
Marblehead, was now president of Harvard
College, and it was probably expected that he

GOVERNOR SHIRLEY'S HOUSE, ROXBURY

BOSTON PUBLIC LIBRARY

would exercise pastoral oversight over this maiden he had known so long.

To do Frankland justice, however, it should at once be said that his intentions at the start seem only to have been those of a friendly guardian. If the heir to Sir Thomas Frankland is seized with a benevolent impulse and wishes to undertake the expense of educating a young person of humble parentage, who is there to say him nay? Mrs. Shirley might laughingly shake her finger at him and tell him to " beware " on one of those occasions when Agnes has looked unusually charming while dining with her and her daughters at Shirley House in Roxbury, but Frankland would of course protest his excellent intentions, — and the matter would be dropped.

It seems to me, indeed, as I examine the evidence, that the relation between these two continued to be that of ward and guardian until Agnes was well over eighteen, the age at which a girl becomes legally her own mistress. For several years she is taught reading, writing, grammar, music and embroidery by the best tutors the town can provide, and though she grows steadily in beauty and maidenly charm she still retains that childish sweetness and simplicity which first won Frankland's heart.

Then these two suddenly discover that they are all in all to each other. The thought of being separated is insupportable to them both. But Frankland has been suddenly elevated to the baronetcy and is no longer his own master. Agnes's father, on the other hand, has died and there is no one to take the matter firmly in hand on her behalf. And so it comes about that this low-born girl and this high-born man find themselves in a situation for which Agnes is to pay by many a day of tears and Sir Harry by many a night of bitter self-reproach. Of course he paid in money, too. How else can one understand his purchase, for the sum of fifty pounds " lawful money," at the close of the year 1745 of Mrs. Surriage's " right and title to one seventh part of a vast tract of land in Maine " inherited by her from her father? Frankland never did anything with this land and the grantor's title to it was none too clear. One can only conclude, therefore, that this transfer of fifty pounds was by way of delicately making a substantial gift to the widowed mother of the girl the baronet felt himself to be wronging.

We caught a hint from Dunton's letters that Boston morality had been somewhat vitiated

by the introduction of the habits and standards
of crown officials. By Frankland's time many
a thing for which a man would have had to
suffer the stocks and women the ducking-stool
— or worse — in the old days was winked at
because the parties concerned sat in high
places. The heart of the people was still sound,
however, and those Puritan maidens who had
been Agnes's school-fellows, naturally shrank
from her when they came to realize that she
and the collector of the port of Boston were
unwedded lovers. Gradually, too, the ladies
whose good opinion Frankland valued grew in-
dignant at him. Thus it was that at this stage
of the story he decided to live in rural Hopkinton rather than in censorious Boston.

Already a former rector of King's Chapel,
the Reverend Roger Price, had purchased land
and started a mission church in this charming
village of Middlesex county. From him Frankland bought nearly four hundred acres, building upon them (in 1751) a commodious mansion house. The following year he and Agnes
took up their abode on the place. Here it was,
then, that Frankland wrote the greater part of
that interesting Journal, which is still preserved in the rooms of the Massachusetts Historical Society, of two hundred hand-written

pages and which reflects so strikingly the
man's varying moods. Of politics there is here
and there a dash, of horticulture one finds a
great deal, of current events there are interesting mentions; but the bulk of the book is given
over to philosophical reflection that bears witness to the strain of introspection in Frankland's temperament and stamps him at once as
far removed from the careless libertine some
writers would make him out.

Under the date of March 17, 1755, we read:
" Mr. Coles gathers anemone seed. Wrote by
packet to mother; Park and Willis for shoes.
Paid for shaving in full for this and the next
month.

" Nothing considerable can ever be done by
the colonies in the present disturbed state.
The plan of union as concerted by the commissioners at Albany, if carried into execution,
would soon make a formidable people. . . .

" The uneasiness thou feelest; the misfor-
tunes thou bewailest; behold the root from
which they spring, even thine own folly, thine
own pride, thine own distempered fancy. . . .

" In all thy desires, let reason go along with
thee; and fix not thy hope beyond the bounds
of probability, so shall success attend thy un-
dertakings, and thy heart shall not be vexed
with disappointments."

Horticulture was Frankland's delight and he introduced upon the Hopkinton estate a great variety of the choicest fruit, — such as apples, pears, plums, peaches, cherries of excellent quality, apricots and quinces from England, — and upon the extensive grounds of the place he set out elms and other ornamental trees, embellishing the walks of his garden with box lilac and hawthorn. The interchange of gardening advice and of recipes was the favourite amenity of the day and we find a Boston acquaintance sending to the baronet with a box of lemons, these lines:

" You know from Eastern India came
    The skill of making punch as did the name.
    And as the name consists of letters five,
    By five ingredients is it kept alive.
    To purest water sugar must be joined,
    With these the grateful acid is combined.
    Some any sours they get contented use,
    But men of taste do that from Tagus choose.
    When now these three are mixed with care
    Then added be of spirit a small share.
    And that you may the drink quite perfect see
    Atop the musky nut must grated be."

That Sir Harry's Arcady never came to bore him was very likely due to these diversions and occupations. Moreover, he had his dozen slaves to oversee, there was good fishing as

well as good hunting, — and Agnes had a mind
able to share with him the enjoyment of the
latest works of Richardson, Steele, Swift, Addison and Pope, sent over in big boxes from
England. The country about Hopkinton was
then, as to-day, a wonder of hill and valley,
meadow and stream, while only a dozen miles
or so from Frankland Hall was the famous
Wayside Inn where his men friends could put
up by night after enjoying by day the hunting
and wines he had to offer. Then the village
rector was always to be counted on for com-
panionship and breezy chat. For that worthy
seems not to have felt it his duty to admonish
Frankland. And Sir Harry, on the other hand,
carefully observed all the forms of his religion
and treated Agnes with all the respect due a
wife. He still continued, however, to neglect
the one attention which would have made her
really happy. A close approach to death was
needed to bring this duty home to him.

I have elsewhere [1] told the story of the visit
these two made to Lisbon in 1755 and of
Agnes's heroic action in her lover's behalf during the earthquake of that year. Frankland's
awful suffering it was, at the time when he
lay pinned down by fallen stone and tortured

[1] See " Romance of Old New England Roof-Trees."

THE CLARKE HOUSE, PURCHASED BY SIR HARRY FRANKLAND

BOSTON PUBLIC LIBRARY

almost beyond endurance by the pain of the
wound in his arm, that brought him to himself.
He then solemnly vowed to amend his life and
atone to Agnes, if God in his mercy should see
fit to deliver him, and he wasted not a moment,
after his rescue, in executing his pledge to
Heaven. His spirit had been effectually chas-
tened, as the Journal shows. For he there
writes down " Hope my providential escape
will have a lasting good effect upon my mind."

The summer of 1756 was passed by the
knight and his lady at Hopkinton but the
following October Frankland purchased of
Thomas Greenough, for the sum of twelve hundred pounds sterling the celebrated Clarke
mansion on Garden Court street, Boston. This
is the house described in Cooper's Lionel Lincoln (although there incorrectly said to stand
on Tremont street) and it adjoined the far-
famed Hutchinson house whose splendour it
was intended to rival. The site was all that
could be desired and the house itself was, for
that period, very elegant and commodious. It
was built of brick, three stories high, and contained in all twenty-six rooms. It had inlaid
floors, carved mantels and stairs so broad and
low that Sir Harry could and did ride his pony
up and down them with safety. This amuse-

ment was probably a feature of those stag-
parties held during his wife's absence in Hopkinton, in the course of which Frankland used
his famous wine-glass of double thickness, a
possession which enabled him to keep sober
long after all his guests were under the table.

The kind of congratulatory letters received
now by Sir Harry and his Agnes may be
guessed from the following, for the use of
which I am indebted to Mrs. S. H. Swan of
Cambridge. The writer of this letter was Edmund Quincy, father of Hancock's Dorothy,
who lived from 1740 - 1752 on the south side of
Summer street, Boston, — in which house his
famous daughter was born May 10, 1747.

" BRAINTREE, Nov. 30, 1756.
" To SIR H. FRANKLAND:

" As ye unhap. situation of my affairs [he
had been unfortunate in business] has dep'd
me of ye satisfaction of long since waiting
upon yourself and lady & personally congrat-
ulating your safe & happy return into this
prov. after so remarkable a protection wh ye
G't Author & preserver of all things was
pleas'd to afford you at Lisbon, on ye never to
be forgotten 10th of Nov. last, I hope yr good-

ness will excuse an epistolary tender of my sincerest complements on ye pleasing occasion.

" I'm agreeably informed that you have purchased ye mansion of ye late Mr. Clarke, &
I hope with a view to settlement for life in ye
town of Boston, whose very declining state ren-
ders ye favor you may have done that town in
ye choice ye more distinguished. As testimony
of my respect & gratitude I have taken ye freedom to send you, a trifling collection of some
of ye fruits of ye season produced on the place
of my birth, on which (tho' mine no more!)
I have yet a residence. It asks yr. candid acceptance, if more & better I sh'd be ye more
pleased. *Tel qu'il est,* permit me ye pleasure
of assuring you that it is accompanied by the
sincerest regard of, Sir, Yr. most obedient &
very humble S't   E. Q."

As Lady Frankland Agnes was cordially received by those who had formerly looked coldly
upon her, and the spacious parlours, with their
fluted columns, elaborately carved, their richly
gilded pilasters and cornices, their wainscoted
walls and panels, embellished with beautiful
landscape scenery, were the background for
many an elegant tea-party and reception. The
Inmans, the Rowes, the Greenoughs and the

Sheafes were constantly entertained at supper
and dinner here, and Dr. Timothy Cutler, first
rector of Christ Church (built in 1723 when the
Episcopalians of the town became too numerous to be accommodated in King's Chapel) was
a frequent and an honoured guest. Very likely
the good old man many a time talked over with
Lady Frankland in a quiet corner of her own
sitting-room the best ways of launching in life
the children of her sister Mary, whose guardian she had become. All in all it was a good
and gracious life that the humbly-born Marblehead girl led in her noble mansion-house on
Garden Court street.

Warm weather, of course, found the family
often at Hopkinton. Once they had a narrow
escape from a tragic end while making the
journey from their country to their town house.
The account of this may be found in the New
Hampshire Gazette of September 2, 1757:
" Boston August 20, 1757. Thursday last as
Sir Henry Frankland and his lady were coming
into town in their chariot, a number of boys
were gunning on Boston neck — notwithstanding there is an express law to the contrary, —
when one of them discharging his piece at a
bird missed the same, and almost the whole
charge of shot came into the chariot where Sir

Henry and his lady were, several of which entered his hat and clothes, and one grazed his face but did no other damage to him or lady.''

Frankland's health, however, was not rugged and in July, 1757, he sought and obtained the post of consul-general to Lisbon, a place for which he was well fitted by reason of his knowledge of the language and customs of the country. The entries in the Journal concerning the articles which he determined to purchase in London '' for Lisbon '' are interesting: '' silver castors; wine glasses like Pownal's; two turreens; saucers for water glasses, dessert knives and forks and spoons; common tea-kettle; jelly and syllabub glasses; fire-grate; long dishes; tea cups etc., clothes etc., for Lady Frankland. Consul's seal; combs; mahogany tray, press for table-linen and sheets; stove for flatirons; glass for live flea for microscope; Hoyle's Treatise on Whist; Dr. Doddridge's Exposition on the New Testament, 16 handsome chairs with two settees and 2 card tables, working table like Mrs. F. F. Gardner's.''

Our hero, it will be observed, has now become a thorough-going family man. It is greatly to be regretted that his Journal no longer deals with Boston and its affairs, for he seems in a fair way to become as gossipy

as the delicious Sewall. Once he puts down
the weight of all the ladies taking part in a
certain pleasure excursion, — we thus know
that Lady Frankland weighed 135 pounds at
the age of thirty-six, — and again he tells us
that linseed oil is excellent to preserve knives
from rust!

The year 1763 found the pair back once more
for a brief visit in Boston and Hopkinton. But
Frankland could not stand our east winds and
so the following winter he returned again to
the old country, settling down at Bath to the
business of drinking the waters. In the Journal he writes: "I endeavor to keep myself
calm and sedate. I live modestly and avoid
ostentation, decently and not above my condition, and do not entertain a number of para-
sites who forget favors the moment they depart from my table. . . . I cannot suffer a man
of low condition to exceed me in good manners." A little later we read that he is now
bed-ridden. He died at Bath, January 2, 1768,
at the age of fifty-two and was, at his own request, buried in the parish churchyard there.

Agnes almost immediately came back to Boston and, with her sister and sister's children,
took up her residence at Hopkinton. There
she remained, living a peaceful happy life

among her flowers, her friends and her books
until the outbreak of the Revolution, when it
seemed to her wise to go in to her town house.
The following entry relative to this is found
in the records of the committee of safety:
" May 15, 1775. Upon application of Lady
Frankland, voted that she have liberty to pass
into Boston with the following goods and articles for her voyage, viz. 6 trunks: 1 chest:
3 beds and bedding: 6 wethers: 2 pigs: 1 small
keg of pickled tongues: some hay: 3 bags of
corn: and such other goods as she thinks
proper."

So, defended by a guard of six soldiers, the
beautiful widow entered the besieged city about
the first of June and thus was able to view
from the windows of her mansion the imposing
spectacle of Bunker Hill. With her own hands,
too, she assuaged the sufferings of the British
wounded on that occasion. For, of course, she
was an ardent Tory. Then, too, General Bur-
goyne had been among her intimates in the
happy Lisbon days.

Rather oddly, neither of Lady Frankland's
estates were confiscated, but she herself found
it convenient soon to sail for England, where
she lived on the estate of the Frankland family until, in 1782, she married Mr. John Drew,

a rich banker of Chichester. And in Chichester she died in one year's time. It is greatly to be regretted that no portrait of her is obtainable, for she must have been very lovely, —and she certainly stands without a rival as a heroine of Boston romance.

THE DAWN OF ACTIVE RESISTANCE

No institution in the life of early Boston played a more important part in promoting the break with the mother-country than the tavern.[1] The attitude of a man towards England soon came to be known by the public house where he spent his evenings, and from the time of the establishment of the Royal Exchange (1711), which stood on the southwest corner of Exchange and State street, a line of cleavage between kingsmen and others was faintly to be discerned. When Luke Vardy became landlord here the place took on the colour which has made it famous. It was then the resort of all the young bloods of the town, who, brave in velvet and ruffles, in powdered hair and periwigs, swore by the king and drank deep draughts of life and liquor. This tavern was distinctly the resort of the British officers and many an international romance is connected

---

[1] For further data on this subject see " Old New England Inns."

with the house, — notably that of Susanna
Sheafe (eldest daughter of the Deputy), and
the dashing Captain Ponsonby Molesworth,
whom the maiden saw marching by with his
soldiers as she stood in the balcony of the inn.
Molesworth was immediately captivated by her
beauty and pointing her out to a brother officer exclaimed, "Jove! that girl seals my
fate!" She did, very soon after, a clergyman
assisting.

The Bunch of Grapes, too, though later associated with many a Revolutionary feast, was,
in the early part of the eighteenth century, a
favourite resort of the royal representatives.
It stood on what is now the west corner of
Kilby street, on State street, and hither Governor William Burnet was enthusiastically escorted by a large body of citizens upon his
arrival in 1728. Governor Pownall, too, frequented the house, and there is a pleasant
story of a kiss which he once delivered, standing on a chair there. Pownall was a short,
corpulent person but a great ladies' man, and
it was his habit to salute every woman to whom
he was introduced with a sounding smack upon
the cheek. One day a tall dame was presented
and he requested her to stoop to meet his proffered courtesy. "Nay, I'll stoop to no man,

GOVERNOR POWNALL

BOSTON
PUBLIC
LIBRARY

— not even to your Excellency," exclaimed the
lady, with a haughty toss of her head. "Then
I'll stoop to you, madam," readily retorted the
gallant governor, and springing to a chair beside her he bent over to do his obeisance.

Ere long, however, there came a time when
a scarlet coat was an inflammatory signal in
the tap-room of this inn. Pownall was rather
less to blame for this, though, than any of the
governors who had preceded him. Our gallant
hero had been in Boston twice before, in the employ of Shirley, before he came to the town as
governor (August 3, 1757), and he really had an
intelligent idea of the underlying causes of the
then smouldering American resentment. To be
sure, he stood calmly and firmly for the pre-
rogative of the king; but he appears to have
divined tendencies, already at work, towards
throwing off the yoke of royalty. At his own
request, he was recalled, after a short term
of service, and it so happened that from 1768-
1780 he was a member of Parliament. Thus
he was able to use, in our behalf, the experience he had gained while here. But his advice
and protests were not regarded in England
and he lived to see us take a place among the
nations in fulfilment of his own prophecies.

After Pownall had sailed back to England

(June 3, 1760) Thomas Hutchinson, the lieutenant-governor, had a chance to try his hand
at the helm. To relieve him there soon came
Sir Francis Bernard, who seems to have been,
personally, a very delightful gentleman, but
who, as the king's representative, had a most
unhappy time of it while in Boston. Before
his appointment to Massachusetts Bernard had
been the successful administrator of affairs in
New Jersey and he had high hopes, therefore,
of getting on well with the Puritans. Writing
to Lord Barrington of the matter he said, " As
for the people, I am assured that I may depend
upon a quiet and easy administration. I shall
have no points of government to dispute about,
no schemes of self-interest to pursue. The
people are well disposed to live upon good
terms with the Governor and with one another;
and I hope I may not want to be directed by
a junto or supported by a party; and that I
shall find there, as I have done here, that plain-
dealing, integrity and disinterestedness make
the best system of policy."

This optimistic vision was destined speedily
to be dispelled by the facts. Though he was
met, near Dedham, on his journey from New
Jersey, by a number of gentlemen in " coaches
and chariots," the new governor had hardly

BOSTON PUBLIC LIBRARY

SIR FRANCIS BERNARD

reached the seat of his province when things began to look blue for him. In his first speech to the Assembly (which came immediately after the fall of Montreal), he maladroitly put his hearers in mind of the blessings they derived from their " subjection to Great Britain, without which they could not now have been a free people; for no other power on earth could have delivered them from the power they had to contend with." Hutchinson, in his narrative of this and succeeding events relates that " the Council, in their address, acknowledge that to their relation to Great Britain they owe their present freedom. . . . The House, without scrupling to make in express words the acknowledgement of their subjection, nevertheless explain the nature of it. They are ' sensible of the blessings derived to the British Colonies from their subjection to Great Britain; and the whole world must be sensible of the blessings derived to Great Britain from the loyalty of the Colonies in general, and for the efforts of this province in particular; which, for more than a century past, has been wading in blood and laden with the expenses of repelling the common enemy; without which effort Great Britain, at this day, might have had no Colonies to defend.' "

The truth was that gratitude to Great Britain was an emotion very remote, just then, from the mind of Boston. For two enactments of long standing, — but which, from disuse, had not hitherto been oppressive, — were now being very unpleasantly brought home to the people. The Navigation Act of Charles II and the Sugar Act of 1733 had been far from acceptable to the New Englanders, but so long as there seemed slight disposition to enforce these statutes nobody minded them much. Then Pitt fell, and there came into power new men who were only creatures of the young king (George III), — and an era of experimentation, so far as the colonies was concerned, was immediately inaugurated.

Governor Bernard was especially instructed to see that the decrees of the English Board of Trade in regard to the collection of duties and the restriction of commerce were enforced. He therefore ranged himself with Hutchinson and Charles Paxton when there came a question of assisting customs officers in the execution of their duty. Hutchinson, as it happened, was Chief-justice of the superior court as well as lieutenant-governor, and it was, therefore, within his power to issue what came to be known as the Writs of Assistance, permits by

JAMES OTIS

means of which officers could forcibly enter
dwelling-houses, stores and warehouses in
search of goods which they believed, rightly
or wrongly, to be smuggled. Charles Paxton,
head of the Boston Custom House, who insti-
gated the granting of these writs, was hung in
effigy from the Boston Liberty Tree as a sign
of the hatred his act inspired in the people.
James Otis, on the other hand, a part of whose
duty as advocate-general it would have been
to support the cause of the customs officers,
resigned his position under the Crown and engaged himself to argue, for the suffering merchants of Boston, *against the legality of the
writs!*

Thus there stepped upon the stage of the
world's history, for the first time, one of the
most brilliant men America has ever produced.
The scene of the now-famous trial, in which
Otis played so important a part, was the coun-
cil-chamber of the Old Boston Town House,
an imposing and elegant apartment at the east
end of the building, ornamented with fine full-
length portraits of Charles II and James II.
Hutchinson presided and there were also in
attendance four associate judges, wearing
great wigs on their heads and rich scarlet
robes upon their backs. Throning the court-

room were the chief citizens and officers of the Crown, all of whom well understood that a matter of enormous importance was to be debated.

Among the young lawyers who were present on that important day was John Adams, a fresh-faced youth who had come up from his home in Braintree to hear what should be said. In his old age he wrote to William Tudor a description of the scene, which brings vividly before us the actors and the parts they took: " Round a great fire were seated five judges, with Lieutenant-Governor Hutchinson at their head as Chief-Justice, all arrayed in their new fresh rich robes of scarlet English broadcloth; in their large cambric bands and immense judicial wigs. At a long table were all the barristers-at-law of Boston and of the neighboring county of Middlesex, in gowns, bands and tie-wigs. They were not seated on ivory chairs, but their dress was more solemn and more pompous than that of the Roman senate, when the Gauls broke in upon them. Two portraits of more than full length of King Charles the Second and of King James the Second, in splendid golden frames were hung up on the most conspicuous sides of the apartment. If my young eyes or old memory have not deceived me, these were as fine pictures as I ever

saw; . . . they had been sent over without
frames in Governor Pownall's time, but he was
no admirer of Charles or James. The pictures
were stowed away in a garret among rubbish
until Governor Bernard came, who had them
cleaned, superbly framed and placed in council
for the admiration and imitation of all men,
no doubt with the advice and concurrence of
Hutchinson and all his nebula of stars and sat-
ellites.''

The case was opened by Jeremiah Gridley,
the king's attorney, who defended the validity
of the writs on statute law and English practice. To which Oxenbridge Thacher replied in
a strong legal argument which showed that the
rule in English courts did not apply to America. Then the Advocate of Freedom began to
speak, confounding all his opponents by the
splendour of his eloquence.

'' Otis,'' says John Adams, '' was a flame
of fire. With a plenitude of classical allusions,
a depth of research, a rapid summary of historical events and dates, a profusion of legal
authorities, a prophetic glance of his eye into
futurity, and a torrent of impetuous eloquence,
he hurried away everything before him! . . .
Every man of a crowded audience appeared to
me to go away, as I did, ready to take arms

against writs of assistance. Then and there was the first scene of the first act of opposition to the arbitrary claims of Great Britain. *Then and there the child Independence was born!"*

For Otis had made a passionate appeal on the ground of human rights. He had said that the writs of assistance were instruments of slavery and villainy, and that he was standing there on behalf of English liberties. He declared that a man's house was his castle and that this writ destroyed the sacred privilege of domestic privacy. Thus for four hours he poured out a stream of eloquence which, if it did not avail to convince the Court (who ultimately sustained the legality of the writs), served admirably to bring home to the Boston people the rank iniquity of taxation without representation. The fight was on!

Governor Bernard did not appreciate this fact, though, and when he opened the legislature, the following autumn, was once more singularly unhappy in his choice of speech-making material. For he now recommended the members to "give no attention to declamations tending to promote a suspicion that the civil rights of the people were in danger." Otis had just been elected a member of the body, and it was, of course, recognized that these words

were aimed at him. The representatives replied to them with scarcely concealed resentment. Speedily, too, Governor Bernard found
out that he would have to be very circumspect
in order to avoid the adverse criticism of this
clever lawyer to whom he had thrown down the
gauntlet.

In the summer of 1762, during a recess in
the sessions of the legislature, Governor Bernard, with the approval of the Council, expended a comparatively trifling sum in fitting
out a vessel with which to quiet the fears of
Boston merchants who wished protection from
the French for their fishing-boats off New-
foundland. Instantly opponents of the administration remonstrated against his " unwar-
ranted outlay." The protest came through a
committee of the legislature of which Otis was
chairman! In the remonstrance it was said
that " no necessity can be sufficient to justify
the House of Representatives in giving up
such a privilege; for it would be of little consequence to the people whether they were subject to George or Lewis, the king of Great
Britain or the French king, if both were arbitrary, as both would be if both could levy taxes
without a parliament." When this passage
was read out, a member cried " Treason!

treason!'' in much the same way that it was
cried against Patrick Henry, three years later.
Yet it was only with considerable difficulty that
the governor prevailed upon the House to ex-
punge the passage in which the king's name
had been so disloyally introduced. Poor Francis Bernard! Well must he have understood,
by this time, that Massachusetts was to give
him anything but '' a quiet and easy administration!''

Yet if his official path was not always smooth,
Governor Bernard was made very happy in
his home life and in his social intercourse.
He had three residences, one in Jamaica Plain,
one at '' Castle William '' and one, of course,
in the Province House. His youngest daughter, Julia, who was a baby when the family
moved from New Jersey to Massachusetts,
afterwards wrote down, for the information of
her descendants, her recollections of Boston in
her girlhood and the resulting manuscript is
freely quoted in '' The Bernards of Abington
and Nether Winchendon '' by Mrs. Napier
Higgins. From that delightful work I reproduce by permission: '' During the hot months
we resided at the beautiful spot, Castle William [Castle Island], a high hill rising out
of the sea in the harbor of Boston, where a

residence was always ready for the Governor, a twelve-oared barge always at call to convey him backwards and forwards. . . .

" My first recollections were of the large Government House, with a great number of servants, some black slaves and some white free servants; a peculiar state of intercourse with the inhabitants, everybody coming to us and we going to nobody, a public day once a week, a dinner for gentlemen, and a drawing-room in the afternoon when all persons of either sex who wished to pay their respects were introduced, various refreshments handed about, and some cards, I can remember. We had a man cook, a black, who afterwards came to England with us. My Father had a country house also a few miles from Boston. . . .

" The cold in winter was intense, but calm and certain; it set in early in November, and continued — a hard frost, the ground covered with snow — till perhaps the end of March, when a rapid spring brought in a very hot summer. During the winter all carriages were taken off the wheels and put upon runners, that is — sledges; and this is the time they choose of all others for long journeys and excursions of pleasure. It was a common thing to say to a friend: ' Yours are bad roads; I'll come and see you as soon as the snow and frost set in.' The travelling is then done with a rapidity and stillness which makes it necessary for the horses to have bells on their heads; and the music, cheerfulness and bustle of a bright winter's day were truly amusing and interesting. Open sledges, with perhaps twenty persons, all gay and merry, going about the country on parties of pleasure, rendered the winter a more animated scene than the hot summers present."

Concerning the house at Jamaica Plain Miss Bernard wrote that it was built chiefly by her father himself and that " there was a considerable range of ground, and a small lake [of] about one hundred acres attached to it with a boat on it. . . . This was called Jamaica Pond. To this residence we generally moved in May, I think, and here we enjoyed ourselves extremely. My Father was always on the wing on account of his situation. He had his own carriage and servants, my mother hers; there was a town coach and a whiskey for the young men to drive about."

Governor Bernard's personal appearance is thus described by his daughter: " My Father, though not tall, had something dignified and distinguished in his manner; he dressed su-

perbly on all public occasions.'' Of her mother
she adds that she was tall and that '' her
dresses were ornamented with gold and silver,
ermine and fine American sable.'' Miss Bernard tells us also that her father was musical
and sometimes wrote both tune and words for
a song he and his friends would after enjoy
together. His was the age of toasts and it is
interesting to know that the bitterly-hated
royal governor originated the following amiable sentiment:

" Here's a health to all those that we love,
  Here's a health to all those that love us ;
  Here's a health to all those that love them that love those
  That love them that love those that love us."

Events in the mother country were now taking place, however, which were bound to make
Massachusetts people hate the royal governor,
no matter how engaging that functionary might
be in his private capacity. Charles Townshend
had been made first Lord of Trade in England
and secretary of the colonies. He proposed to
grasp and execute absolute power of taxation.
Whereupon George Grenville came to the front
and planned a colonial stamp act designed to
pay the expenses of the British army! Naturally the colonists protested. Yet it was not

so much, now or at any time, unwillingness to
pay their part of England's current expenses
as unwillingness to help support a government
in which they were not represented that we
should see in ensuing events. " It was not the
taxation of the Stamp Act that alarmed them,
but the principle involved in it."

In this " strike " of the Bostonians as in
many a strike since there were — unfortunately — outbreaks of mob violence as well as
calm and effective opposition. And the very
men who condemned unlawful measures were
credited, just as they often are to-day in similar circumstances, with " standing for " the
particular measure involved. Hutchinson favoured neither the Stamp Act nor the Sugar
Act. He believed that the government, whose
loyal servant he tried faithfully to be, was
making a great mistake in instituting such
measures in the colonies. But he regarded with
the utmost horror what he saw to be a growing
tendency towards revolt from the mother-
country. His whole attitude in this matter is
expressed in a quotation which he selected as
the title-page motto of his " History of the
Revolt of the Colonies: " I have nourished
children and brought them up and even they
have revolted from me " (Isaiah). In other

words he was a Loyalist in every drop of his blood.

Nobody, however, except Samuel Adams, looked with favour upon revolt at this stage of the game. What Otis and Franklin desired was Parliamentary representation for the colonies. But the redoubtable Adams had for twenty years been thinking along revolutionary lines. When he was graduated from Harvard he had taken for the subject of his master's thesis the question, " Whether it Be lawful to Resist the Supreme Magistrate, if the Commonwealth Cannot Otherwise Be Preserved? " and from this beginning he had followed a methodical scheme of advance in pursuance of which such men as Otis, John Adams, Dr. Joseph Warren and John Hancock were enlisted as his co-workers.

Hutchinson had had the misfortune to receive an office which James Otis had wished given to his father and he never recovered from the idea that all the Otis opposition was based upon personal resentment. Otis, on the other hand, was firmly persuaded that Hutchinson was a rapacious seeker of power and so failed, on his part, to do justice to a strong and commanding personality glad of much work to do because conscious of ability to do

it. That the brilliant young orator had a great
principle on his side when he asserted, again
and again, that judicial and executive power
should not be invested in the same person we
of to-day clearly recognize. But Montesquieu's
doctrines are now well-established where he
was then an author known in America only to
Otis and a few choice others. So, though
Hutchinson was conscious of no offence in ful-
filling at one and the same time the functions
of lieutenant-governor, president of the Council, chief justice and judge of probate, Otis
could and did make capital out of his Pooh-
Bah-like personality. The result was that poor
Hutchinson, as we shall see, had to pay very
dearly for his honours.

The hated Stamp Act received the king's
sanction March 22, 1765, and the news of it
arrived in Boston on the twenty-sixth of the
following May. The act was not to be opera-
tive until the following November, however, so
the people had five months in which to resent
its enaction and plan their modes of resistance.
The office of distributor of stamps was accepted
by Andrew Oliver; he was promptly hung in
effigy from the branches of the Liberty Tree.
Later, on that memorable fourteenth of August, the effigy was burned in view of Mr. Oli-

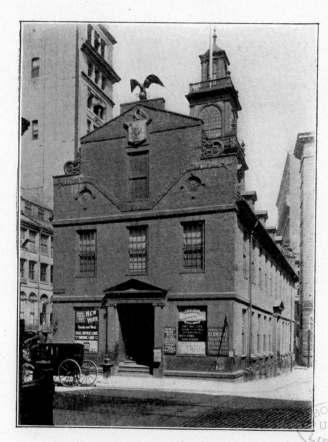

THE OLD STATE HOUSE

BOSTON PUBLIC LIBRARY

ver's residence and he himself was set upon by the crowd. The next day he resigned. It began to be seen that there would be no great demand for the stamps. Yet business could not go legally on without them. Vessels could not enter or go out of a harbour without stamped papers, colleges could not grant their degrees, marriages could not be made legal, and newspapers and almanacs would require this " mark of slavery " ere they could circulate undisturbed.

While feeling was at fever heat a sermon preached against violence was interpreted by a half-drunken mob, who seem to have heard only rumours of it, as urging people forcibly to resent the Stamp Act. And then there followed what is, without exception, the most disgraceful scene in Boston's history, the outrageous pillaging of an official's house by a mob frenzied with liquor. The story as told by the victim in his Autobiography is not a bit too prejudiced to be reproduced as narrative here:

" *To Richard Jackson*

" Boston, Aug. 30, 1765.

" My dear Sir, — I came from my house at Milton, the 26th in the morning. After dinner

it was whispered in town there would be a mob
at night, and that Paxton, Hallowell, the cus-
tom-house, and admiralty officers' houses
would be attacked; but my friends assured
me that the rabble were satisfied with the insult
I had received and that I was become rather
popular. In the evening, whilst I was at supper and my children round me, somebody ran
in and said the mob were coming. I directed
my children to fly to a secure place and shut
up my house as I had done before, intending
not to quit it; but my eldest daughter repented
her leaving me, hastened back, and protested
she would not quit the house unless I did. I
couldn't stand against this and withdrew, with
her, to a neighboring house, where I had been
but a few minutes before the hellish crew fell
upon my house with the rage of devils and in
a moment with axes split down the doors and
entered. My son, being in the great entry,
heard them cry: ' Damn him, he is upstairs,
we'll have him.' Some ran immediately as
high as the top of the house, others filled the
rooms below and cellars, and others remained
without the house to be employed there.

" Messages soon came, one after another to
the house where I was, to inform me the mob
were coming in pursuit of me, and I was

obliged to retire through yards and gardens to a house more remote where I remained until four o'clock by which time one of the best finished houses in the Province had nothing remaining but the bare walls and floors. Not contented with tearing off all the wainscot and hangings, and splitting the doors to pieces, they beat down the partition walls; and though that alone cost them near two hours they cut down the cupola or lanthorn, and they began to take the slate and boards from the roof, and were prevented only by the approaching daylight from a total demolition of the building. The garden-house was laid flat and all my trees etc broke down to the ground.

" Such ruin was never seen in America. Besides my plate and family pictures, household furniture of every kind, my own my children's and servants' apparel, they carried off about £900 in money, and emptied the house of everything whatsoever, except a part of the kitchen furniture, not leaving a single book or paper in it, and have scattered and destroyed all the manuscripts and other papers I had been collecting for thirty years together, besides a great number of public papers in my custody.

" The evening being warm I had undressed me and put on a thin camlet surtout over my waistcoat. The next morning, the weather being changed, I had not clothes enough in my possession to defend me from the cold, and was obliged to borrow from my friends. Many articles of clothing and a good deal of my plate have since been picked up in different quarters of the town, but the furniture in general was cut to pieces before it was thrown out of the house, and most of the beds cut open and the feathers thrown out of the windows. The next evening I intended with my children to Milton, but meeting two or three small parties of the ruffians, who I suppose had concealed themselves in the country, and my coachman hearing one of them say, ' There he is! ' my daughters were terrified and said they should never be safe, and I was forced to shelter them that night at the Castle.

" The encouragers of the first mob never intended matters should go this length, and the people in general expressed the utmost detestation of this unparalleled outrage, and I wish they could be convinced what infinite hazard there is of the most terrible consequence from such demons, when they are let loose in a government where there is not constant authority at hand sufficient to suppress them. I am told the government here will make me a compen-

sation for my own and my family's loss, which
I think cannot be much less than £3000 sterling.
I am not sure that they will. If they should
not it will be too heavy for me, and I must
humbly apply to his majesty in whose service
I am a sufferer; but this and a much greater
sum would be an insufficient compensation for
the constant distress and anxiety of mind I
have felt for some time past and must feel for
months to come. You cannot conceive the
wretched state we are in. Such is the resentment of the people against the Stamp Duty,
that there can be no dependence upon the General Court to take any steps to enforce, or
rather advise to the payment of it. On the
other hand, such will be the effects of not sub-
mitting to it, that all trade must cease, all
courts fall, and all authority be at an end. . . . ''

The picture made in court, the day following
the riot, by the stripped Chief Justice was a
very pathetic one if we may trust the Diary
of Josiah Quincy. The persecuted king's officer, clad in tattered and insufficient garments,
then protested in language which can leave no
doubt as to his sincerity, '' I call my Maker to
witness that I never, in New England or Old,
in Great Britain or America, neither directly

nor indirectly was aiding assisting or support-
ing, — in the least promoting or encouraging,
— what is commonly called the Stamp Act;
but, on the contrary, did all in my power and
strove as much as in me lay to prevent it.''

The mob violence visited upon Hutchinson
was, of course, abhorred by Adams and by the
soberer inhabitants generally. At a meeting
held in Faneuil Hall a unanimous vote was
passed calling upon the selectmen to suppress
such disorders in the future. Hutchinson, however, states grimly that many of the immediate actors in the orgies of the night before were
present at this meeting! The Stamp Act itself
was, of course, roundly denounced on this occasion, notable as one of the first through which
this fine old landmark came to be identified
with the cause of liberty. The original building
given by Peter Faneuil in 1740 to be a market-
house and town-hall had burned in 1761, but
the edifice had been rebuilt the following year,
and it was, therefore, in the hall substantially
as we know it to-day (though the place was
enlarged in 1805), that Liberty first found itself. The beautiful mansion-house of the hall's
donor stood on what is now Tremont street,
opposite the King's Chapel Burial-ground.

As was to be expected no stamps were sold

PETER FANEUIL'S HOUSE

BOSTON PUBLIC LIBRARY

when November first dawned. The ports were closed, vessels could not sail, business was suspended. The news of all this naturally penetrated speedily to England, where Pitt soon stood up in Parliament and declared that he " rejoiced that America had resisted." In May accordingly there came to Boston news of the Act's repeal and every one was so glad of this tidings that no attention was paid to the Declaratory Act accompanying the revocation, an act of enormous importance, however, in that it maintained the Supremacy of Parliament in all cases whatsoever not only in the matter of taxation but in that of legislation in general. It was in the train of this permissory measure that there followed the first steps of active revolution. For Samuel Adams had now been joined in the Assembly by John Hancock (who, through the death of his uncle, had just come into the largest property in the Province, and was beginning to visit with particular assiduity the daughter of Edmund Quincy, now a blooming girl of nineteen). Confronting these distinguished " patriots," as they soon came to be called, were Bernard, Hutchinson and the Olivers, henceforward widely branded by their enemies as " Tories."

From this time on the influence of the chief

town in the province grows, day by day, to be more and more important. In a speech delivered in Parliament by Colonel Barré, one of the staunch friends of Massachusetts, the Bostonians were characterized as "Sons of Liberty," and this name was soon adopted by a society comprising about three hundred active patriots, many of whom were mechanics and labouring men. The public gatherings of the society were held in the open space around the Liberty Tree, and Samuel Adams was the leading spirit of all that went on there and in the private sessions of the club. Both he and Otis encouraged the people to celebrations on anniversary days of significance in the development of the Revolutionary idea, and at these gatherings and the dinners which followed them Bernard and his colleagues were invariably stigmatized as calumniators of North America and now and then pronounced worthy of "strong halters, firm blocks and sharp axes."

The people now saw clearly that they had really gained nothing by the repeal of the Stamp Act inasmuch as this hated measure had only given place to Townshend's Bill, so-called, a measure levying duty on glass, paper, painters' colours and tea. In the excitement following the announcement of this bill's passage